C902867345

D0585114

From My Heart

Linda
NOLAN

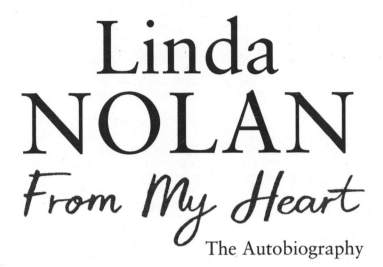

From My Heart

The Autobiography

SIDGWICK & JACKSON

First published 2018 by Sidgwick & Jackson
an imprint of Pan Macmillan
20 New Wharf Road, London N1 9RR
Associated companies throughout the world
www.panmacmillan.com

ISBN 978-1-5098-7634-1 HB
ISBN 978-1-5098-7637-2 TPB

1 3 5 7 9 8 6 4 2

A CIP catalogue record for this book is available from the British Library.

Typeset by Palimpsest Book Production Ltd, Falkirk, Stirlingshire
Printed and bound by CPI Group (UK) Ltd, Croydon, CR0 4YY

Visit www.panmacmillan.com to read more about all our books
and to buy them. You will also find features, author interviews and
news of any author events, and you can sign up for e-newsletters
so that you're always first to hear about our new releases.

For 'my Brian'
You showed me how to love and be loved.
I miss you.
From 'your Linda'

And for Bernie,
who showed me how to live, love
and smile through adversity.

Contents

Prologue

I lay on the cold white bed, covered in one of those hideous blue patterned hospital gowns, staring up at the ceiling tiles above me.

'Here we go again,' I whispered to myself.

And then I felt the bed gradually start to edge backwards through the CT scanner. The machine is like a giant Polo mint and my job is to lie absolutely still on the bed as it slides through the hole in the middle. It's a bit like being on the conveyor belt at the till in Asda. Beep . . . beep . . . beep . . . one Nolan coming through. All I need is a bar code stamped on my behind.

The scanner sends rays through my body seeking out the cancer I know is hiding there.

It's definitely there. And it's not going away, either. That's the thing with secondary breast cancer – it's there for good. Well, for bad, I should say.

'Treatable not curable,' is what the doctors said when they found it back in March 2017. It's exactly what they said to my little sister Bernie when her breast cancer came back. My darling, vibrant, full-of-life Bernie who had more fight in her than anyone I've ever known had died just ten months after her breast cancer came back.

'If anyone can beat this it's you,' I told Bernie that day she came home from hospital saying the cancer had spread through her body. But even Bernie couldn't fight the inevitability of secondary breast cancer. So I'm well aware of what it all means. But I'm also well aware that some women can live two years, five years, ten years, even more before it takes them.

And at the moment my tumour is sitting quietly in my hip bone, behaving itself. Not trying to spread its cruel tentacles around my body or upping and flying to another bit of me.

Every three months I go through the giant Polo mint scanner to see if that's changed.

Every three months I go through a mounting sense of anxiety as the scan date gets closer. Then even greater worry in the fortnight that follows until the results come through.

But it's OK – it's just the way life will be for me from now on. I take tablets every day to try to squeeze the tumour and stop it from spreading. And then there are the scans with the turning of every season.

The leaves were changing colour and blowing around the streets in Blackpool when I went for my last scan.

'I'll come with you, Linda,' my sister Denise said that morning.

'It's OK, Denise,' I replied. 'Thanks, but I think I can do it myself this time.'

And so I got a cab to the hospital and trotted down the corridor to the CT waiting room all on my own. That probably doesn't sound much to most folk. But for me it was a huge achievement. Through the last ten years I have leant so heavily on my amazing family. It was their love and determination which dragged me through the darkest of times. But now I'm getting stronger. And that trip to the hospital proved it.

I sat in the waiting room alongside an older guy who looked even more worried about the whole process than me.

The nurse called across to us: 'Can Alan and Linda come up now, we're ready for you.'

We both trotted up to the front desk.

'Hello. I'm Alan by the way,' the guy said gravely to the nurse.

I looked at him and across to the nurse. 'Well, I'm pleased I shaved this morning so they didn't get us muddled up,' I said, giggling.

All three of us started to laugh and by the time they took us through to the scanning machine I think me and Alan had both forgotten how scared we were moments earlier. And so that's where I was, still smiling to myself, as a nurse injected me with the dye which spotlights any hiding cancer, as I trundled down the conveyor belt through the CT scanner.

Still smiling, that's what I am. Still smiling and still standing (albeit with a crutch some days!) after everything I've been through.

I don't know how much longer I have left in this world. And that has changed me.

There have been many times in my life when I was so sad, so grief-stricken and so depressed that I didn't want to be alive any longer. Now I have a violent determination to cling to life. I am desperate it isn't snatched from me quite yet.

While I don't have any choice in how long I have to live, I do have a choice in how I spend the time I do have. And I've chosen not to spend it constantly stressing about cancer. Or stressing about anything, in fact.

I've chosen to live and enjoy every moment life has to offer me still. I've chosen to enjoy the little things: a pub meal with my brothers and sisters, watching a movie on the sofa with my great-nieces and -nephews, a walk in the park where we played as kids.

I've chosen to laugh. And I've chosen to look back on my life and thank God for it – the good bits and the bad. Because there's been some massive highs, and some terrible lows. But that is life. Sometimes I feel blessed that I've had my diagnosis because it has given me the ability to appreciate my life in a way I don't think I ever did before. Like most people I just got on with it; got up every morning, went to bed every night, worked hard and laughed a lot in between. But I didn't think about it much more than that.

Now I'm savouring what I've achieved in the past and every moment of the present. The future can look after itself. Writing this book has helped me do this. Looking back at my life has made it crystal clear what it's all been about – and what really matters. And actually, what's important is so very simple . . .

To love and to be loved.

One

Early Days

I clip-clopped up Maryville Road, wobbling all the way, but feeling like a million-dollar movie star. Even limping along in one of Mum's sparkly stage stilettos (I could only wear one at a time, couldn't balance in both!) I wasn't more than three feet tall. Not even four years old but what I lacked in years I more than made up for in style. And volume.

Mum used to call me our street's alarm clock. And I suppose I could make a bit of a racket singing my version of 'Molly Malone', dressed in my big sisters' frocks and Mum's 'hee-highs' as I called her high heels.

The stage may have been the pavement of our street running through Dublin's St Anne's council estate, but in my mind it was the grandest theatre on earth. Performing was what I did before I even knew what performing meant. As the sixth child to my parents Tommy and Maureen Nolan, performing was a bit like breathing. And if you wanted to get noticed in the chaos of our house you really had to make quite a bit of noise.

Big families are unusual now but back then in Dublin we were quite small compared with some of the neighbours nearby. Down the road one family had fourteen kids. At ours, Tommy was the eldest, the sensible first-born who arrived in 1949, followed by Anne a year later. Next up was Denise in

1952, Maureen two years later and Brian the year after her. Then came me, just as a watery sun was beginning to break through a slate-grey Dublin winter, on 23 February 1959.

I'm guessing that after five kids Mum knew all the signs of labour. But even though she was heavily pregnant and the pains starting to come she still decided there was time to give the kitchen floor a thorough Monday morning scrub. I wasn't due for another few weeks but Mum knew I was on my way. Unperturbed she finished scouring the floor then got up, put on her best coat, asked a neighbour to keep an eye on the other kids then hopped on the bus to Hollis Street Hospital. That's where I burst into the world a few hours later. Where was Dad? Who knows? Probably working. That bit never made it into family folklore. But then men rarely made it as far as a hospital ward in those days.

It's impossible to imagine a woman doing all that now.

Back home I soon slotted into Nolan family life, perched up in my big pram, being fussed over by my brothers and sisters while Mum got on with the endless round of cooking and cleaning and trying to keep some kind of order. It must have been tough for her. In fact when I think about it now, I think life was pretty tough on Mum all round.

She was beautiful-looking when she was young with dark, dark hair, pale skin and greyish-green eyes. She was very, as they say, 'Irish-looking'. A bit like my sisters Denise and Coleen nowadays. But just as beautiful as her looks was her voice. She would sing to us all when we were little and in my mind I can still hear her singing Brahms' 'Lullaby' and 'Five Pennies'. She had a voice that could send any of us to sleep or calm any nightmare. It was simply perfect. How she managed any of that with a rabble of kids running around is a mystery to me.

Mum had grown up in a very traditional working-class Dublin family. Her dad, two sisters and brother were all extremely musically talented and would put on shows around the city. At seventeen she became the youngest girl ever to be offered a scholarship to the Irish Academy of Music. She had a soprano voice which the college obviously thought had huge potential. It was an enormous achievement but in the end she turned the offer down.

When we were growing up she'd talk about it sometimes. We all thought it sounded so glamorous but she'd just shake her head and say, 'Oh, it wasn't for me. I wanted to do more light musicals than opera.' Looking back, I'm not sure if that was the only reason or whether her family depended on the money she was bringing in from performing in clubs. But I don't think she regretted her decision. At least, she never said so, although I've often wondered what she might have achieved if she'd taken the scholarship. The Nolan Sisters would probably never have existed, for one – because not long after turning down the scholarship she was performing four shows a week in theatres and clubs around Dublin.

One of the other popular entertainers around the city in those days was a handsome, skinny young fella called Tommy Nolan. One night one of the female singers in the band was poorly and Mum was asked to stand in for her. The rest, as they say, is history. Our history.

Dad must have been quite a catch in those days. He was twenty-three – the same age as Mum, and he looked and sounded the spitting image of Frank Sinatra, his idol. I can imagine why Mum fell for him hook, line and sinker. I'd like to say our dad fell in love with Mum in a second across that musical hall stage too. But who knows? What we do know is that a few months after they started going out, Mum had fallen pregnant with Tommy – and everything changed for ever.

Dad had had a very different childhood. His family were quite well off and I reckon they thought their Tommy could do better than our mum. Dad was also hugely talented and was by then in big demand as a singer in dance halls all over Ireland.

Getting pregnant out of wedlock was still a big deal in Ireland back in those days and Mum knew her family would be horrified. Not only was there the shame in a still staunchly Catholic country, there was her entire career and future she'd be throwing away. I imagine Dad was just terrified how Mum's parents were going to react when they found out.

So it seems Mum and Dad cooked up a plan to run away to England, where they could start a new life together. Mum was to get the boat over first with money she and Dad had saved up from their shows and then Dad would join her a few days later. It must have been horrific for Mum – sneaking away from her family, getting on the boat alone like a fugitive, then finding a train to London and finally booking into a boarding house where she waited. And waited. And waited.

Dad never turned up – he'd abandoned her pregnant and alone in a foreign country. It must have been utterly heartbreaking for Mum. And also terrifying, to be abandoned, utterly alone. When she told us about it years later, I just felt incredibly sorry for her.

After a few days the lady who ran the boarding house must have worked out what was wrong with this tearful young Irish girl with the swelling belly and managed to coax Mum into telling her the story. Secretly she then wrote to Mum's parents – remember this was before everyone had phones so it all took weeks. My granddad then got the boat over and fetched Mum home. Goodness knows how Dad thought he was going to get away with behaving like that. But he didn't. He was told in no uncertain terms: 'You will marry my daughter.'

So Mum had a husband and a father for her unborn child. But it can't have been a happy start to married life. And we always wondered if, somehow, that's where Dad's resentment lay. Maybe that was the beginning of the darker side of Dad which was to emerge much later. He'd already been blocked by his family from travelling to London to perform when he was younger so that he could stay home and support the family. And now he was married with a kiddie on the way. He was very, very handsome and had all the screaming bobby-soxers in Dublin going mad when he performed on stage. He was close enough to stardom to see what a great life it could be – but it was always just slightly out of his reach. And so rather than living the high life in casinos and exotic locations he spent his days trudging through Dublin fog to work as a bookkeeper, his head stuck in boring balance sheets, before finally at the end of the day he got to put his stage suit on and perform in the way he loved.

Like most folk, though, Mum and Dad got on and played the cards they were dealt. After they married and set up home in a little semi-detached house on the St Anne's Estate in Raheny, they continued to perform together in the clubs all over the city and were a popular act. They'd gaze deeply into each other's eyes and sing the most beautiful harmonies. It must have looked and sounded like a great love affair. But then they'd go home where Mum would be hand-washing a pile of cloth nappies and Dad would be lighting the kitchen fire.

When they weren't performing together Dad would be out on his own singing at one of the clubs in town. Or out somewhere. Goodness knows what he was up to a lot of the time. Certainly when Mum had been pregnant she'd found out the hard way he had a wandering eye. I don't know who told her but she discovered that Dad had been carrying on with another woman while performing around the country.

And while Mum may have been a trooper who got on with whatever was thrown at her, she was no doormat. Oh, no.

'What do you think you've been doing with my husband?' she yelled at the woman, after turning up on her doorstep. 'Tommy Nolan is my husband and this . . .' she paused, pointing at her stomach, 'is his baby.'

'And this is his too,' said the other woman, pointing at her stomach too.

Poor Mum. How awful. How totally crushing that must have been. But she got to keep Tommy Nolan and the other woman didn't, so I suppose there was some victory for her.

It means of course that somewhere out there is another Nolan brother or sister. We'd all love to meet her or him but I doubt we ever will now – maybe they don't know themselves. Of course there may be other Nolan brothers and sisters out there too. There was probably a lot of Dad's gadding about in those days that Mum knew little about, stuck at home looking after us.

Mum was the permanent fixture in our lives. Always there. Stirring a pan of porridge in the morning as clothes hung over chairs dried in front of the fire. Then she'd be getting the older kids dressed for school and spend the day cleaning the house while me and the little ones toddled around her before she embarked on the mammoth task of cooking tea for when everyone piled back through the front door again.

Us kids were pretty much left to our own devices – most kids were back then. We'd flit in and out of each other's houses or play in the street until Mum came out screaming it was time for bed. It seemed there were children everywhere – of course there was no contraception; and not much on the telly either!

I can only just remember life in Dublin but we lived in a small council house a stone's throw from the beautiful St Anne's Park to the north of the city. We would go for walks across the park then look out over the North Sea to where the ferries chugged their way to England. I don't ever remember wondering what lay on the other side of that flat, grey sea. But my parents must certainly have been wondering, for soon after I turned four there we all were, wrapped up in wool sweaters, heavy coats, hats, gloves and scarves, on board one of the big boats spewing yellowy foam behind us as we headed for Liverpool.

I don't remember any conversations about moving away. It was one of those things that just happens when you're a kid and because you're a kid you really don't think much of it. But looking back, again it must have been so tough for Mum, packing up her home, saying goodbye to all her family, then getting seven kids – baby Bernie had turned up by then – all on a boat to England. Being Mum, though, she just got on with it.

All I can remember of the journey was that the sea was terribly rough. It was really frightening – but exciting too. I didn't realize we were going for ever. And I was far too young to worry about where we'd live or whether Dad would find work. For me and the other kids it was just an adventure.

What we kids didn't know was that work had been drying up in the clubs for Dad. It was the start of 1963 by then and a teenager's idea of a good night out was no longer smooching to Sinatra in a Dublin dance hall. Dad was hoping he'd have more luck in the working men's clubs and dance halls which were still popular all over the north of England.

After landing in Liverpool we headed straight to Blackpool – I'm not sure why there, but why not? It's been my home pretty much ever since.

At first we all piled in, bags and all, to the house of a man we were told firmly to call Uncle Fred and to be on our very best behaviour with. He was being good to us and there was to be 'no messing'. To this day I'm not sure whether Fred Daly was a real uncle or just one of those people we were endlessly introduced to as kids who we referred to as 'Uncle' or 'Aunt' to be polite. I think he may have been an old friend of Dad's family who'd moved to England years earlier. There were a lot of Irish families living in Blackpool at that time.

Uncle Fred was tall with a gentle, smiley face. He lived alone in a four-bedroom house in Ascot Road in Blackpool and unbelievably generously he'd agreed to let us all stay with him until we got ourselves on our feet. He must have been either very kind or a little bit mad to let a young couple and seven raucous kids move into his house for eighteen months. It must have been chaos.

Us girls all bunked down in one room with four of us lined up in one enormous double bed. The boys slept in a box room and I can't even remember how Mum and Dad slept. Maybe they didn't!

I was old enough to start school soon after we arrived in Blackpool and was beside myself with excitement about it. St Kentigern's was a five-minute walk down Ascot Road and I remember Mum marching me there on my first day, my face freshly scrubbed and my blonde hair neatly tied back. Tommy, Anne, Denise, Maureen and Brian were already at school and they always seemed to have a right old laugh there so the thought of it didn't bother me one jot. I trotted to the classroom alongside all the other new starters clinging on to their mothers' hands. Then our parents gave us a kiss goodbye and left. The door was locked behind them to make sure there were no deserters! Well, you should have heard the wail that went up. I looked around mystified at all these other kiddies desolate at being abandoned by their mammies. I'd grown up surrounded by people and noise and other kids. School didn't faze me for a moment. It was just a whole new playground.

My first teacher was Mrs Bridges, and she was the most beautiful, elegant lady I'd ever seen. She had a refinement and serenity which must have been hard to maintain amid a mob of five-year-olds in Blackpool. She smelt of Estée Lauder, and even now when I walk past a spray of it in Superdrug I'm transported back to St Kentigern's, sitting on the carpet and listening to a story about bears or wolves or some other slightly terrifying characters.

Bernie was just eighteen months younger than me so was only one school year behind. We both slipped effortlessly into life at St Kentigern's because we were so young and it's easier at that age to make new friends. It was harder for the older ones going into the junior school, with their strong Irish accents and feeling very different to the other kids.

Mind you, Mum always used to call me 'Dublin Molly'

because I had a really deep, strong Irish accent. And with my blue eyes and mop of curly blonde hair I looked like a little Molly Malone.

Bernie and I were so close in age that we had played together from the time she could walk. One favourite game for Bernie and me was 'schools'. Bernie of course was the teacher; she was always super-confident and capable, even when we were tiny. I'd sit at an old desk in the garage at the side of our house, pretending to be the diligent pupil, while Bernie marched up and down teaching me my times tables.

We hadn't any furniture or possessions and only a handful of clothes in Blackpool and we were still living off a virtual stranger's charity, but I never remember feeling hard done by. Everything was just fun. Music had already played a huge part in my childhood but in Blackpool there was more and more. Mum and Dad would be out most nights of the week performing their stage show, which was going down a bomb locally. They could sing beautiful harmonies together and I think audiences liked the idea that they were a real-life couple too.

After about two years in Blackpool, as Anne, Denise and Maureen reached their early teens, they also became part of the act. It had sort of happened by accident in the first place, as they stepped in when Mum was pregnant with Coleen and couldn't go on stage. Anne was fifteen by then and it was already clear that all three of the big girls had great voices. And the audiences loved it, so even when Mum came back after having Coleen it just carried on from there. When I'd see them getting ready, putting on their frocks and styling their hair, I'd be so jealous. It was like a night out – on a school night! And singing in front of a crowd was what I wanted to do more than anything.

I was six the year *The Sound of Music* came out and I was utterly crazy about it. All us sisters were. The older girls would take me to watch it over and over again down at the Palladium on South Shore in Blackpool. We knew all the words, could sing all the harmonies, perform the dance routines. 'We could do that,' we told each other over and over. (Well, without the mountains.)

It was round about then, after we'd been in Blackpool a couple of years, that we finally moved out of Uncle Fred's house into our own home. It was a four-bedroom terraced house in Waterloo Road, just a ten-minute walk (fifteen minutes if you dawdled with an ice cream) up the hill from the beach at South Shore.

All the Nolans were present and correct by then, which meant one bedroom was for Tommy and Brian, another had two sets of bunk beds for Anne, Denise, Maureen and me, another had Mum, Bernie and Coleen, and then Dad had a little box room to himself. Mum and Dad weren't sleeping in the same room by then. Mind, after that many kids I can't blame them. But they were only just forty, so it was young for them to have given up on that side of their marriage. At the time I didn't think there was anything strange about it, but looking back there were clearly far bigger problems in their marriage than we younger kids were able to see.

The bathroom at Waterloo Road was the size of a postage stamp and the boys would go round to our neighbours, Mr and Mrs Fleck, to have a bath rather than wait on all us girls to finish ours. It was cramped and noisy and chaotic. But it was home. And actually felt like a palace to us having spent two years bunking down at Uncle Fred's.

We spent a lot of our time out and about anyway. We loved

wandering down to the beach. In summer it was incredible. Blackpool was still in its heyday and holidaymakers and day trippers would flock there in summer from all over England. We'd look down the hill onto the beach and it seemed like it was covered in ants, there were so many folk there. And while Blackpool was a place of once-a-year dreams for the holiday-makers, for us it was home. We were so proud to live there. Mum would pack up jam sandwiches and bottles of fizzy pop and we'd go down to the beach for the entire day in summer, paddling in the sea, burying each other in sand and watching all the goings-on.

But if life was like one long summer holiday for us kids, it must have been a very different story for Mum. She still had an old-fashioned twin-tub washing machine, which you had to stand over before hauling all the clothes across into a spin-ner. Once a week that would come out and the kitchen would be full of steamy, soapy air. And then she had to mangle the clothes dry. And for a long while in that house we didn't have central heating, so the kitchen was constantly lined with school uniforms and Dad's shirts drying in front of the fire, which Mum had already laid and lit.

Poor Mum never stopped working – and most evenings she was out performing with Dad on stage too. After she'd spent the day scrubbing and cooking she would sit in front of the mirror in her bedroom and put on her make-up and turn herself effortlessly from harried housewife into serene stage star.

I'd perch on the bed watching as she prepared herself at the old mahogany dressing table. First she'd dab on a strong pan-stick foundation so she didn't go shiny in front of the stage lights. Then she pencilled on her blue eyeliner before choosing what shade of eyeshadow best suited the dress she was wearing that night. Most of her full-length evening gowns were from charity shops round Blackpool, but to me when she was all dressed up she was the epitome of glamour – like the Baroness in *The Sound of Music*!

Mum's hair was piled up in a beehive for most of the 1960s, as far as I can recall. She went to 'get a piece put in' up at the hairdresser's in town then kept it in day and night (with the help of a hairnet when she was in bed).

Then, when the hair and make-up were completed with a bright red lipstick, Mum would take her huge powder puff, dab her face, then tap me on the nose with it, leaving me in a haze of her powdery scent.

She'd look critically back into the mirror, saying: 'Now, am I beautiful?'

'Oh yes, Mummy,' I'd reply. And she was. Then Dad would appear at the bottom of the stairs, always pausing in front of the mirror to comb his eyebrows. Just 5 foot 7 inches, never a sliver above 10 stone, and with a cigarette hanging out the corner of his mouth, he looked more like Frank Sinatra than Sinatra did by then! Dressed in his tuxedo you could see why he'd sent all those girls crazy back in Dublin.

Mum's sister, Auntie Theresa, had moved to Blackpool by then, so she'd babysit if all the girls were out performing with Mum and Dad. If they weren't then Anne and Denise were left in charge. I'd be fast asleep by the time they came home but Mum always came into our rooms to check we were fine and to give us a goodnight kiss. I'd smell her panstick foundation in my dreams and know Mum was home for the night, that everything was OK.

Two

Born to Perform

'You joining us tonight, Linda?' Mum asked me one evening.

It was another long hot summer in Blackpool and the town was throbbing with holidaymakers enjoying their week of freedom. Dad had landed all five of us girls and Brian a summer season at the Central Working Men's Club, which was packed every night.

I was included because for weeks I'd been begging them to let me join in. 'Just for one song, Mum?'

Everyone had known it was going to happen sooner or later, so why not sooner? It was just before we'd moved to Waterloo Road and I was only five, but I could still belt out a song like a kid twice my age. And we all seemed to have been born with a natural talent for harmonies. Coleen was just a baby but even before she'd been born people hadn't asked if it was going to be a boy or a girl, they'd asked if the baby would be able to sing.

Since arriving in Blackpool, we had quickly built up a reputation as good family entertainment. Mum would do some light opera, Dad sang some Sinatra numbers, then the whole family would sing together as an act. At first I only made the occasional performance. Probably just to stop me pestering them to have a go. But at that time I was still the youngest on stage so I guess I had the 'cute factor' going for me.

By the age of nine I was performing frequently with the older girls. Dad landed us all a summer season at the Brunswick Club in Blackpool. Bernie, who was then seven, would come on stage too and even little Coleen made an appearance at just four.

By the time I was at junior school I even had my own solo song – Shirley Bassey's 'Big Spender'. It's a big song for a little girl which needs to be belted out but that didn't worry me in the slightest. For me it was like play-acting, and I'd throw myself into the song, owning the stage with the confidence of a fully grown woman. Mum made me a dress for performing in and when I stepped out in front of the crowd, clutching a microphone, it felt the most natural place in the world.

You wouldn't be allowed to put children on the stage late at night nowadays, but back then no one bothered about it. I had a brilliant time – it was clear even then I'd never do anything else.

And if I wasn't performing on stage in a club I'd only be doing it at home anyway. Ever since we'd moved to Waterloo Road, me, Denise, Anne, Maureen and little Bernie had created our own shows in the garage at the side of our house. We'd sling old blankets over a girder in the roof and that was our stage curtain. Then we'd sweep the floor and collect up any chairs we could find around the house for the audience.

Backstage we'd practise for hours before Mum, Dad, Auntie Theresa and any passing neighbours could be press-ganged into attending the big show. The older girls would open the performance with 'Keep Your Sunny Side Up' and then me and Bernie would join in too. After we'd seen *The Sound of*

Music countless times all those songs became regulars in our garage shows, and soon became the main plank of our professional performances too. It gave us a chance to sing the harmonies that we seemed to pick up naturally. Maybe it was because we were related and spent so much time together but somehow we instinctively found the right key and sang together effortlessly.

By the late 1960s we were performing so often – every summer season, weekends and week nights – that we were known as 'The Singing Nolans' and our business cards said 'Blackpool's Own Von Trapps'.

And maybe in some ways we were like the Von Trapps. Certainly Dad could be just as strict as the Christopher Plummer character, particularly with the older girls. While most girls then were parading around Blackpool with skirts skimming their backsides, Anne, Denise and Maureen were still wearing knee-high socks and knee-length frocks. And he had very high standards for when we were performing. It didn't matter that we were still kiddies, on stage we were professionals.

Oh yes, Dad was very strict. And while Mum would scream and shout at us for making a racket or leaving our clothes lying around the house, Dad only had to give us one look and we'd know we were in trouble. We never wanted to make Dad angry. He had a way of making you feel like you'd let him down and there'd be a simmering fury which was terrifying.

As I went up the years at junior school I could see that Dad's moods were becoming more unpredictable. More scary. I don't think anyone ever told me he was drinking too much. Certainly the word 'alcoholic' was never used. But I knew if he came home late it was best to be well out of his way. I'd hear him and Mum yelling at each other downstairs. Sometimes there were thuds and crashes. I tried not to think what those noises meant. Me and my sisters didn't talk about it, but we all knew the back of Dad's hand was something to be avoided when he was in a fury.

So, yeah, sometimes he could be an ogre.

But other times he was the most fabulous Dad ever. He made everything magic. He was holding down three jobs – one as an accountant, another in a printer's, and he was doing the shows at night. So he wasn't around much. But when he was and he talked to you he had the ability to make you feel like you were the only person on earth who mattered. I guess that's what they call charisma. He would read us bedtime stories and ask loads of questions about what we'd been up to at school. But he wasn't like other adults who ask 'How was school?' without even waiting for an answer. He'd listen, and the next time would remember what we'd told him we'd been learning and ask what had happened next. He was so enthusiastic and interested in what you were telling him that it made you feel special for that moment.

Sometimes at weekends he'd take some of us down to the beach. Or we'd all pile in the car and go to Lytham St Annes along the coast. Mum would pack up a picnic which we'd eat sitting on the long grass banks overlooking the sea before a game of rounders. With a family our size, we had two full teams!

A few times he took me, Bernie and Coleen camping too. There is one occasion which stands out clearly in my mind. I was eleven by then, so Bernie was nine and Coleen was six. He took us to a campsite about five miles up the road and we spent most of the day trying to erect this huge white tarpaulin tent, like one of the old scout tents. Us girls loved it and we were running around, playing ball games and having the time of our lives. We'd been there a few hours and it was early evening when Dad said, 'I'm just popping out for a bit.'

By the time night fell he hadn't returned.

'Nothing to worry about,' I said breezily to Bernie and Coleen. 'Let's just get our pyjamas on and get into our sleeping bags. He'll be back soon.'

As the oldest of the three of us I instinctively took on the role of protector – in a big family where Mum and Dad have a million things on their minds, you learn to do that early.

Although that night I think Dad had only one thing on his mind – booze. I can't be sure, because he never said a word about it, but I've wondered since if he got locked up for drink-driving and forgot we were alone. Either way he didn't come back all night. It may sound strange but we weren't unduly worried. We were used to Dad coming and going so we simply fell asleep in the tent, far from home with no mobile phone, no adult and just a pint of milk and a couple of dried-out bread rolls to eat.

'He's not back then?' Bernie said the next morning.

'He will be soon,' I replied. 'He's not just going to abandon us here, is he?'

And despite everything, I knew that was true. Sure enough, soon afterwards a dishevelled-looking Dad pulled up at the campsite. We were a loud, loving family but there were a lot of things in the Nolans which were never said. Where Dad disappeared to that night was just one more of them. We didn't even tell Mum what had happened. None of us would ever want to create one of those yelling matches which ended with bangs and thuds in the night.

But that incident pretty much summed up the two sides of our dad. He could be the most fun, adventurous, interested, exciting person in the world, who made you feel utterly special. Or he could just forget you existed. We were learning fast that when he'd been drinking he was a very different person.

I don't remember him drinking at home, it was just when he went out. And he went out a lot in those days. He'd be gone most nights and then on a Saturday he'd head out before lunch for a few pints before going to the football. By the time he got home it was late and most often he was drunk and in the mood for a row. Us girls would often stay up late on a Saturday, squashed up on the sofa, watching telly with Mum. But once we heard Dad's key in the door we knew it was time to scarper up to bed.

It's only quite recently that I've accepted Dad was an alcoholic at that point. For years I thought an alcoholic was someone who you passed in a shop doorway, out of their heads and covered in filth. Now I understand someone can be dependent on drink and it can shape their lives, but they can still function on a day-to-day level. And I guess that was what Dad was doing.

It must have been a huge strain for Mum, who must have known exactly how much her husband was drinking. And who increasingly was on the wrong end of his terrible furies. To make matters worse, Dad's mum, Nana Nolan, moved in for three years. I was sleeping in the box room with Bernie and Coleen by then, in bunk beds, leaving the big girls to themselves. There was barely room to swing a cat in there but then we didn't have a cat – or many possessions at all. Dad moved into the boys' room so his mother could have his room. And poor old Mum slept on the couch.

Nana Nolan was a bit of a grumpy old woman. She wore those stout leather boots with zips up the side and her personality was a bit like the boots. She seemed to spend a lot of time staring disapprovingly about our house, despite the fact that her daughter-in-law was running around after her and sleeping on the couch every night. It was quite clear she thought Dad had married beneath himself. After three years she returned to Dublin and I was still no clearer why she'd moved in in the first place.

Mum wasn't a victim to Dad or his family, though. Oh no. When her hackles were up she loved a good row too. In fact us kids would be willing her to let some minor disagreement lie, in case it got nasty, but Mum couldn't do that either and that's when things became bad.

Once it all became too much for her. I guess she'd had enough of eight kids and a boozing husband and the endless round of cooking and cleaning. After one row too many she stormed out of the house in her carpet slippers with nothing but a thin cardie over her dress.

Years later, she told me: 'I thought, "And where in God's name do you think you are going now? You've got eight kids back in that house, your family are in another country and you haven't a penny in your pocket." So I walked back home again. This was my life and I had to get on with it.'

And that was pretty much Mum's way of dealing with all of it – just to get on and make the best of a situation.

I think Mum also loved Dad deeply. Until her dying day she did and she could forgive him anything. She would never have wanted to leave him, she just didn't want things to be quite so hard. And it can't have been easy knowing that her children adored the fun side of their father and were so desperate for his attention and approval. For while Mum was brilliant, she was always so busy, cooking, cleaning and running the house, she just didn't have time to do fun things with us.

She was, I suppose, a typical Irish mother. She did everything and ruined us. We were totally spoilt – even though there were eight of us to spoil. And at the time we really didn't appreciate it.

'What's for tea, what's for tea?' we'd all yell as we poured in the door from school.

'Bees, knees and spiders' ankles,' she'd laugh as she chopped up lumps of beef and peeled enough spuds for a small army.

Mum would spend hours cooking a big dinner for ten of us every night (eleven during the years when Nana Nolan had moved in) but then quite often while we were all tucking in, she'd perch at the end of the table with a sandwich.

'What's that, Mum?' I'd ask.

'Oh, it was all I fancied after cooking all day,' she'd reply.

At the time I was too daft to realize that there wasn't enough dinner to go round but she put us before herself. And then when we'd finished eating our dinner, we'd all just get up from the table and go to watch telly, leaving all the plates lying on the table. Mum would spend another hour clearing and doing the washing-up. But she never asked us to help and Dad never did either – I'm not sure he even noticed how much work Mum had to do. So we grew up not even thinking about it.

I remember the first time I went round to my friend

Suzanne's house for tea. Her mum was instructing Suzanne and her brother Alan to lay the table. Then afterwards it was, 'Suzanne, you wash up, Linda, you dry and Alan, put away.' Helping their mum was second nature in Suzanne's family but it had never occurred to us. I've often wondered over the years why Mum, with such a big family, never asked for more help.

Mum was a great cook – very plain, but great. On a Saturday there'd always be a big pot of stew. She'd make it with both stewing steak and meatballs and it would be on the stove slowly cooking all day while the boys were out at football and us girls were at friends' houses or out shopping. Then on a Sunday we would have a traditional roast dinner. Some week nights we'd have boiled bacon, cabbage and mash. But even cooking all that for ten of us, Mum would be saying: 'And what do you want with yours?' to each of the kids. So Denise might have mince with hers because she preferred it to the bacon and Tommy wanted peas instead of cabbage – and so it went on and on. I don't know how she had the patience. But she just got on with it. She had her moments, of course, where she lost it, and she was a real shouter. We used to laugh because suddenly it would be: 'Anne, Denise, Maureen . . .' and then she obviously ran out of energy and just yelled, 'EVERYONE, come down here!'

Neither Mum nor Dad were great when it came to things like parents' evenings at school – they were always too busy to turn up. Or I thought that was it. Maybe they just weren't that interested. It was already assumed that we'd be going into entertaining so perhaps they didn't think it mattered how we got on at school. But I hated the morning after a parents' evening as the other kids would rush into class saying: 'What did Miss so-and-so say about you?' or 'Did your mum and dad go mad when they got home?' Of course my parents hadn't gone and I never knew how to reply.

I wasn't great academically and all I wanted to do was perform – when I wasn't daydreaming about being a beautician. But I think me and my brothers and sisters could have achieved more if we'd been encouraged and it's a shame that didn't happen.

The one subject I was good at was English, which I think was because we did a lot of reading at home. Mum and Dad bought us loads of books. We started out on the Disney story books – Cinderella was my favourite. Then when I was older I charged through all the Four Marys annuals and Malory Towers books. I loved them and used to dream about going to boarding school.

'Well, that's all very fine,' Mum would say, 'but I can promise you it wouldn't all be horse riding and midnight feasts, you know.'

The Fleck family had moved in next door in Waterloo Road when I was ten. I poked my head out of the window one morning and saw a girl about my age lugging stuff into the house. The following day we started chatting over the garden wall.

'What's your name?' I asked.

'Suzanne,' she replied in a strong Scottish accent, explaining her family had moved down from Glasgow and she didn't know a soul.

'How old are you?'

'Ten,' she said. 'Eleven next February the 23rd.'

'Same as me – we're exactly the same age!' I shrieked. 'Want to come round to play?'

Nearly half a century later Suzanne and I are still best friends.

We both went to the same secondary school – St Catherine's – and spent almost every spare moment together.

'We might as well knock a hole in the wall so you don't have to keep walking round,' Suzanne's mum, Mrs Fleck, used to laugh. And she was right. If I couldn't be bothered to go home after we'd been sitting in Suzanne's room all evening listening to music and flicking through magazines, I'd just sleep over. It was my second home. (And my brothers' bathroom, of course!)

Soon there was a little gang of us. Me, Bernie, Suzanne, her brother Alan and another boy from the road, Peter Bond. After dinner we'd play out in the street until it got dark and all our mums stood at the front gates yelling at us to come in.

The best game was Relievio where one of us had to be 'On' and had to count to 20 while the others hid and then tried to sneak back to 'Home' without being spotted. Other times we'd play Two Balls up against the chip shop wall in the alley at the end of the road. Sometimes in the summer we'd play tennis in the alley, pretending we were stars we'd seen at Wimbledon on the telly.

One afternoon in the summer holidays we decided to pick ourselves some apples from a tree in one of the neighbours' gardens. We thought we were so big and brave.

Peter climbed up the tree then threw the apples down one at a time while I stood at the bottom catching them and dropping them into an old bucket.

All of a sudden this old man emerged from the house, ranting and raving: 'Where did you get all those apples from?'

'We found them,' I spluttered.

'All of them?' he yelled, glaring at the bucket. It didn't seem sensible to prolong the explanation so we all just turned and legged it down the road as fast as we could go. We thought we'd got away with the crime of the century!

Other days we'd ride round the streets on our bikes, just being kids the way kids used to be kids.

If it was raining outside – which it did quite a lot in Blackpool – me, Bernie and Suzanne would play dressing up indoors. The house in Waterloo Road had a long landing which was just perfect for a Miss World catwalk. Me, Bernie and Suzanne used to raid the older girls' and Mum's wardrobes for anything that looked suitably sparkly and spangly. Then one of us would be the commentator and the other two would be contestants.

'Good evening, and who are you?' I'd ask Suzanne as she wobbled down the hall landing in a pair of Denise's platform shoes with a towel wrapped round her head and one of Mum's dresses hooked over her like a sari.

'I'm Miss India,' she'd reply.

'And don't you look stunning tonight,' I'd say, doing my best Eric Morley voice.

We could play for hours. Well, there was never anything on television and there weren't any computer games, so we had to make our own entertainment.

Suzanne and I both had our first major love affair at the same time too . . . with Donny Osmond. We were both mad for The Osmonds. I had posters on my bedroom wall, a Donny Osmond pillow case which had been a Christmas present from Mum, and all the albums. Suzanne and I were even members of the Osmonds fan club.

Obviously, sharing a bedroom with Bernie and Coleen

meant the Osmonds shrine was confined to one wall. Above her bed, Bernie had huge posters of Elvis and David Cassidy. Coleen, meanwhile, had posters of horses and dreamed of one day being a vet.

One summer afternoon I was playing out in the garden when Mum yelled out: 'Linda, quick, quick, The Osmonds are on the telly.' I went sprinting up to the back and pushed the porch door open – only for my hand to go straight through the glass. I don't think I even noticed the blood pouring from the cuts as I sat there glued to the television.

I was soon performing with my family at least twice a week – usually once on a school night and again at weekends. Most of the time I loved it. I loved the getting ready, putting on the outfits Mum and Auntie Theresa had sewn for us, then hearing the applause of the audience and feeling the heat of the lights on my face as I walked out on stage.

'Don't you get scared?' kids at school sometimes asked me. But that never occurred to me. I was surrounded by my family. All the way to the gig we'd be laughing and joking and singing and then we'd just go out and sing some more in front of a load of people who liked us. It felt like the most natural thing in the world.

We'd perform at working men's clubs, British Legion clubs, dance halls and theatres all across Lancashire, Yorkshire and up into Scotland. Most of the time me and Bernie just thought it was all an incredible adventure. But there were sacrifices too. Other kids would be off to birthday parties or out on a trip to the cinema but I would never be allowed to go if it was show night. Dad made it clear from the beginning that work came before everything. And while Mum would be running around making hot drinks if we felt poorly or dabbing

us better with TCP if we'd fallen over and cut our knee, with
Dad there was never any question that whatever had happened the show must go on.

I can see now it must have been even harder for my older
sisters and brothers. They were well into their teens but had
no say at all in whether they spent all their spare time travelling around the country to perform in nightclubs with their
kid sisters when they'd probably far rather have been out on
the town with their mates.

For me, though, the performing was the most fabulous feeling on earth. But all the hanging around that comes with it was
a whole lot less fun. When we were doing a club we would
usually be booked for two hour-long spots so we'd have to
wait around between our couple of appearances. More often
than not the dressing room in a working men's club was the
size of a shoebox, which meant we'd spill out onto corridor
floors, tired, bored and grouchy. Other times we'd go outside
and chase each other up and down the street.

We were introduced into an adult world very soon. On one
occasion that was particularly scary.

Often at the end of the evening I used to enjoy going round
the club collecting dirty glasses and stacking them behind the
bar. It made me feel like one of those super-glamorous bar-
maids of the time. One evening, when I was about eleven, I
was still tidying glasses when I realized Mum and Dad and
all the others had left the club and gone out to the car. I guess
when you've got as many kids as they had it was quite easy
to forget about one. I ran into the dressing room to collect
my belongings, scared I was going to be left behind. But in
the dressing room was another of the entertainers. He was in
his thirties and we'd worked with him lots of times so I knew

him well. He'd been chatting to me and my sisters earlier in the evening but this time he seemed very different.

'Where's your mum and dad?' he asked, staring intently at me.

'They've gone. I've got to catch them up,' I said, grabbing my costume and shoes from a hanger.

Suddenly I became aware of him right up close to me. He was pushing his body closer and closer to me and I felt myself being squeezed between him and the wall. I really had no idea what was happening. Then suddenly his face was pushed into mine and he'd forced his tongue into my mouth. I was so utterly stunned by what was happening that I didn't even try to stop him.

I was very innocent – all us Nolan kids were – and I didn't even realize that was how people kissed. To me it was just bizarre as well as disgusting that a grown adult would want to stick his tongue in my mouth. But I knew it was wrong. Instinctively, I just knew. I squirmed out of his way and ran out the door as fast as I could. I sprinted to the car, shaking with fear, but no one even seemed to have noticed I was missing.

'Jump in, Linda,' Mum said. And that was it. I was far too embarrassed to mention anything about it to Mum or my sisters. I would have been mortified for them to know what had happened and I wouldn't have dared talk about such a thing.

It was another confusing aspect of adults' lives. Like Dad and his drinking. Every night when we were performing he'd insist on drinking as much as he could. And even after we'd finished and the club was shutting up Dad would almost always still be there at the bar, chatting to whoever was still around. Mum would be pleading: 'Tommy, please can we go now, the children are shattered.' But still he'd carry on drinking and talking.

And then of course he'd get back in the car and drive us all home. Mum would bring a pillow for me and Bernie to put our heads on while she somehow managed to hold Coleen and doze herself. Anne and Denise would be squeezed into the front alongside Dad in the driver's seat. We had a minibus at one point, which meant Mum could make beds up for us in the back of it. We'd only wake up as we pulled up outside Waterloo Road. Then we'd drag ourselves out into the cold and up to bed, sometimes at two or three o'clock in the morning. Four hours later and we'd be back up for school.

Several times I fell asleep at the back of the class. Goodness knows what the teachers thought but I don't ever remember them calling in Mum or Dad to ask what was going on. Maybe they understood. It was a different time.

And the touring and performing wasn't all bad, by any means. On our way to a show we'd play games or sing together. Anne, Denise and Maureen were in the school choir and they'd teach us the hymns and all the harmonies that they could do. The girls taught us to do three-part harmonies for Brahms' 'Lullaby' in French, German and Irish. It was great practice.

We'd been doing the summer season at the Brunswick Club for a few years, and I was about eleven when the law changed, which meant that Bernie and I would no longer be allowed to perform every night. I guess the legislation was to prevent kids being exploited – but at the time I was outraged. Instead of staying at the club with the older kids, me and Bernie had to be fetched home by Auntie Theresa as soon as our first eight o'clock spot was over.

'This is totally unfair,' I shouted, stomping off the first time me and Bernie were packed home to bed. But after a few weeks we both quite liked it. We still got our moment on stage but then we were free. And Mum soon trusted us to get ourselves home, so we'd walk up to the bus stop on our own, stopping for chips and gravy on the way. What a treat.

Even our holidays weren't holidays as such. During the six-week summer break or at Easter and half term we'd be off on a tour round Scotland or Wales.

It was while we were on a tour around Scotland that I met a lad called Neil Reid who was also touring up there. He'd won *Opportunity Knocks* and had a number-one-selling album. In his act he'd dress in traditional Scottish tartan kilt and flouncy shirt. He was hugely popular at the time and everyone loved him. But he was also just a normal kid too. He was a skinny little thing with floppy dark hair and a sweet face. In between shows we'd get chatting and when we were travelling from show to show we'd sing together in the back of the minibus. Then when we got to venues we'd play It out in the street with Bernie. It was strange: we were living that crazy life of performing every night but we were all still just normal kids too. I was twelve and he was probably a couple of years older. We didn't so much as kiss but in my head he was 'my boyfriend'. Young love, eh?

Dad would have exploded at the mere thought of the word 'boyfriend'. 'Not for my girls,' he'd say. Even the oldest girls, Anne and Denise, weren't supposed to be doing that sort of thing, so me and Bernie definitely weren't.

But within a couple of years there wasn't any stopping us!

Or so we thought. One day Suzanne and I sneaked out while our mums were busy to meet up with a crowd of boys we'd got chatting to in the town one Saturday. Their school, St Thomas's, was right next door to ours so it felt like fate!

We all went to the indoor funfair, had a few goes on the rides and just hung around in the way young teenagers do. But by the time we got home to Waterloo Road both our mums were standing on their front steps in full-on furies. 'Oh God, here it comes,' I mumbled to Suzanne as we both darted past our mums as they started yelling at us. You could never get away with anything in Blackpool because it was such a close-knit town then. And because everyone knew me and my sisters from the singing, it was harder than ever.

By the time I was thirteen, my eldest brother Tommy was twenty-three and out at work. He had long hair and a Fu Manchu moustache, spent weekends playing his drum set in his bedroom and was seriously into heavy metal music. The pounding beat of Black Sabbath coming from the boys' bedroom drove Sinatra fan Dad potty. 'Get that off,' he'd yell, 'it's just noise.'

Brian was three years older than me so we were closer. That said, we could fight like cat and dog too. When we were performing we'd duet on a collection of songs from *Mary Poppins* but he was becoming more independent by then and wasn't so keen on being part of the Nolan Family. He'd rather hang out with his friends, all done out in their Ben Sherman shirts and braces. Me and Bernie used to mill around the front room as they prepared to go off to watch football together, giggling and trying our best to flirt with them.

And then there were my sisters. Anne was the eldest and very much the leader. She was nine years older than me so by then she had a job as Dad's secretary. The pair of them were very close. Although it was only much later that we would discover how close – and how terrible – that relationship had become when Anne revealed to us all that Dad had abused her from when she was eleven. But back then there was nothing, nothing at all, which could have made us suspect anything other than a close relationship between a dad and his eldest daughter. Anything more would have been too much for us to even imagine.

Every Friday when she got paid, Anne would return home with a comic book for all the kids. Brian got the *Beezer*, I got *Bunty*, Bernie got *Jackie* and Coleen had *Teddy*. That was typical of Anne – always thinking about the little ones and getting us all organized.

Denise, who was seven years older than me, was like our Mother Hen. When Bernie and Coleen were babies it was Denise who quite often bundled them into the pram and took them for walks down to the seafront on South Shore. And she was a great storyteller. She could make up the most amazing tales in her head to get us off to sleep. She was brilliant at fairy stories, but some of her descriptions of people breaking down in their car on a dark night and having to beg for help at a spooky house (very *Scooby-Doo*!) certainly didn't help us drop off. When we were older she'd blow-dry my and Bernie's hair after we'd had our bath. She was very loving.

And then there was Maureen. She was the quiet, gentle one. Always laid-back and beautiful, inside and out.

Anne, Denise and Maureen were an incredibly tight little threesome. They did everything together and felt a lot older than me. Bernie remained my closest playmate in the family, although we could have the most terrible fights at times too.

I guess that's the thing about a big family. There's always someone to chat and have a laugh with – but there's generally someone to fight with too! It was certainly a noisy house, from first thing in the morning until last thing at night. I speak quite loudly anyway, and just as well – in our house it was the only way to be heard.

It was strange being the sixth child. Everyone else seemed to be special in some way. Anne was the eldest of us girls, Denise had the amazing voice and Maureen was the beautiful one. And by then they were out performing most nights in clubs with Mum and Dad as The Singing Nolans. At home they'd be chatting about make-up and boys and things I wasn't involved in. So I wasn't part of that group and of course I wasn't in with the boys either, who were off doing whatever it was boys did. And then Bernie and Coleen were the babies.

Mum was always busy and I wasn't a Daddy's Girl either. Not like Bernie – she and Dad got on so well. I just didn't quite fit in anywhere; I was stuck in limbo as the middle daughter, which I think is just one of those things in big families. I don't blame anyone for it. But in the family I got a bit of a reputation as an attention-seeker. Once, when we were still living at Uncle Fred's, Brian and I were chasing each other round the house. I was holding a toy floor brush and in the rough and tumble I clonked him over the head. There was blood everywhere and I was in terrible trouble for 'showing off'. To this day, I say I was just excited and behaving the way excited little girls do. But somehow the idea that I was a show-off became my label.

Looking back, I don't think I was showing off, I was just hoping that someone, anyone, might notice me. Sometimes I feel sad for that little girl. I've got a photo of me, Bernie and Brian standing by a piano, taken in a studio. It's a lovely photo but when I look into my eyes in the picture, all I see is a small girl who didn't want to be called bossy or a show-off. She just wanted to be noticed.

I don't ever remember Mum or Dad saying they loved me, although that's perhaps more an issue of their generation. I'm certain they did love me. But something was sort of missing. If we'd been performing a show late at night and we were bundled on the back seat on the way home, Coleen would be sat on Mum's knee and Bernie would be cuddled up next to her. I remember thinking: 'What about me? I'm tired too.' But I didn't say anything of course. And I'm not complaining now. With eight kids to look after, Mum barely had time to stand up straight, let alone make a fuss over me. And Mum and Dad were good parents. But maybe, just maybe, I wanted to feel special too.

Each week Mum and Dad would take one of us, on our own without brothers and sisters, to dinner at the Golden Egg restaurant in Blackpool then on to the cinema for a film of our choice. Every couple of months, when my turn came, I felt like I'd won the golden ticket. I remember them taking me to see *The Wizard of Oz*. The film was brilliant, but having Mum and Dad to myself was perfect. For me, that really was the end of the rainbow.

Three

Success and Secrets

Behind the sugar-sweet harmonies and the whiter-than-white Von Trapp image, there were things going on at home which were beginning to feel far darker.

I think Dad's frustrations at life had grown greater and he was drinking more and more. On the nights we weren't performing as a family Dad would still go out to the clubs. Sometimes Mum would be performing with him, sometimes he went alone. Either way he was clearly around alcohol more than was good for him. I was too young to fully understand that then. All I knew was that when he came in late he'd most often be in a foul temper. If he'd been drinking, the whole mood in the house changed the moment he walked in. He'd appear in the front room all edgy and ready to pick an argument with anyone who irritated him. He could turn at the flick of a switch – and it was terrifying. A little bit of saliva would form at the corner of his mouth and we knew he was building up for something. It's funny how that detail lives with you so many years later.

It was particularly difficult for the older girls because they wanted to be out enjoying themselves but Dad was still putting them under huge pressure to do the singing jobs, whether they wanted to or not. And he was just as strict about what they could do and wear even when they were in their late teens and working. Some nights the girls would wait until Dad went off to one of the clubs, then sneak out of the house to meet their friends at a disco. Mum would let them but then she'd be fretting all evening that Dad would get back before them and there would be a terrible row. One Monday evening Mum got a message that Dad was coming home early and she sent Brian out at top speed to find Denise and Maureen at the disco and drag them home. Meanwhile, she stuck pillows under their bedspreads in the hope that if Dad looked in he'd be fooled into thinking they were already in bed. Fortunately he never checked; the girls slipped back in after he was asleep and another volcanic eruption was avoided.

As a special treat Mum sometimes let us younger ones – me, Bernie and Coleen – stay up with her and fall asleep on the couch. One night I woke up on the sofa to the sound of terrible shouting. This was even worse than the thuds and bumps we'd heard from our beds in the past. Dad was screaming and shouting at Mum and she wouldn't back down, so it went on and on. I was terrified he was going to hit her but had no idea what to do. I felt completely lost and powerless to stop this horror going on around me. Soon after that there was another blazing row after Dad had been drinking and I did see him lash out at Mum. I'm not sure what he did, it's almost like I've blocked out some of those memories, but I do remember blood gushing from her leg. It was horrifying.

Another evening, me, Bernie and Coleen were up in our room, chatting, giggling and messing on, the way sisters do.

'Will you girls be quiet up there and get to sleep,' Mum yelled up the stairs. Five minutes later she was having to shout up to us again as we were still fooling around.

There was no third warning. The next thing we knew, Dad had stormed into the room and by the look on his face we instantly knew he'd been drinking. I heard the most terrific slap as he lashed out on the back of Bernie's legs as she lay on the bed. Then I felt the stinging pain as he did it to me. Finally he smacked little Coleen, who really hadn't been messing around at all.

He knew Coleen had been lying there quietly but he still did it – and that was what seemed so unforgivable afterwards. All three of us cried ourselves to sleep into our pillows. Poor Coleen was so devastated she was too scared to even get out of the bed, and wet herself in the night. I don't think she ever forgot about that night. None of us did.

Another time Anne was insisting on watching some programme on television she'd been looking forward to. Of course it was the days of one TV set per house and you either had to compromise on what you watched, or lump it. On this occasion Dad said there was 'no way' we'd be watching the programme Anne wanted. He'd clearly had a few drinks and was like a bomb waiting to go off but Anne refused to back down. We were all willing her just to turn the telly over and forget it but she was determined. The row went on and on until Dad suddenly lashed out at Anne, hitting her across the face with the back of his hand. She was so brave, refusing to cry in front of him. It was awful, terrifying. I just wanted to disappear from the room.

But still, despite the drinking getting worse, Dad could be the most loving father you could ever hope to have when he was sober. He had the ability to make the most ordinary moments magical. As for Christmas, well that truly was magical in our house.

Christmas is special in any family but with so many kids, aunties and uncles it seemed extra special at ours. When we were very young Dad would always take us on Christmas Eve to Lewis's department store in the town centre to see Santa Claus. And then we'd spend the next few days gathered around the television watching Disney movies. We were all reared on Disney in our house.

You can imagine how many presents were piled up in the front room when we were all very little – it would be like a toy shop. One year alone there were three bikes, two prams and two train sets. Mum was clever, though, because she said Santa never wrapped presents. If he did she would have been there all year doing it! How on earth they afforded it all I don't know.

Even when us kids were all in our teens, the magic of Christmas in our house remained the same. There was still the enormous pile of presents in the front room and then as many people for Christmas lunch as we could squeeze round the table. And then some more as well. Our Auntie Theresa always came for Christmas Day lunch and often there were other members of Mum's family and Dad's mum and sisters too. One year there were twenty-two of us perched round the table on chairs of every shape and size, most borrowed from neighbours.

And what a feast Christmas dinner was. Prawn cocktail or melon for a starter, then turkey, roast potatoes, mashed potatoes, the best mushy peas on earth, sprouts, stuffing, homemade bread sauce, carrots and gravy. All that on a four-ring cooker! And of course all followed by homemade Christmas cake.

I think a big reason why Christmas was always so special

was that it was the only time of the year when we didn't work and were like any other family. Mum and Dad had a cast-iron rule which we all loved: 'The Nolans don't work Christmas.'

Because Christmas Day was so special to Mum and Dad as well as us kids, we knew there was no way Dad would agree when we were asked to perform one year at the Cliffs Hotel in Blackpool. The boss of the place had come round to see him, pleading with him to bring us along for a special show at lunchtime on Christmas Day. Apparently a guy from London called Joe Lewis, who was managing director of the Hanover Grand entertainment company, was coming to stay and they wanted to put on the best show Blackpool could offer.

'No, not doing it,' Dad said first off without even thinking.

But then the boss of the Cliffs Hotel came back and offered even more money.

'Still no,' Dad replied, sucking on the endless stream of cigarettes which were in and out of his mouth. Despite being the ultimate entertainer and showman he really believed Christmas should be about family not work.

Finally the boss of the Cliffs Hotel came back and said: 'OK, Tommy, name your price.'

'All right then,' Dad said, laughing. He asked for an enormous sum of money – we'd never been paid anywhere near that to perform. Dad must have been fairly certain they'd turn him down flat.

'Done,' came the reply.

Dad was flabbergasted. 'Well it'll pay for Christmas, I suppose,' he said, smiling at Mum.

So that Christmas Day lunchtime we were all lined up at

the Cliffs Hotel wearing knee-length socks and matching frocks hot off Auntie Theresa's sewing machine, singing a selection of songs from *The Sound of Music*. We closed with 'Danny Boy' which by then had kind of become our signature tune. What I didn't realize then of course – none of us did – was that Christmas Day, 1973, was to be the beginning of our professional careers.

After the show Joe Lewis, a slight but sharply dressed man, only about the same height as Dad, rushed over to us.

'You've got to come to London,' he said, bubbling with energy. 'These girls are going to be stars. Mega stars.'

Of course us girls were incredibly excited as we heard this dapper Londoner promising the earth to Dad; it really was like all our Christmases had come at once.

Years later Joe Lewis's entertainment industry expanded such that he became one of the world's richest men, with a £6 billion fortune. At the time he must have seemed to Dad like just another sharp-talking southerner peddling dreams. But what could he deliver?

Dad was worried about moving to London. He'd never have admitted it to anyone back then, but now I wonder if he was scared. In Blackpool he was a big fish and able to control everything we did. In London he'd be a small fish in a very big pond. And he wasn't daft. He knew that in London there'd be all sorts of wheelers and dealers wanting to get involved in our careers. And take their slice of the profits. Could he still protect us in that environment? Perhaps he wasn't sure that he could. And perhaps he also wondered what a move to London would mean for *his* career and *his* dreams. And his family. Because another big issue was that Mr Lewis, as we always referred to him, was interested in just the six girls performing an act in his cabaret theatre, the London Rooms, in Drury Lane.

In Blackpool it had been us girls along with Mum, Dad, Tommy and Brian. Going to London would mean breaking up the family – both on stage and in reality. The boys didn't want to move to London so someone would have to stay with them in Blackpool. It was a huge dilemma. But Joe Lewis wasn't the kind of guy who took no for an answer. Which I guess is why he ended up one of the richest men on the planet. For weeks there were messages going backwards and forwards between London and Blackpool and lots of whispered late-night conversations between Mum and Dad.

We girls were desperate for our parents to sign Mr Lewis's contract. But for ages it looked like Dad just wasn't going to agree. 'I'm just not sure about it,' was all he would say.

We knew Mum was our best hope. She was always easier to win over in an argument than Dad, so the five of us older girls piled on the pressure. Coleen wasn't bothered about going. She was still young and wanted to stay in Blackpool with her friends at school. But Bernie and I never stopped pestering.

'Please Mum, please Mum, pleeeease can we go to London, we're going to be famous,' I'd whinge and whine day and night.

Mum was nervous. And rightly so. Anne was almost twenty-four by then, Denise twenty-three, and Maureen nineteen, but I was just fourteen and Bernie had turned thirteen. And London seemed like another world. She must have been terrified about what might happen to her daughters once they'd hit the bright lights. But she also knew how much we loved performing and how standing in our way could have led to a lifetime of regrets. And she knew all too well what regrets can do to someone.

There were more meetings with Mr Lewis's agent from London. Gradually it was agreed that Mum would chaperone us at all times and we'd even live in Mr Lewis's home with his wife and daughter when we first moved down south. And so finally Mum agreed to sign the contract. Dad never really agreed, but he stopped opposing the plan too.

The deal was done. We were to be paid £1,000 a week, which seemed like a fortune. There were to be the regular gigs at the London Rooms, a recording contract and even the chance of TV shows. It was all our dreams come true, and more. It truly was the chance of a lifetime and I instinctively understood that, even though I was only fourteen.

Of course I didn't have the first clue what a West End night-club would look like, but in my mind I imagined a lot of gold leaf and red velvet fittings. It sounded like the pinnacle of glamour and a world away from sitting in the corridors of working men's clubs, which we'd been doing for nearly ten years.

We were on our way to the big time . . .

Four

The Big Time

Bernie and I looked at each other across the vast double bed. The sheets were thick and ice white. You didn't need to have seen expensive bed linen to work out this was what expensive bed linen looked like! On the walls were huge oil paintings in gilt frames and the floor was covered in a carpet so deep we sank into it as we walked. And best of all, gazing out of our bedroom window in our new 'home' at Joe Lewis's mansion in Wentworth, Surrey, we could see the family's huge swimming pool and tennis courts.

That first morning at the Lewis mansion felt like we'd left Blackpool and been airlifted onto the set of a Hollywood movie. There was even a cook and a butler. Bernie and I had unpacked our suitcases and stashed them under the bed within minutes. There was no way we were going home any time soon!

The older girls were sharing another bedroom and Mum had her own room too. It was incredibly kind of Mr Lewis, his wife Esther, son Charles and daughter Vivienne to take us all in. Even though it was a huge house it must still have been a shock to suddenly have five noisy young women and their mother descend upon it. And really, it was the Lewises' kindness, far more than the swimming pool and snooker room,

47

which encouraged us to stay in London. Although, to be fair, the swimming pool helped. Especially for me and Bernie, who loved swimming. We thought we'd died and gone to heaven! And Vivienne and I became good friends as we were the same age.

It was strange our family being cut in half, though. It was decided Coleen was too young to be performing every night, and she was happy to stay in Blackpool as she enjoyed school, horse riding and her friends at home. Bernie and I would never have agreed to be left behind but Coleen didn't love performing in quite the same way we did. While we were away she moved in with our Auntie Theresa and Uncle Jim. She quite liked having a break from all the late-night shows and general chaos of our family life.

Tommy and Brian had stayed back too – Tommy was in his mid-twenties by then and had landed a good job as a sales-man, and Brian was about to finish school and start work too. Dad's day job as a bookkeeper meant he also needed to remain at home, but he was constantly travelling backwards and forwards to London to see how we were getting on.

Although The Nolan Sisters would be performing every night at Mr Lewis's cabaret club, because Bernie and I were younger we could only legally do two or three performances a week so we alternated them between us. The venue was hugely popular with tourists and Londoners who wanted a special evening out with good food and a range of cabaret entertainment. Sometimes it could be booked out for months in advance.

But as well as performing live, Mr Lewis still had big dreams of getting us a record deal. Within days of arriving in London we were in a recording studio working on possible singles with a small label called Target Records. Each night we went home dreaming of one day being on *Top of the Pops*.

'We need to sort out the girls' image,' Mr Lewis said, looking us up and down, soon after we arrived in London. Back in Blackpool we'd still been performing in matching frocks and knee-high socks. But if we were heading for the big time, we needed to look the part.

Mr Lewis brought in a manager called Robert Earl who'd been a famous singer himself during the fifties. He and his wife Daphne were charged with creating an image which would sell. They hired costume designers who went away and a couple of weeks later reappeared with our first stage costumes – white halter-neck catsuits with 20-inch flares. Embroidered in diamanté on the flares were the initials NS for Nolan Sisters, as we were now to be known.

There were little jackets to match, again with the diamanté NS logo. I know none of this sounds great now, but, bear with me, it was 1974 and this was the height of fashion. And it was a whole lot better than my St Catherine's school uniform which I'd been wearing the week before.

We were also presented with matching lemon chiffon floor-length frocks. We weren't so keen on those but at least we finally looked like pop stars of the day.

Robert and Daphne Earl also hired a choreographer – Nigel Lythgoe, who later became a household name in *Pop Idol* – to help us work out some simple dance routines for our shows. Nigel was in his mid twenties then and hugely famous as part of the BBC's Young Generation dance troupe which performed on all the big shows. He was ever so handsome and I think all of us sisters had a little crush on him. Whenever he was teaching us a new routine and he had to hold our arms or waist to get us into the right body position we'd all have a little giggle.

The management team also brought in professional make-up artists to show us how to do our stage make-up.

While all that was going on we spent six weeks solidly rehearsing our London Rooms show. Alyn Ainsworth was our musical director and Stewart Morris, a top BBC producer, put together a sixty-minute spot. We were to be on stage with a live band which we'd never worked with before, so it took some practice. And the dance routines had to be perfect. We were in no doubt we were now in the big time and there would be no room for mistakes. Fortunately Mum and Dad had brought us up to be utterly professional about our work. We were girls who loved a laugh and a joke but when it came to performing we were dead serious.

After all that preparation, finally we were ready for our launch night at the London Rooms in Drury Lane. I thought the London Rooms were the epitome of glamour – just like the clubs we'd seen in all those Hollywood movies. It was decorated in deep shades of red with gold cloths and napkins on the tables, which were arranged in tiers around the stage. The audience were able to come in for an entire evening of dinner, drinks and then the cabaret. It was very classy and the idea of performing there in the heart of the West End was still hard to believe. That first night we were dying of nerves. To make things worse, Maureen came down with a terrible sore throat.

But Maureen is a trooper and there was never any doubt the show would go on. We had been rehearsing for weeks and knew exactly what we were doing so there was no reason why anything should go wrong. But that didn't stop us panicking that it might, not least because we knew there were record executives and showbiz producers coming to watch us.

Our opening number was The Four Tops' 'Reach Out and I'll Be There'. When we finished the audience all cheered and clapped for ages. What a relief. They liked us. And the more we sang, the more they seemed to like us. Cliff Richard was actually in the audience, as our unveiling at the London Rooms had been hyped up for weeks in the gossip columns and across the London showbiz world. I think I might just have managed to say 'hello' to Cliff as he was swept past by his entourage, but the whole evening was a whirl. It was all desperately exciting.

When we finished our final song, which was an old Osmonds number, there was a standing ovation from the audience. We'd done it. We were all euphoric. We went back to our dressing room, which was packed with bouquets of flowers, and were literally jumping up and down and squealing with excitement.

All we had to do then was wait for the all-important critics' reviews in the press the next day. Fortunately they loved us. From then on the customers kept coming and we kept singing.

Again, Bernie and I had the best of both worlds, in that we were performing two or three times a week but on our enforced nights off we were able to go to the theatre or cinema with Mr Lewis and Vivienne. Or else we'd stay home and watch their massive TV on their sumptuous sofas.

It was a win, win, win situation for us.

For the older girls, performing until late six nights out of seven probably wasn't quite so much fun once the novelty had worn off. Yes of course it was glamorous and had opened up a whole new world, but it was also pretty relentless.

Occasionally at weekends and in school holidays Coleen would come down and join us. It was a strain on all of us, living at different ends of the country.

We were being talked about by promoters in the entertainment world and it was clear we wouldn't be going back to Blackpool any time soon so Mum and Dad decided we should find our own home.

After a few months of looking Mum found a house in Granville Road, Ilford, east London. It was a bit of a comedown from Mr Lewis's mansion but it was a beautiful, huge double-fronted house which had previously been a doctor's surgery. There were grand steps up to the front door and high ceilings. Oh yes, and a conservatory. We were definitely going up in the world!

Bernie and I still shared a room with twin beds and the older girls had their own room. Dad was still flitting back and forth between Blackpool and Ilford but when he was down south he and Mum remained in determinedly separate bedrooms.

Mum and Dad enrolled me and Bernie at a private school in Ilford – Clark's School for Girls. We'd missed a lot of schooling by then and it was decided it would be better to go into a private school with small classes which could cope with us being a bit behind our peers, rather than hurling us into exam year at a big comprehensive nearby. We made friends there and when Coleen moved down she joined too and loved it. But I was coming up for sixteen by then and really any hope of my getting a decent education was long gone. The only thing I cared about was performing and I left school as soon as I was allowed.

In many ways Mum and Dad were more relaxed about

everything since we'd moved to London. Dad wasn't drinking so much and there were fewer of the late-night yelling matches. He could still blow a fuse at times but generally life seemed calmer. Maybe coming to London had freed us from his control and changed the dynamic. The spell had been broken.

As part of our contract, Dad sometimes sang at the London Rooms too. It wasn't the regular work he'd had in Blackpool and I wonder if he felt he'd just got the spot as a sweetener so he'd agree to let us girls come to London. But he enjoyed it and I think he realized that things had changed once and for all.

Mum and Dad knew they were giving their girls incredible opportunities. It didn't get much better than being chosen to perform on Cliff Richard's new show for the BBC. Playing in one of the most famous clubs in London was thrilling – but television? This was amazing. We were all beside ourselves with excitement.

It was a six-week pre-recorded series and in each show we'd been booked to do a different song and then a big medley finale with Cliff. It meant lots of rehearsals, getting the harmonies and choreography absolutely perfect. During the weeks of rehearsals us girls would get a train from Ilford to Gants Hill, and be on the Central Line tube before the rush hour had even started. Six of us would be sat in a row, all asleep on the next one's shoulder. We'd somehow wake up just in time for our stop at North Acton where the BBC rehearsal studios were based.

We first met Cliff there in the rehearsal rooms and he was fabulous. He remembered us each by name and was incredibly professional. We still felt like a bunch of kids from

Blackpool and we were performing with one of Britain's best-loved stars – it was incredible.

Almost as incredible was going to the rehearsal rooms canteen. At that time the biggest show on telly was *Poldark* (the first time around!). All of us girls were mad about it. Christopher Biggins played Osborne Whitworth, 'the most hated man on TV'. And who was in the lift with us that very first day? Only dastardly Osborne Whitworth! We all gasped in horror the moment we saw him – we even managed to do that in harmony.

Another day, next to me alongside the trays of veg and shepherd's pie in the canteen was George Chakiris, the leader of the Sharks from *West Side Story*. I nearly choked on my chips.

All of Cliff's shows were pre-recorded and we just had to sit back and wait for them to be screened. For the first night of the show Mum had invited Auntie Theresa down and the house was full of friends and relatives. We were sick with nerves, even though we'd already filmed the whole show and knew full well nothing was about to go wrong. But when we saw ourselves on the screen in our floor-length frocks and television make-up, we all started screaming in a mix of excitement and confusion – it still didn't really feel this could be happening to us.

By the end of the third episode of the six-week series we were getting recognized in the street in Ilford and whenever we went on the tube. There were only three channels in those days so viewing figures were much higher. And because we all went everywhere together it made us even easier to spot.

Our next big break came when Stewart Morris heard that Frank Sinatra was looking for a new support act for his

European tour. He used an American comedian for the English-speaking shows but but needed a musical act in cities where there was a language barrier. We were one of five different bands put forward for the gig and Frank Sinatra, yes, that's FRANK SINATRA, looked at videos of the groups to make a final decision. And he chose us.

It's hard to explain what a big deal that was. We'd grown up with Dad singing Sinatra songs every night. He was Dad's idol. He'd helped shape our entire musical lives. And now we were going to be sharing a stage with the great man.

We were screaming when we found out, and Dad stood in the centre of the room, shaking with the shock of it all.

We saw every show and when we met him he was wonderfully courteous and generous. One evening we took Dad backstage.

'Mr Sinatra, this is our dad,' we said.

'Good evening, Mr Sinatra,' Dad croaked.

'Good evening, Mr Nolan,' he replied, shaking Dad's hand.

All his life Dad had dreamed of being like the man stood in front of him. It must have been extraordinary to meet him in the flesh.

The Sinatra tour took us to places we'd only previously heard of, like Vienna and Frankfurt. We'd been on an aeroplane when we were kids when we visited our grandparents in Ireland, but this time we were travelling with a full orchestra. Our bags were carried for us and we were greeted by chauffeur driven cars at every airport. We stayed at some of the best hotels in every city we visited. They were all four- or five-star places with huge bathrooms, deep carpets and fancy lightshades. We felt that we were being treated like royalty.

Fairly soon after that tour Dad packed in his job and moved to London. But even with him living under the same roof as his girls again, Dad's rule of iron was over. After years of trying to control everything the older girls did and everywhere they went, he seemed to have simply given up. To be fair they were grown women by then and loving the London life. As soon as they'd finished work at the London Rooms they'd be off out on the town to clubs with new friends they'd met. There were limousines and handsome men, disco dancing and fun, fun, fun. Not only that but Mum and Dad were paying us £150 a week each in cash. The first time I received my envelope I thought I'd won the Pools. It was probably an average wage for the time but I was still just a teenager with nothing much to spend it on than clothes and shoes, so for me it felt a fortune.

Once I'd turned sixteen I was adamant that if I could work as late as my older sisters, then I could party as late as them too!

The older girls quickly became regular fixtures on the London nightlife scene – their pictures would be in the gossip pages of the newspapers and they had a string of admirers. All the blokes fancied Maureen – she was beautiful, fun and sweet. But she was still very innocent too. Maybe that's why the men adored her so much.

Our regular haunts were Samantha's nightclub and The Valbonne in Soho. We didn't drink much, we just chatted and danced and lapped up the atmosphere. Afterwards we'd go on for something to eat at a place called Mike's Diner in Greek Street and then we'd roll home at dawn. Mum used to leave a key out in the milk bottle for us. And as we didn't have to be at work again until the following evening we could lie in bed the next morning for as long as we wanted.

It was round about then that Denise started dating Tom, who was a drummer at the London Rooms. We could all tell very soon that he was the one for Denise. They were a great pair – and forty-seven years later they still are!

I'd been going out on the town for a few months with my sisters and Linda Fleck, our Blackpool neighbour who had moved down to London to stay with us, when we all went out to celebrate at The Valbonne – and that's when I met this drop-dead gorgeous Persian guy called Mehrdad.

'Do you fancy coming for lunch tomorrow?' he asked, gazing at me with chestnut eyes you could swim in.

'Er, I'll have to ask my friend,' I said.

A minute later back with Linda I was begging her to come for lunch with me, Mehrdad and a friend of his the following day. 'Pleeeease,' I pleaded. 'He's absolutely gorgeous.'

Linda agreed and we went for the most lovely lunch. After that we started dating regularly. Mum and Dad knew about it but realized it wasn't too serious

Mehrdad was twenty-five, lived in a penthouse flat over-looking Hyde Park, and came from a hugely rich family. I'd go round to see him before our show at the London Rooms – or sometimes afterwards. I was convinced he was my first love but it was incredibly innocent. I only ever kissed him. We'd been dating for about eight months when Mehrdad announced he was moving to America.

'Come with me, Linda,' he said.

How fabulous to be asked, and I thought he was amazing, but of course I didn't go with him. I was too young to take such a big step with someone I hardly knew. Besides, performing was my life. At the same time, I was utterly heart-broken when we kissed goodbye at his flat for the final time. I went home in floods of tears. I was devastated – for all of about two days! I was having way too much fun to be sad about that for too long. And I still had my only one true love – and that was performing.

The next few years were a whirl of TV and tours. We did a six-week series of *The Two Ronnies*, then a series with Val Doonican, and another with Vince Hill. They were the biggest shows on television back then and it meant everywhere we went we'd be recognized as 'those singing sisters off the telly'. Then we did our first summer season with Ronnie Corbett in Eastbourne. The theatre was packed every night and Ronnie was lovely to us.

We were also chosen to do a two-week show with Engle-bert Humperdink in New York. We'd never been to America before and it was so exciting – New York looked just like the movies, right down to the yellow cabs and steam spewing out of the pavement. Dad hired a car and we toured the sights, ogling at the Statue of Liberty and Wall Street. One morning we went to the top of the Empire State Building. I couldn't believe how fast the lift went up – it didn't feel like there was anything like that in England.

We had a fabulous time on that show. At the end of each night we'd sit out at the stage door with the rest of the crew, cooking burgers on a little barbecue someone had found.

During that period somehow we became household names. OK, so we had a very sweet image, six Irish Catholic girls, but the millions of ordinary Brits who watched the Saturday night family shows on which we appeared loved us.

I think being sisters helped keep our feet on the ground. We knew each other so well that anyone who ever tried to get above their station quickly got slapped down – usually with a well-timed joke. And when you're still bickering over whose turn it is next in the shower and why no one put the lid back on the butter, it prevents it all becoming too serious.

Sometimes it could feel odd when we went back to Blackpool to see Tommy, Brian and Auntie Theresa. For us it felt like nothing had changed at all but we became aware that some people thought we'd got a bit full of ourselves. Some guys were horrible to Coleen one night in a club and it really upset her. But our real friends were only ever thrilled for us. And we were only ever thrilled to be back home. When I walked back down Waterloo Road the first thing I did was to go round to Suzanne's house and we'd sit in her front room gossiping as if I'd never been away.

In 1977 all six of us – Coleen was with us by then – toured South Africa with Rolf Harris, the comedian Stu Francis and ventriloquist Ray Alan and his hugely popular puppet Lord Charles. It was a fourteen-hour flight back then, which was the longest we'd ever been on an aeroplane. Poor Maureen was as sick as a dog. When we arrived they took us up onto the roof of our hotel in Johannesburg to take some publicity photographs and even then Maureen had to keep dashing off to throw up in a corner.

We were in Johannesburg for three weeks then on to Cape Town for a fortnight before moving on to East London and Durban. We were staying at a beautiful hotel in Johannesburg and the morning we arrived all of us girls decided we'd try out the gym facilities. Truth is we weren't really gym people and the following morning we were so stiff from all that exercise that we could barely walk. We decided to recover by lolling in the sauna for a while. We were all sat there, covering our modesty with fluffy white towels, when who should walk in but . . . the world's most celebrated womanizer of the time, Tom Jones.

He walked in, looked at us and burst out laughing. 'Oh my goodness,' he said. 'Don't move a muscle – can you imagine what the tabloids would make of me being in a sauna with six Nolan sisters!'

He was lovely and we sat and chatted for ages but I can report there was absolutely no scandal for the tabloids to miss.

There was a little romance for me, though. Us girls spent quite a bit of time with Tom Jones's orchestra as we were all staying in the same hotel. They were great fun to hang out with in the evenings and so when Mum, Dad and Coleen booked a safari, I decided to stay in the city with my sisters and our new friends. There was a sax player who was gorgeous and I really fell for him. When he asked me out to the cinema I was thrilled. It was very, very sweet and innocent though – we didn't even kiss.

I celebrated my seventeenth birthday on that tour so I was still very young. Which is what made one aspect of that trip so upsetting. And looking back now it feels far more sinister than I ever realized at the time.

During the tour we hadn't spent much time with Rolf Harris, who was there with his wife. They kept themselves to themselves during the daytime but they were both very friendly when we did see them.

One evening I was in a bathrobe in the dressing room at the theatre just putting on my make-up when I decided to quickly pop down the corridor to use the loo. I don't remember seeing Rolf when I went into the toilet, but when I came out of it, there he was facing me in the corridor.

'Hello, Linda,' he oozed.

'Hi, Rolf,' I replied, knowing what was coming next. My sisters and I had already clocked that he was incapable of walking past any of us without lurching in for a hug. But some blokes were like that.

That night was different though. He pulled me towards him in the corridor and wrapped his arms around me so tightly that his hands came all the way round until they were groping my boobs. Then I could feel his tongue licking my neck as he pushed himself against me.

'Stop it, Rolf,' I said, trying to push myself away from him. But still it went on. 'Please, Rolf, no,' I said, feeling more and more stressed about what was going on. I pushed again and after what felt like a lifetime he took a step back.

'I was only joking, Linda,' he said, smiling. And then instantly I felt silly for making such a fuss. It definitely hadn't felt like a friendly hug. 'But maybe I'm just being oversensitive,' I thought as I walked back to our dressing room.

And because I really didn't understand exactly what had happened there I didn't mention it to a soul. But I made sure I was never alone with Rolf for the rest of that tour – and I wouldn't let Coleen, who was still just twelve, anywhere near him.

Early in 2013, I was round at Maureen's when a report came on the radio.

'Police have arrested a TV entertainer in his eighties for a number of historic sexual offences,' the newsreader said.

'I bet that's Rolf Harris,' I said, turning to Maureen.

'How can you possibly know that?' she replied.

'Because he did it to me,' I said simply.

'What?' she said. 'What do you mean?'

And I told her the whole story. Of course what happened to me was nothing compared with the terrible ordeal he put some of his young victims through – but it showed what he was capable of, given the opportunity.

It was a different world back in the seventies and women didn't normally complain about being groped by dirty old men. I guess that's why they went on to abuse more and more women; and with the more vulnerable ones they were able to get away with the most awful things.

Apart from that incident it was a great tour. In fact all the tours and the TV appearances were the most tremendous fun. But what we all wanted then more than anything else was for one of our singles to do well in the charts. We'd recorded seven by then and each one had flopped.

We had a reputation of being a bit sickly-sweet goody-two-shoes. That had been brilliant for Saturday night light entertainment shows but it wasn't the sort of music teenagers would buy with their own money. Still, we kept on trying and I kept on hoping one day we'd make it onto *Top of the Pops*.

But not all of us felt the same.

'I've got something to say,' Denise said one day as we sat in the big front room of our house in Ilford. 'I want to leave the band.'

'Oh, Denise, no,' I said. It wasn't entirely surprising, Denise had been mulling it over for a few months. But announcing it like this was still a shock.

Denise had – and still has – the most incredible voice. If we were doing a cabaret show and it wasn't going brilliantly it would be her voice that saved the night. She would go out and sing 'This Is My Life' or 'I Who Have Nothing' and make the hairs on the back of your neck stand up. But when we'd been recording pop songs it tended to be me or Maureen who did the slower ballads while Bernie took the lead in the up-tempo tunes. On top of that Denise had never enjoyed all the choreography we needed to learn for the TV shows. And by then she'd met Tom, they were happy together and she felt ready to go it alone on her own terms. So we all understood her reasons. And there was no animosity or falling out. But it was still terribly sad to think she wouldn't be on stage with us any more after all those years.

The first time we performed without her felt like we were missing a limb. But then Coleen joined the band full time and so we carried on. And we still saw Denise all the time too. There was no bad feeling. I think she was just twenty-six and ready to take control of her life.

Maureen was dating the West Ham footballer Billy Jennings by then. Anne had a few boyfriends though nothing serious and I was out partying most nights of the week. Although none of the others had any plans to leave the band it was clear we were all pushing the boundaries towards greater independence.

We were no longer girls, we were women.

Five

Falling in Love For Ever

Christmas stockings hung around the enormous fireplace of our house in Ilford as my sisters and I stood there singing a Christmas song in close harmony. Fairy lights twinkled in the background and it felt utterly magical. In fact that evening was to become the most magical of my entire life.

It was December 1979, and me and the girls were filming the *Nationwide* Christmas Special in the front room of our home. As Britain's favourite early evening magazine show, *Nationwide* was watched by millions of people. But it turned out there was just one paying special attention to me.

A guy called Brian Hudson.

He was stood just off camera as filming began but I could feel his eyes on me the entire time we were singing.

Brian was Denise's new agent since she'd gone solo. He was about 5 foot 11 inches tall with thick dark hair, blue eyes and a smile that sparkled like sunshine on sea. He was gorgeous.

There was just one hitch. He was also married.

'He's only coming for the *Nationwide* show because he wants to meet you,' Denise had teased me earlier in the day.

'Get out,' I laughed. 'He doesn't know a thing about me.'

'Maybe, but he seems pretty certain you're the Nolan sister that he wants!'

Although Denise had left the group we still did occasional performances together like that night. And at Christmastime it was great to all be together again.

Denise had first mentioned Brian a couple of weeks earlier.

'I know someone who fancies you,' she'd laughed over dinner.

'Who? Who?' I'd demanded.

'Brian – my new agent,' she replied. 'In fact he is totally crazy about you – constantly asking what you're interested in, where you like going, what you enjoy doing.'

'Hasn't he got a wife, though?' I asked, pointing out the fairly obvious flaw in any such suggestion.

'Well he is still married,' said Denise. 'But I don't think they're actually "together", if you know what I mean.'

I didn't really, so I put the whole conversation right out of my head. But when I saw him that night at the Christmas show I could feel there was something there. It sounds corny, but there just was. I'd got home from a holiday in Florida with Bernie and Maureen the previous day so I was tanned and my hair was bleached white blonde. I was wearing a white dress and so, yeah, I was looking pretty good. I could feel Brian's eyes all over me.

After we'd finished filming I wandered into the kitchen to fetch a drink and there he was in front of me. I took one look at him close up and thought: 'Oh, hel-lo. You really are nice.'

When he'd left I said to Bernie as casually as I could manage: 'So, Denise's new agent seems nice.'

'Do NOT come crying to me,' Bernie said in a heartbeat, raising her eyes upwards.

'I only said he was nice,' I spluttered in mock outrage.

'Hmmm . . .' was Bernie's only response to that.

We always had a huge party on Christmas night at the house in Granville Road. Dozens of friends, neighbours and people we'd met in the entertainment industry since moving to London were all invited. It was set to be a great night. What I didn't know, however, was that Denise had also invited Brian, his wife Caroline and their little boy Lloyd, who was then four. As her agent it was only polite Denise should have invited them. But from the moment he stepped over the entrance to our house that night it was clear nothing was ever going to be the same again.

I was still just nineteen. I'd had boyfriends since moving to London but nothing serious and I was still very innocent. My last relationship had gone horribly wrong when I found out the guy who'd been leading me on for months and months had a wife safely at home. 'Avoid married men from now on,' I'd told myself. And I meant it. But Brian changed everything.

That night he started chatting to me in the kitchen and we got on so well. He was thirty-two, so thirteen years older than me, but he was gorgeous to look at and he made me laugh. He asked me about the band and what work we'd been doing and then told me about his life too. He'd grown up in Plaistow, east London, and started out playing drums and singing in harmony bands such as Tony Rivers and The Castaways, Capability Brown and Sparrow. Then he decided he wanted to go into music agenting and that's how he'd ended up working with Denise.

It was after midnight and most of the guests, including Brian and Caroline, were preparing to leave. Suddenly I found we'd been separated from the others and we were alone in the back room. He looked at me intently and said quietly: 'You and I are going to end up together.'

I just smiled at him. I mean, how do you answer that? And when he wandered down the front path I was a bit flabbergasted. He was clearly a confident kind of guy. And very attractive. But his wife was gorgeous, curvy with blonde hair and lovely to chat to. And there was no way on earth I'd do anything to upset the life of their gorgeous little boy.

Months later Brian told me he'd always fancied me when he'd seen me on television in the band. And then he said he just 'fell into my eyes that night'. I know that sounds daft to some people but there was an intensity to my relationship with Brian from that first evening.

Less than twenty-four hours later he had rung me at home.

'Hi, it was great seeing you last night,' he said.

'You too,' I replied. 'But you've got to understand – I'm really not interested in married men. I'm just not that kind of woman.'

'It's over between me and Caroline,' he said. 'Look, I know blokes always say that but it really is. We fell out of love a long time ago and have just been trying to do the right thing for Lloyd ever since.

'I really need to see you,' he went on. 'Please can I see you?'

I was already in deep. Way too deep. I was fascinated by this guy and unbelievably flattered by his attentions but I really, really was not the kind of girl who'd been brought up to help myself to other women's husbands. Plus, if my dad found out he'd go stark, staring mad.

'No,' I said firmly. 'I'm sorry, but no.'

That, however, wasn't the last I heard from Brian Hudson. He called me every day from then on. Sometimes dozens of times a day. I'd try to make an excuse that I was just going out or couldn't talk but other times we'd chat. Just for five minutes. Or maybe ten. The problem was we always seemed to have so much to talk about.

'Please, can I take you out,' he said one evening. 'Just the once.'

'Oh goodness,' I replied feeling flustered and knowing my resolve was melting like margarine in August. 'All right, but really, just this once.'

He drove over to pick me up – although obviously he couldn't knock on the door as I'd made up some colourful cover story to avoid telling my parents the truth about where I was off to. He'd booked a table at a little Italian restaurant in Hampstead, north London, and we spent the entire evening chatting and laughing. But unlike most other blokes I'd met up until that point he actually listened too. He seemed fascinated by everything I said. He seemed fascinated by me. Not just another Nolan. Me. We both loved music, we both loved entertaining, we both loved talking. We had so much in common.

I couldn't leave, though, without asking for the full truth about what was going on with his wife. It was pretty obvious we were serious about each other even though we hadn't even kissed. And certainly wouldn't be doing so until I could get to the truth.

Brian told me everything. How he'd first married a woman when he was very young and had a daughter, Sarah, who'd been adopted by his ex-wife's new partner. That was back when Brian was constantly on the road touring. He admitted he probably hadn't been ready for the commitments of either marriage or parenthood. But he'd never forgotten about Sarah and still desperately missed her.

Soon afterwards he'd met Caroline but after a time things there had fallen apart too and they'd agreed to live separate lives while still sleeping under the same roof.

'She wouldn't mind about *this*, you know,' he said, touching my arm softly. 'She'd like to meet you properly and talk.'

Firstly, there was no '*this*'. Yet.

Secondly, it sounded like the worst idea in the world.

And even if his wife didn't mind about us seeing each other, I could pretty much guarantee my dad would. My parents might have become more lax in recent years but the mere thought of their nineteen-year-old daughter going out with a twice-married older man with two kids who was still living with his wife would send them into a full-on meltdown. They were still staunchly Irish Catholic in their faith and values (even if Dad rarely made it to mass). A married man was not what they had in mind for any of their daughters.

At the end of that first date Brian drove me home. We sat in the car just far enough away from our house not to be spotted, and chatted for hours.

'Better be off then,' I said finally.

'I love you, you know,' he said simply.

'Yeah, of course you do,' I laughed nervously, not quite knowing what to believe.

And then he leant across and kissed me. It was incredible.

Some people might have thought my falling in love with someone so utterly at odds with my parents' moral code was the ultimate act of rebellion. But it really wasn't. I was just falling, literally falling, into something enormous that I'd never known before and there seemed nothing I could do to stop it. I felt physically sick with nerves and excitement and happiness for days.

Brian and I began seeing each other in secret as often as we could. My parents were used to me going out most nights and so they rarely questioned what I was up to. I'd take a cab from home to nearby Gants Hill tube station and he'd be there waiting for me in his car.

And it really did seem that his wife was relaxed about our relationship. It sounds bizarre, but it was true. I'd even call him on his home number and Caroline would answer and chat for a bit before handing the phone over to Brian. Once, Brian was working abroad when we did a series of *The Mike Yarwood Show* and Caroline videoed the whole thing for him to watch when he got home. Of course I can't be absolutely certain what was going on in their marriage because I wasn't in it. And Brian still went home every night.

He was the first man who made me feel totally special. He was the first person in fact who'd ever looked at me as someone important in my own right. It felt incredibly liberating. I never ever wanted to be apart from him.

We saw each other and chatted on the phone whenever we could but it was so difficult because I was still living at home and Mum and Dad must have worked out I was up to something. I knew if it was going to continue I was just going to have to tell them the truth. I was scared because I knew they would be furious – but also genuinely worried about what I was getting myself into. But I couldn't bear to keep lying to them all the time, and, most importantly, I wanted to spend all my time with Brian. I couldn't do that unless I told them exactly what I was up to.

'You what?' yelled Dad. 'You're doing what with who? He's married.'

Mum just looked so sad.

'This is only going to end in heartache,' she said. 'And you'll be the one who gets their heart broken.'

Dad's view was more straightforward.

'No,' he said simply. 'He's married.'

I felt dreadful. I wasn't angry with my parents because I could understand why they were reacting that way. I was just desperate for them to like Brian as much as I did.

But no matter how often I told them about Brian's marriage being over and him and Caroline just being together for their son, it made no difference. As far as our dad was concerned, no man was good enough for one of his daughters. Let alone a married one.

I couldn't give him up, though. Couldn't. As the weeks went by I carried on sneaking out to be with Brian whenever I could. And as I was travelling back and forth to work every evening by then there was nothing much my parents could do to stop me.

Eventually, Dad would pass the phone over to me when he called. Then Mum would answer the door to him when he called to pick me up on a date. But they weren't happy about it. The only thing I could do was keep telling them that Brian's marriage really was over and try to persuade them to accept him. Gradually I think they saw how serious Brian was about me and the amount of time we were spending together meant he really must have split from his wife. And so, little by little, they welcomed him into our home. The girls all got on with him and we were inseparable.

He would ring me twenty or thirty times a day and if I was

away on tour we would send each other two or three tele-grams a day. He would send flowers and teddies and the most beautiful love letters.

A few months after we'd been together I had a bit of a wobble and wondered if it was all just a bit too intense. I knew he was the man I wanted to spend the rest of my life with but I was still so young. Brian was devastated at even the thought of us splitting up.

'How can I make her really fall in love with me?' he asked Bernie one night.

'Stop bloody phoning all the time and give her some space,' she snapped back. If you ever needed honest advice, Bernie was your woman!

And of course it worked. Brian stopped phoning all the time. Then one evening he offered to give Denise, me and the other girls a lift into town. He joined us for a quick drink then said, 'Right, I'm off, see you soon,' and got into his car to drive off.

There was something about the moment when the car pulled away that crystallized everything for me. I thought: 'Oh my God. I love that man.' I turned back into the bar where the girls were waiting and announced: 'I'm going to be with him for the rest of my life.'

It was like a lightning bolt. And that was it. From then on I was in deeper than ever before. And there was no doubt it was for ever. Even spending a night without Brian had me pining. He'd stay over on a day bed in our downstairs cloak-room but there was so much sneaking between bedrooms in the middle of the night that in the end Mum said: 'For good-ness' sake, why don't the pair of you have my double bed when he's here and I'll move into the box room.'

It was a miracle!

Brian was the first man I'd been intimate with and it was special. Magical.

'Mum, could Brian move in, do you think?' I asked one morning soon after. 'He spends so much time here he might as well.' Amazingly, she and Dad agreed.

Then in the autumn of that year Brian said he'd seen a little flat near Mum and Dad's which would be perfect for us. The idea of having him all to myself day and night certainly sounded perfect to me. I wasn't much bothered what the flat looked like!

So we moved in soon after my twenty-first birthday. I guess it was all very serious and very fast. But I wasn't an idiot and certainly felt very mature. I'd been living and working in London since I was fifteen and had travelled round the world. Maybe everything in my life was just a bit accelerated.

From the very beginning I was the doting 'wife'. And he was the adoring 'husband'. Even if I'd been out singing in a club until the early hours I'd make sure I got up when he woke for work next morning and make him tea and toast. Then as soon as he'd gone to work I'd go back to bed. Often I'd get the tube into the centre of town to meet Brian at his office in the afternoon just so I could come home with him again in the car. It might sound a bit too intense for some people, but it was a very strong love and we needed each other in an almost addictive way.

I've always gone for older men. Maureen can spot the kind of guy I'll fancy at first glance – mature, confident, centre of attention. And Brian was all of these things. Perhaps I was looking for a father figure. Maybe. From the beginning he treated me like a princess. He looked after me. I wasn't to worry about anything because he would sort it. I know some women would find that suffocating but I loved it.

I felt safe with Brian. Secure. And I adored him.

He and his wife had begun the process of getting divorced and they were both so civilized and grown up about it that it meant Lloyd didn't suffer any more than he had to. At weekends he would come to stay with us and I loved helping to look after him. When his mum came to collect him she'd pop in for a cup of tea and it meant little Lloyd never felt he was growing up in a battleground.

Brian was invited for the big Nolan Christmas of 1980. All the family were there in Granville Road and there was the usual mass of presents, laughing and chaos under the tree. Brian was desperate for me to open his present and I was smiling as I opened the wrapping paper and saw it was a box of my favourite Rive Gauche perfume. Except it felt rather light for a bottle of perfume. I felt my stomach spin. I knew exactly what was coming next. I knew everything Brian thought and felt – just as he did with me.

Inside the box was the most beautiful sparkling engagement ring. One large diamond in the middle, a cluster of smaller diamonds around it. I started squealing, my sisters started screaming. Everyone was hysterical. I leapt on Brian and wrapped my arms around him. And there was no need for an answer because, like I said, he knew everything I thought and felt. And the answer was only ever going to be yes.

Even Mum and Dad were delighted. I was still young and the relationship may not have started out the way they might have hoped, but they could see how happy I was.

On 28 August 1981, just twenty months since we'd first met, Brian and I were married at the register office in Blackpool followed the next day by a beautiful ceremony at the town's St Paul's Church. I wore a lace and diamanté meringue dress (think Princess Diana – it was the same year!) which cost Dad more than £3,000 from a boutique in London. There was no expense spared. But I was in no doubt this was going to be a once in a lifetime experience for me.

Things got off to a slightly rocky start when Brian took a call from Mum in the morning.

'Tell Linda her dad has flushed his teeth down the toilet,' she said. 'He won't be able to make his speech.'

Brian started laughing. 'It's not funny!' Mum said.

It turned out that Dad had been out celebrating the night before with family and friends, got home late and while going to the loo he sneezed and his false teeth fell into the toilet. It was a bank holiday weekend, and so it took him a whole morning of phoning round to find an emergency dentist who was open and could sort him out. He was forty minutes late picking me up, which was a bit stressful but at least he had teeth when he walked me down the aisle! Dad did have a little whistle whenever he spoke which Brian and his best man John Parker found hilarious.

In the church my sisters sang 'May Each Day' and Mum sang 'Ave Maria' and there wasn't a dry eye in the house. She was still only fifty-three and had the most beautiful voice. Two hundred were invited for the church ceremony and another hundred for the reception in the evening. Even Brian's ex-wife Caroline was there.

When Dad walked me down the aisle towards Brian I felt I was heading for exactly where I'd always been meant to be. But as soon as I stepped into the car taking us from the reception to the airport for our honeymoon, I burst out crying.

'What's the matter, Linda?' Brian said, looking slightly panicked.

'I'm just so happy but it all feels so weird,' I tried to explain. 'We're married now. I'm Mrs Hudson and it's a whole new life. It's too much to take in.'

I think I was probably just a bit overtaken by emotion. Not to mention champagne!

Fortunately I was able to sort out my smudged mascara before we got to the airport, because on arrival there was a press photographer waiting to get snaps of the new Nolan bride and her new husband. Next day they were all across the front page of the *News of the World*.

Our honeymoon was to be Brian's surprise and I had no idea where we were going until we got to the airport and he showed me two tickets to Paris. That was me off weeping with happiness all over again!

What a week we had in Paris. It was late summer with the trees just starting to turn in the parks as we ambled along hand in hand. We visited the Eiffel Tower and Notre-Dame, wandered along the river and enjoyed long lazy dinners in the evening and long lazy mornings in bed. It could not have been more perfect.

Even when we got home the honeymoon wasn't over. Dad had asked Brian to become tour manager for The Nolans so we were together 24/7 – just the way we liked it. I'm sure my sisters couldn't understand why we wanted to be together day in day out but when I wasn't with Brian it felt that something was missing.

Like a jigsaw, we were two pieces of the same picture. We belonged together.

Six

In the Mood

While I'd been busy falling in love with my husband, I had also been really busy with work as The Nolans went from strength to strength with a succession of tours. And finally we had some chart success too. Up until 1979 we'd still struggled to have much luck with our singles. We were with the Warner Brothers record label who'd had high hopes for us but nothing seemed to work. Then we'd recorded an album of cover versions called *20 Giant Hits*. The sleeve picture still had us all lined up in matching pink floor-length dresses, which was hardly rock 'n' roll. But despite that it sold well. It made it to number two in the charts and stayed there.

We then moved to Epic Sony-CBS Records and had our first hit single, a ballad called 'Spirit, Body and Soul' which crept in at number thirty-four – our highest chart entry so far and high enough to get us on *Top of the Pops*. Finally, all those years after me, Bernie and Suzanne had crowded round the programme every Thursday night, it was happening to us.

We'd done tons of TV before but there was something super-exciting and nerve-racking about *Top of the Pops*. Finally we were being accepted as proper pop stars. We'd been out and got new dresses specially for the show. Bernie and I were in black and the other girls were in a deep pink. We had our hair and make-up done and then there was a bit of fussing around with the dresses to make sure full cleavage was on show. We were ready for action.

It was pre-recorded and we gave it our all. I watched with Suzanne when it aired a couple of days later. It really was like all those millions of times we'd watched the show before – but now me and my sisters were on it!

A couple of months later we released a pop-ish dance song we really weren't too sure about at first. It was called 'I'm in the Mood for Dancing' – and it was the song which was to make us famous around the globe and for the rest of our lives. It was in the charts for fifteen weeks, peaking at number three. And again we were back on *Top of the Pops* at the start of 1980. This time we were in coordinating jumpsuits. It was fabulous.

More singles followed, although we never matched the success of 'I'm in the Mood' which had become a hit across the world. It was number one in Japan and we were immediately booked to tour there. We'd never travelled that far before and had no idea what to expect. About an hour and a half before landing we were warned by the crew on board the plane: 'Oh, just to let you know, everyone in Japan is very excited about your visit. There will be members of the press at the airport.'

That was fine – we were used to having our pictures taken in the British tabloids. But when the plane doors opened on the airport runway I gasped in amazement. There were dozens and dozens of photographers snapping away at us. And beyond them, thousands of screaming fans. You know when you see those pictures of The Beatles landing in America – it was like that. Truly.

'Oh my goodness, Bernie,' I gasped. 'This is something else.'

Japan had two pop charts – a domestic one and an international one. We were number one in both and over an eighteen-month period we sold 8.2 million records there.

I think the Japanese liked us because we were an 'acceptable' face of pop music. We weren't going to be doing drugs or throwing TV sets out of hotel windows. And because it is a society with huge respect for family and moral values they liked the idea that we were sisters *and* singers. They also adored Coleen with her fair skin and dark hair, which I guess is a similar colouring to their own. They all said she was '*kawaii*', which means 'cute'.

And, to be fair, I think they liked our music. It certainly seemed to be playing everywhere we went. Our faces were on the front of cereal boxes and we were invited on endless TV shows. The scale of attention from fans was something we'd never experienced before – if we left our hotel we would be mobbed. They even managed to get past the reception desk on occasions and up to our room. They were very polite when they met us but were just so insistent that we sign their autograph books, or even just talk to them. It felt like they went everywhere in groups of twenty, and once you got trapped by a group there was no escaping.

'They're knocking on the door again,' I remember Coleen saying, looking quite rattled by it all. It was pretty intimidating and after a while we just stayed in hiding in our rooms, waving at fans out of the window occasionally. After two weeks holed up in a hotel room I was going demented.

'If we don't get out of here soon I really will be throwing TVs out of the window,' I laughed. When we asked if we could go for a wander round a local department store it was decided the only safe way was to close the shop as otherwise we'd be mobbed again.

Fortunately Brian was our tour manager by then and he looked after everything so we didn't have to worry about a thing. We had a fabulous time and the Japanese made us feel incredibly welcome. It was so successful that a thirteen-week tour was planned for the following year – including the country's enormous Budokan Stadium. Tickets sold out within two hours.

But before then the group changed again when Anne decided to leave to have her first daughter, Amy. The previous year she'd married Brian Wilson, a lovely guy who was a footballer playing for Blackpool. Anne worked right up until she was eight months pregnant – still on stage weeks before the birth at the Opera House in Blackpool.

But then Amy was born and Brian got a transfer to Torquay United and Anne decided she wanted a break to spend more time with her new family. And who could blame her? She'd worked so hard for so long and now she had a family of her own. It was only right she wanted to spend a bit of time enjoying it.

The band carried on touring, recording and doing TV shows. We were so lucky because for a few years we really were living the dream. When we weren't working we'd get invited to showbiz parties and premieres. Next day we'd often wake up to see our pictures in the gossip columns of the papers.

The newspapers could be tough on us, though. I'm not moaning because we understood we needed publicity for the band, but we'd been pigeonholed as a bit of a cheesy sickly-sweet act. And no matter what we did it seemed impossible to break out of that image.

We once had two reporters from the *Daily Mail* come and live at home with us for two days to write a fly-on-the-wall feature. They seemed lovely when they were there and we all went out of our way to make them feel at home so when we read the finished article we were horrified. It had things about how we cried ourselves to sleep with unhappiness and were anxious about everything. It was just ridiculous. And frankly, untrue.

Increasingly we felt the papers were trying to catch us out. Because we'd started off with the reputation as a group of Irish Catholic sisters who all dressed the same and were terribly innocent it was like they were constantly searching for things which didn't live up to the wholesome image. And to be honest, there were plenty! But we'd never attempted to hide it. We loved a drink, we smoked, we partied late, we had boyfriends, we swore. Yes, swore! In fact we were pretty much like every other young woman in the country at the time. But somehow it was regarded as a matter of national astonishment if we weren't acting like angels.

Although we weren't as boring and bland as people had first assumed – thank goodness – it's not like we were living a Sex and Drugs and Rock 'n' Roll lifestyle. Even if we'd wanted to, we wouldn't have been able to afford it. We weren't rolling in money at all – in fact we were still on the same £150 a week each in cash which Dad had first given us when we moved to London.

To be honest we'd been victims of some bad management over the years. We sold a lot of records and did a lot of gigs during that time but saw very little of the money. I think, sadly, our dad was slightly out of his depth by that time in London and some of the other people we worked with took advantage of him. When Brian became more involved in our tour management he could see how certain people had been making money out of our naivety and pocketing the bulk of our earnings.

Soon after Brian took over and we were due to be touring, the record company rang up demanding that an album be finished in the next two days. It meant that after performing a live TV show we would have to go straight into a recording studio through the night and lay down another three tracks. Dad would just have agreed but Brian played hard ball. 'This is going to cost you,' he told the record company. And it did. A couple of weeks later we each received a cheque for £25,000 for money they owed. It was a small fortune back then and allowed me to put a deposit down on my dream house in the country.

It was a four-bedroom detached house surrounded by fields in Great Dunmow, Essex. The village was close to where Brian had been living before we got together and so we had got to know the area quite well. It was our first 'grown-up' home together and everything I could have hoped for. I bought some beautiful dusty pink velvet curtains for the front room and had the bathroom all done out with a burgundy suite. I spent my weekends choosing carpets and furniture. I loved it out in the countryside because it felt like being miles from anywhere, surrounded by trees and fields, and yet we could still be at my parents' house in half an hour. There was a little pond in the centre of the village and five or six local pubs where we'd go for a quiet drink in the evenings. Mike Reid, the comedian who went into *EastEnders*, and his wife

Shirley lived nearby and we became best friends. Then there were two other couples – Paul and Mary, and Carol and Derek who were landlords of the Kings Head pub – who we hung around with. We would have parties and so much fun. We had a great set of friends, my family close by, a beautiful home and money coming in. They were lovely times.

And of course even when I was touring around Britain, Brian was with me as tour manager. In that job he was the consummate professional. Nothing was ever left to chance. He fussed over all us girls like a Mother Hen. I loved it because he was my husband and, yes, maybe I did like someone willing to make a fuss of me. But my sisters weren't so keen. I thought it was great that Brian wouldn't let us carry our bags off a tour bus when we arrived at a hotel for a gig. But increasingly the girls found it irritating. 'We can lift a bag on our own, you know,' they'd say.

And Brian didn't like it if the girls went out for a walk around town on their own before a gig.

'Don't think you should be doing that,' he'd say.

'Well we are,' they'd reply then stomp off.

It was only because he worried about them and felt he was responsible for absolutely everything that happened while we were on tour. But I can see how they found it suffocating at times too. There was clearly a tension building up.

Two years after leaving the band to have her daughter, Anne felt the time was right to come back. We were delighted to have her back too, it was great. But things had changed since she'd been away. As the eldest we'd always felt like she was the boss but now Brian was there too there was inevitably going to be friction.

When she said she wanted to come back, Brian was straight

on the phone to her to say how happy he was about it and how great it was going to be.

'Well I want you to know, I don't trust you,' she replied.

He came off the phone completely bewildered. 'What was all that about?' he asked me.

'I haven't got a clue,' I replied. And I truly hadn't.

Of all my sisters I was least close to Anne. She is nine years older than me, which is a lot when you are kids. When she'd been in the group before, she'd always acted like she was in charge so I'd thought there might be some issues over the way things had changed while she'd been away. But I never thought she'd hold it personally against Brian. Our family has always been one for big flare-ups and then it's all forgotten, but I was certain it was going to take me a long while to forget about how she'd spoken to Brian that day. It didn't bode well for the future.

I think Anne and my sisters had grown up believing the only person who could look after us and have our best interests at heart was Dad. So there was a suspicion about anyone who wasn't a blood relative. I don't think my sisters ever really got how much Brian loved The Nolan Sisters and that he simply wanted us to succeed. Relations within the group became more and more strained.

One day as he fussed around us, getting out of a car, Bernie snapped: 'Brian, we are grown women. We can get ourselves out of a car.'

'He's only trying to help,' I snapped back. There was a bad atmosphere for the rest of the day. I hated falling out with my sisters but no one was going to criticize the man I loved.

Another day the girls wanted to go shopping before we moved on with the tour.

'No time I'm afraid,' Brian said. 'We'll be late.'

'Stop bossing us around,' came the reply. It was getting worse.

Dad was still very involved with our management, with Brian supposedly just dealing with tour arrangements, but that relationship had become tense too. Brian felt Dad could be protecting us better and getting us better financial deals. And I guess Dad thought Brian was interfering.

To make matters worse, Brian had introduced an old friend of his called Elaine to Dad and she'd begun working as his secretary. Within weeks her relationship with Dad had grown very close and she'd turned on Brian. Very soon Elaine had huge influence on Dad, which made me feel very uneasy.

Things felt increasingly fraught and each day I could feel Brian and the rest of my family taking opposing sides – with me left floundering in the middle somewhere. All over again I felt a bit lost in the middle of the family, a little bit of the outsider. Only Brian still made me feel special.

Since Denise and Anne had left the group I'd always known that was an option for me one day – but it was never one that I wanted. Yet as the weeks and months went by I felt that was the way I was being pushed. I couldn't bear the endless frosty atmosphere on the tour bus with Brian and me sitting together slightly apart from all the others. And, I started to think, if I did go solo then Brian and I could be together all the time without anyone interfering. But, no, the thought of leaving my sisters horrified me.

Then the decision was taken out of my hands. It all came to a head one night when we were performing at the Golden Garter Showbar in Manchester. 'Can we all have a proper chat tomorrow, at the hotel?' Anne said to me. 'Just us girls.'

'OK,' I replied. But I knew in my gut this wasn't going to be any old chat.

We met in a room of the hotel at lunchtime. I'd arranged to catch up with Brian afterwards. At first no one spoke but then gradually it all poured out.

'We've decided we don't think Brian is right as our tour manager any more,' said Anne.

'Oh,' I replied, instantly feeling my hackles rise. 'Why not?'

'He's fabulous,' Maureen joined in, 'but sometimes he can be just a little bit overprotective.'

'We just think it might be for the best,' added Bernie. Coleen nodded.

So it was all of them. They all wanted to ditch my Brian.

I sat looking round the room at each one of them. I was seething inside. And I could feel tears starting to burn my eyes but there was no way I was going to cry in front of them all.

I felt the room was spinning around me. I knew there was no way I could stay in the group if Brian was sacked as tour manager. And my sisters knew that too. Yet they were still prepared to go ahead with it. I felt sick.

'Well it looks like you've made your decision then,' I said, getting to my feet. 'And you know full well that if Brian goes I go too. But if that's what you want.'

Even then I was desperately hoping someone – anyone – would say that wasn't what they wanted at all. But nobody did. I stormed out of the room feeling utterly crushed.

But how I felt was still nothing compared with how devastated I feared Brian was going to be when I told him. He was waiting in the car for me outside. I took a deep breath as I opened the passenger door.

'Everything all right, Lin?' he said, seeing me shaking with fury.

'Oh no, it's not, Brian,' I said. 'I'm so sorry but it's the girls. They've made a decision. They don't want you as tour manager any more.'

'Oh no,' he said quietly, gripping the steering wheel. 'Why?'

'I don't know,' I said, putting my hand on his arm. 'I really don't know.'

'But what have I done wrong?' he said. 'I must have done something wrong.'

'You've done nothing wrong at all,' I insisted. 'It's them. It's not you at all. But if you're going, I'm going. We belong together.'

Brian was as upset as I thought he would be. We drove to stay with his best friend John Parker, who lived nearby, in almost total silence.

Brian loved The Nolans, he always had. He really thought we were the best thing since sliced bread – that was what he always said. He'd never been in it for himself and never wanted Dad's job or cared how much he earned. In fact he could have made loads more working as a tour manager for other people. He just wanted to be with us and make us as successful as we could be.

Of course Brian didn't want me to leave on his behalf. 'You can't leave the group – it's your life,' he kept saying. But it wasn't even up for discussion. We would be leaving together. Before then, though, we had a six-month tour to finish.

That six months was really difficult for all of us. Brian and I sat together on the tour bus and there wasn't much chat between me and my sisters. We'd do the show every night on stage but then I'd go back to my hotel room with Brian and not see the rest of the girls again until the next night's show. But Brian remained the consummate professional. At each venue he decorated our changing rooms with flowers, cards and mementos, and made sure our stage make-up was laid out.

One night it was scorching hot on stage and there was Brian sliding ice in a tea towel across the stage to cool us down. Or if one of us even looked like we were about to sneeze, he'd already be there with a tissue.

Maureen has since said that Brian was the best tour manager she ever worked with in her entire career. I think probably all the girls felt that but unfortunately at the time they found working with him too much. It was clear that us all working together was over.

One night near the end of the tour Bernie came up to me in the wings and said: 'Oh Linda, why don't you stay. It won't be the same without you.'

We both had tears in our eyes as I shook my head. 'I can't, not without Brian,' I said. 'We need a tour manager and he's the best in the country. But if he has to go then so do I.'

Our last gig on the tour was at the Derngate Theatre in Northampton. The audience knew it was our last show together and our last song that night was 'Goodbye Girl'. As we sang the words I could feel tears bubbling up in my eyes.

As it finished the girls hugged me. It was terribly sad. I'd been singing on stage next to my sisters since those days when I'd belted out 'Big Spender' in a frock Mum had sewn me. And now it was over. Right then it really did feel as if goodbye was going to be for ever.

The prospect of going solo was terrifying. I was always much happier performing harmonies than being out there on my own. But that was going to be my future. I felt devastated but determined to make the best of it.

Then a horrible situation became even worse when Dad handed me a £13,000 pay cheque as sort of redundancy money for my time in the band. It was supposedly my share of everything we had earned – for all the hits, all the TV shows, all the foreign tours; £13,000 – that was all I got. But Anne had received £10,000 when she left a few years earlier and that was before we'd had a single hit. And then she'd come back into the band two years later.

'The girls sat down with the accountants and this is what they came up with,' Dad told me as he handed over the cheque.

I was furious and beyond even wanting to speak to my sisters by then. I wrote them a letter instead.

'I'm not asking for the earth,' I said. 'I simply want the fair amount that's due to me for all the work I've put in over the years.'

They wrote a joint letter back saying it had been worked out as the right figure. Letters went backwards and forwards getting more and more fraught. I felt like I was having to fight for everything – they wouldn't even agree at first that I should get a share of royalties for the hits we'd had.

To add insult to injury I'd just received a tax bill for almost exactly £13,000 so I hadn't a penny to show for all that work. Nothing. And it was my family doing it to me. Looking back now I can see maybe the band just didn't have enough money to pay me out any more. The chart successes had recently stopped, and our popularity was dwindling. The girls were having to perform in bingo clubs or gay clubs, often not going on stage until three in the morning. So in hindsight perhaps they just didn't have any more money to give me. Which is sad, because a lot of people had got rich on the back of The Nolans over the years – unfortunately we weren't any of them. I can understand now that perhaps the pay-out wasn't there for me but at the time I just felt my family were being deliberately mean.

I knew there was nothing I could do to persuade Dad differently. I'd wonder whether, if I'd been one of the other girls, he might have found some more. But I knew it wasn't going to happen for me. I was too hurt and tired to argue. With both Brian and myself out of work it was going to be a long hard battle to keep our heads above water. And no one even seemed to care.

I didn't speak to my sisters for more than a year. I still called and visited my parents and I didn't blame them. I felt by then that Dad was just doing what the girls told him to do. And Mum hadn't any involvement in the band management at all. She was just devastated her girls had fallen out.

All my life I'd been surrounded by my noisy, funny and often maddening sisters, but now they were gone. After years of feeling a little unnoticed within the family I now felt like I'd entirely disappeared without trace. And no one seemed that bothered. None of my sisters phoned to see how I was getting on. It felt they'd just moved on without me.

That was how it felt then but now I can see it differently. I didn't call the girls either and had probably been pretty awkward to be with during those last months on tour. I was angry they'd broken Brian's heart and felt there was nothing to discuss.

It's still painful looking back on that time, because losing my sisters was like losing a limb. It felt so strange. Even now we have never discussed what happened back then. I think it's still too raw. While my sisters and I are very open people in many ways, there are some things which we never discuss . . . me and Brian leaving the group is one of them.

Back then I knew it was going to take a whole lot of water going under this bridge before I'd be able to forget what had happened.

Thank God I had Brian. Always Brian.

Seven

Going It Alone

With just a sheet (almost) covering my modesty there I was draped across page three of the *Sun* under a giant headline: 'The Naughty Nolan'. And with my blonde hair piled high, my lips scarlet and a come-to-bed look in my eyes, it was certainly quite naughty.

'What do you think my dad will say?' I gasped as Brian and I gazed at the pictures.

'Not much,' he mumbled.

But that one photo shoot had got the launch of my solo career more publicity than the rest of the group had had in years. And I needed it. The snaps might have been quite shocking for the supposed sweet and innocent Catholic girl – but I thought I looked pretty good.

On the day it was announced I was going solo Terry Wogan chuckled on his breakfast radio show: 'It's like a Nolan factory.' And that's what the public thought. Denise had left, Coleen had joined, Anne had left, Anne had rejoined, now I was leaving. There had been so much chopping and changing that I needed a point of difference.

Brian understood that. And that was why he'd hired top photographer John Paul for a photo shoot which would make me stand out from the Nolan crowd. Although I don't think any of us had thought I'd be standing out in quite such a risqué way.

We were in the studio all day doing fairly standard pictures of me in long dresses, short dresses, trouser suits and the rest of it. I was knackered by about seven in the evening and popped to the loo, desperately hoping we were nearly finished. When I came back into the room John Paul had had an idea.

'He wants you to get naked and drape the sheet over you,' Brian whispered, looking a little nervous at how I might react.

'You're joking me,' I said.

'Er, no,' he smiled. I don't think he was any too happy about his wife stripping in front of a stranger either.

'OK, I'll do it,' I said, feeling really nervous inside.

My body was pretty good in those days and this certainly would be one way of making people sit up and take notice of me. And the furore after the pictures emerged did just that. Suddenly everyone wanted to interview me about my bold new go-it-alone career. And 'The Naughty Nolan' had a ring to it. In the band I'd been known for my blonde hair and big boobs – so I might as well play on that. It had certainly placed me apart from the traditional Nolan Sisters' saccharine image.

Years later I asked Mum – who, remember, was a staunch Catholic who attended mass every day – if she'd been upset about the pictures.

'Oh Linda,' she laughed. 'I've seen you in less on the beach.'

Having stories in the papers was all very well. But what I really needed was work. Fortunately, having the best agent in the business, my Brian, meant I didn't have to wait long. Brian worked for Neil Warnock at The Agency and they were touring Gene Pitney. My first job was supporting him in his 1984

UK tour. We opened in Belfast. It was tremendously exciting but as I stood in the wings of the city's Opera House I'd never felt so alone. Of course I'd done hundreds of solos over the years. But an entire set without my sisters felt wrong. Empty.

Not one of the girls had sent flowers or a card for my opening night. I tried to pretend I didn't care. But I did. Being cut off from my family hurt like hell.

'I can't do it,' I whispered to Brian, my heart pounding and palms sweating.

'Yes you can,' he said, touching my arm. 'You can do anything.'

And once I got through those first-night nerves, it was fine. Brilliant, in fact. I still missed singing harmonies and I missed the laughing and joking rapport I'd had on stage with my sisters, particularly Bernie, but at the same time there were none of the tensions we'd had on the last tour with all the girls. Increasingly I revelled in the independence of being on stage alone, doing exactly what I wanted and building a relationship each night with the audience. The money for the tour was great too. Brian and I had been totally skint when it started and he arranged for me to get paid in cash for the opening show. We were that desperate. The night the tour manager handed over a brown envelope we took it back to our hotel and tossed the £20 notes in the air like millionaires. We were far from that but at least we could eat!

So I began to really enjoy performing again. Most importantly, I realized I could do it. All those years on stage I hadn't been Anne, the oldest one, Maureen, the pretty one, Bernie, the lead singer, or Coleen, the cute one. I was just Linda, the blonde one. On stage now it was just me. And once I'd got used to my sisters not being there, that felt good. Finally I wasn't 'just another Nolan'. I was a performer in my own right.

It was unfortunate, though, that the days of cabaret shows were on the wane. Brian and I travelled the length and breadth of Britain doing gigs but it was a pretty hand-to-mouth existence. It was no easier for my sisters. The Nolans' star was beginning to fade and we all had to take work where we could find it. Soon after ditching Brian, the girls had also dropped Dad as their manager and put him in charge of running the fan club. I know it devastated him but they felt they needed more professional management. This was exactly what I had suggested, although I wanted our dad to get help, not to be sacked. But by that time the work was less high profile anyway. It happens to every group sooner or later.

It was more than a year before relations thawed between me and the girls. At first I would see one or other of my sisters at Mum and Dad's house or if I was round at my brother Tommy's or Brian's. It was terribly awkward and we'd stick firmly to conversations about the weather or the buffet but gradually it eased, although we all made a big effort to avoid talking about work or anything that might flare things up again.

Brian and I loved the touring life, staying in nice hotels in different towns and going out partying with the rest of the cast. People called us Mr and Mrs Showbiz and the industry was our life. There was a lot of drinking and partying in those days. Looking back I just remember it being tremendous fun. We never had to get up early so there was never any reason to go to bed early. What I didn't consider at the time was that both Brian and I were probably drinking more than was good for us. I loved a few glasses of wine at the end of a show but Brian was drinking his favourite whisky and Coke for longer and longer periods every day. It's very easy to slip into that habit when you're not in the normal day-to-day routine of office and family life. We didn't have kids together so we could pretty much do whatever we wanted, when we wanted.

Not having children is the only regret of my life. When Brian and I first got together I was still really young and it felt like we had ages ahead of us to think about things like that. As the years went by it would occasionally pop into my head and I adored my nieces and nephews when they turned up – I've always loved children – but it seemed the wrong time in my career to be considering kids. I didn't think I could carry on with the touring if I was a mum, and we needed my wages to survive. It wasn't that we decided not to have children – we just never quite got round to it. There was always a summer season or a panto in the diary which would have made it the wrong time. And so one year rolled into the next.

Then, in early 1986, Brian and I started discussing having a family more seriously. I was twenty-seven but Brian was forty-three by then and was worried he would be the oldest dad in the playground and too rickety to kick a ball around with a youngster. He was still excited by the idea though.

'It doesn't matter if you are older than the other dads,' I said. 'You'll give the child your love and humour and know-ledge. And that's all they need.'

We decided to give it a go, so I talked to my GP who gave me folic acid to get my body ready for pregnancy. I called Maureen to talk it over with her.

'We're going to go for it,' I announced.

Maureen instantly started squealing. 'I'm so happy for you,' she said. 'You'll be the best mum ever.'

But it wasn't to be. Not then. Or ever, in fact. And it was all my own doing.

A couple of months later I was chosen to take the lead role in a massive new production being staged in Blackpool called *Maggie May*. It was a big gig and meant good money from May to November. Money had been tight for a long while and this felt like a miracle solution to all our financial worries. However much I wanted children I couldn't do it then. And as I told myself at the time, I was still young. I had years left for babies.

Maggie May was the most fabulous job. The theatre at the end of Central Pier in Blackpool had been recently refurbished. Inside it had been brilliantly designed to look like the Liverpool docks in the Victorian era. The audience would come in and sit at tables, have something to eat and a few drinks while I performed as Maggie May, a 'lady of the night' who hosted an evening of cabaret, sang a few solos and got everyone involved in a big singalong at the end.

My costume for the role of Maggie was a tiny little basque and fishnet tights with a big plume of feathers coming out of my headdress. I still had the blonde hair and big boobs which had been my trademark in The Nolans so was able to carry off the revealing outfit pretty much OK.

The town's landladies loved it because it was so popular among holidaymakers. The acts were all top quality and it was a proper night out for folk. The first year was so successful that it was soon decided there would be another season the following year. If we were going to be spending so much time in Blackpool, Brian and I would hardly ever be at our home in Great Dunmow in Essex. We had credit card debts to clear and after a while decided it made more sense to sell up and rent a smaller place in Blackpool, which would give us flexibility and allow us to get our finances back on an even keel. Mum and Dad had moved back too so it was nice to pop round and see them between rehearsals. All my sisters had left home by then so it was natural for Mum and Dad to come back permanently to Blackpool. And they were happy to be home.

And of course that meant I saw my sisters far more frequently at Mum and Dad's. The wounds of the past gradually healed.

Maggie May ran for eight years in the end before transferring to the theatre on South Pier where it was renamed *Rosie O'Grady*. I took the lead role every night during the incredible run and it was one of the best jobs I've ever had.

During that whole time Brian looked after everything for me. I didn't lift a finger. I'd arrive in my dressing room every night and it would have been totally 'Brian-ed'. Just like it always was on tour. He'd have made sure there were fresh flowers in pretty vases, good-luck cards pinned on the walls, mementos around the mirror and all my make-up and hairbrushes neatly set out on the dressing table. Then he would go and check the theatre to ensure all the chairs were in the right place and nothing had been left out which I could trip over or might upset the performance. Nothing was left to chance. As the years went by he became more involved in the production of the show too. In many ways, Brian and I *were Maggie May*.

After the show had finished we'd sit at the bar with the

crew drinking, chatting or doing something daft like having beer-mat-flicking competitions. Sometimes we'd finally pull up the shutters to go home and it would be daylight. We'd been there drinking and laughing all night. Other times I'd wake in the morning feeling shocking and think: 'What happened last night? What was I drinking? Did we have a row?' We rarely argued – unless we'd had one too many!

Looking back, Brian was probably drinking too much. You'd think that having grown up with a father who was an alcoholic I'd have seen the warning signs but in my mind Brian was the perfect husband who just happened to enjoy a few whiskies. He was never violent or nasty to me. At the time it just felt like fun.

At the end of each season we threw a huge party for the entire cast and crew which was fabulous. And then Brian and I would book a holiday and collapse in the sun for a few weeks before returning to England, at which point it would be time for panto.

Between pantomime finishing and the summer season starting again in May I didn't get paid, and so I guess things were often a bit tight financially. I say 'I guess', because in all honesty I had no idea. I knew absolutely nothing about any of our financial dealings. Brian did all of that. He felt it was his job as my manager and hated me worrying about that sort of thing. He paid every bill, answered every letter, booked every holiday, filled in every form. I didn't even know how to write a cheque because he always did it. Perhaps I should have been more involved and shared the burden but Brian was insistent that I didn't. And I was more than happy with that.

Not only did Brian look after all the business side of things, he also kept the house clean, did the shopping and cooked the meals. I guess that was our deal because I was the one going out to work. If I didn't roll out of bed till mid-morning after a night at *Maggie May*, Brian would already have cleaned the house and filled the fridge.

He'd make me a spot of lunch then we'd hang around together for the rest of the day, reading the papers (him the *Sun*, me the *Mirror*), doing the crosswords and chatting until it was time for me to go to work. Then Brian would come with me to check everything was 'just so' at the theatre and wait for me backstage to finish. And we did that day after day after day.

Maybe it sounds like Brian was a bit of a doormat, but he was far from that. He was a strong, clever man who'd dedicated his life to me and took looking after me very seriously.

'Don't you ever want a break from him?' my sisters would sometimes joke. But I didn't. I really didn't. We belonged together.

That first year of *Maggie May* I was on stage seven nights a week, which was gruelling. When they'd asked for me to go back the following year, Brian told the theatre boss: 'Sure, but she has to have one night a week off this time.' They agreed and that made everything slightly more manageable. But no matter how many times we performed that show, the audience never got sick of watching it. Which is why we carried on for ten years, I guess.

Brian and I had a fabulous time working on *Maggie May* and *Rosie O'Grady*. We worked hard, partied hard and had some gorgeous holidays. But we'd never quite got round to having that baby.

'Maybe we are just too old and selfish now,' I thought to myself as I reached my mid-thirties. I loved my nieces and nephews but I could see how tough being a parent really was. Anne had worked so hard juggling two kids and a stage career and was fortunate her husband Brian was able to become a house husband when they were little. Maureen had kept on working after having her son Danny in 1989 but that was hard too when so much showbiz work means long periods away from home. Fortunately she'd had loads of support from her partner Ritchie's parents.

And Coleen had pretty much given up work entirely when she had her boys, Shane Jnr and Jake, with the actor Shane Richie. He'd been able to keep going with his career while Coleen stayed at home with two little babies.

Brian and I were also so self-contained that it never felt as if we needed a baby to make our marriage complete. It had always been complete. It was beginning to feel that if there was a time when we were going to have kids, it had already drifted past.

Brian's son Lloyd visited us regularly and it was wonderful watching him grow up into a gorgeous young man. And Brian also made contact again with Sarah, his daughter from his first marriage. They looked so alike and had so many similar characteristics that they got on like a house on fire.

The summer season in Blackpool had been dramatically reduced over the last few years of *Maggie May* and *Rosie O'Grady*. Holidaymakers were taking advantage of cheap deals abroad and the entertainments industry was changing. Meanwhile cabaret work during the rest of the year had almost entirely dried up.

For years we'd been living one month to the next on my earnings and we had no savings. So when the work dried up, so did our cash. There were no more foreign holidays, and nights out became a rarity. We were more likely to be sat indoors watching the telly. Shane and Coleen even lent us £2,000 at one point when things were tight.

Brian rarely mentioned to me what was going on, but he must have confided in others. We were very close to a guy called Graham who'd been the stage manager at *Maggie May*. We were godparents to his son who would stay stay the night at our house with his sisters. One day we were sat at our breakfast bar chatting with Graham when he pulled £50 out of his wallet.

'Look, it's all I've got at the moment, but take it.'

I'm not completely daft and knew that with my working less things had become a bit tight financially. But in showbiz it's always feast or famine so I didn't worry unduly. But when Brian simply picked up the £50 and put it in his pocket, thanking Graham over and over, I felt a wave of sickness hit me. I had no idea it was this bad.

'What's going on?' I asked Brian later when Graham had gone.

'Oh, it's nothing to worry about,' he replied. 'We'll be OK. We always are, aren't we?'

And yes, of course I should have asked more questions, I should have got more involved in our financial situation. But that just wasn't how things worked between us.

'You need to start paying more attention and know where all the paperwork is in your house,' my friend Shirley Reid, Mike Reid's wife, said to me once. 'When he goes you are going to be lost.'

'Thanks, Shirley,' I laughed. 'But I have no plans for him to be going anywhere for a very long time.'

Of course she was right. But I only realized that much later.

Although Brian wouldn't talk about his money worries, I wasn't stupid. I could tell something was up but I didn't realize the severity of it. There was no point me constantly quizzing Brian on our cash flow situation as I knew he'd only tell me not to panic. Well, that was what I told myself at the time. Looking back perhaps it was also partly that I just didn't want to hear the truth.

One morning I popped into the town for a wander around the shops. The sales were on and so when I saw a beautiful blue shirt for a tenner which would look lovely on Brian, I picked it up. 'Bargain,' I thought. But Brian clearly thought differently.

'How much was that?' he said, glaring at me and the shirt as I pulled it out the bag, back at home.

'Only a tenner,' I snapped, feeling he was being rather ungrateful.

'Linda,' he sighed. 'We just can't afford it.'

But this was £10 – surely things couldn't be that bad. Turns out, they were.

It was one day in 1995 that I heard Brian on the phone pleading with a guy about something.

'What was that about?' I asked when he slammed the phone down.

'The hire purchase company are saying they are going to reclaim the car,' he explained. 'We missed a couple of payments. I've told them we'll pay just as soon as you start work again next month. I've told them that without a car you can't work and then we won't be able to pay anything, but they're not having any of it.'

A couple of days later two guys appeared at the house demanding the keys. I was mortified. And devastated too.

'How could they do that when we've only missed a couple of payments?' I cried as they drove off in the car. Brian just looked out the window and didn't answer.

Soon after, I heard Brian urgently on the phone again. By then I was becoming more alert to the problems which seemed to be mounting around us. He was talking to someone about a bankruptcy hearing. Despite having stuck my head firmly in the sand for years and years I wasn't so stupid that I didn't realize it must be us he was talking about.

But still I didn't ask. And Brian didn't tell me.

A few weeks later, in the summer of 1995, we were staying with Shane, Coleen and their boys at their house in Middlesex. We often stayed with them if I had a job in London and we always had a fabulous time there. They made us so welcome.

I woke one morning at their house to the noise of someone banging on the bedroom door. The next thing I knew, Shane was in the room, striding round the bed to me.

'You'd better get up – you're bankrupt, darling.'

'What?' I choked. 'What are you talking about?'

Shane was waving a newspaper at me. 'Look, there it is in black and white: "Linda Nolan Bankrupt".'

I thought I was going to throw up.

It was all over our failure to keep up the repayments on the car. For that. For seven and a half grand on a poxy little car, I'd gone bust.

'I'm so sorry, Linda,' Brian said, looking entirely crushed.

I couldn't be angry with him, he looked broken.

'But why didn't you tell me, Brian?' I asked.

'I didn't want you to worry. I thought I could sort it.'

For weeks Brian had become quieter and quieter. He was

withdrawn and he seemed sad. It was hard to get him to snap out of it. And he was still drinking a lot. It wasn't that he would get blind drunk, he just seemed less worried or anxious when he had a drink in his hand. Now I knew why.

The night the bankruptcy story broke in the papers I was due to do a private gig at Warwick Castle. And who was I on stage with? None other than the comedian Ken Dodd, who had been cleared a few years earlier of tax evasion. So he knew all about public humiliation over money matters.

The thought of going out on stage when everyone in the audience would know I was on my uppers was utterly humiliating. I felt ashamed and embarrassed, and was terrified everyone would think I'd never been able to make it on my own and here was the proof. But now I knew exactly how desperate for the money I was, there was no choice but to get out there on stage and perform.

With the bankruptcy order in place the bank immediately froze our accounts. We'd hired another car to get us from Coleen's house to the gig but we couldn't even get money out of the bank to pay for petrol.

Coleen stood in her kitchen and handed over a wad of cash.

'Oh Coleen, I'm so sorry,' I said, tears pouring down my face. 'I feel so ashamed.'

'There's nothing to be sorry for,' she replied. 'And look, tonight's going to be tough. But you can do it.'

We'd grown up knowing the show had to go on regardless of coughs, colds or some other kid's birthday party which you'd rather be at. But bankruptcy? Did it still have to go on through that? Quite simply, the answer was 'Yes'.

Before the show, Ken told me to go on stage and say, 'Yes,

I'm the bankrupt Nolan. My mistake was having Ken Dodd as my financial adviser.'

I loved him for that. So I got up on stage in my long evening gown and waited for the muted opening applause to die down. I knew I had just seconds to get the audience on my side. I picked up the microphone and told the joke. They instantly applauded and I went on with the show. It was OK. I could do this.

Brian had spent the entire day trying to sort out whatever deals he could on the back of the bankruptcy revelations. So by the following morning I was sat with a journalist telling the whole story about my financial woes – in return for a very healthy £17,000 cheque! The only problem of course was I still didn't really understand quite how we had got into such a predicament. I knew that the work had stopped coming in but the bills hadn't stopped arriving. But both Brian and I always believed that the next job that would get us out of trouble would soon be around the corner. It's hard for people who've never worked in showbiz to understand quite how unpredictable it is financially. Brian and I had never known anything different so we always believed it would pick up one day soon. Which it did that day. The newspaper cheque meant we could get ourselves straight with the hire purchase firm, clear a few debts and get back to square one again. The bankruptcy was annulled and so, bizarrely, we were financially in a better position afterwards than we had been before. But the whole episode had shaken me and Brian. I felt like I'd failed publicly. And Brian felt like he'd let me down. And rather than talk about those things we ignored them. Brian withdrew further into himself. I was worried. Nothing seemed quite right any more.

Back home in Blackpool I couldn't bear to leave our flat. Everyone knows the Nolans in our home town and I was convinced people would be pointing and laughing at me. Not because they're deliberately cruel, but because there is something in human nature which can't help delighting in others who've fallen on hard times. The newspaper interview had only made the episode more public – so no one could have missed the news now. But I had to do that for the money it paid.

When I did finally venture out into town I was overwhelmed by how kind people were. One lady tapped me on the arm and said: 'Don't worry about it, luvvie. I had a cheque bounce once and wanted the earth to open up and swallow me. You'll be fine.'

And with the various crises I've been through over the years I've always been amazed and comforted by the incredible kindness of strangers.

Financially we limped along but when *Rosie O'Grady* finally ended in 1996 things were even more precarious. Maybe I should have demanded Brian go out and get a job. He would have swept the streets for me if that was what we needed. But he was my manager and we knew there would be another job along for us at some point. And there *were* jobs – it was just the waiting in between times seemed to be getting longer and longer.

I did gigs at Haven Holidays camps all over the country. Brian and I would go and stay overnight and the audiences were always really good and determined to enjoy themselves because they were on holiday. And then I did a few tours in the clubs in Northern Ireland, which I enjoyed. But it was getting harder and harder to get the bookings because entertainment was changing so much. People were more interested in staying in watching television or going out for dinner than in traditional cabaret shows.

But I could hardly take up a new career. I didn't think there was any other job I had the skills to do. I'd been performing since I could walk. And I kept thinking the next big break was just around the corner. It had to be . . .

Eight

Losing Dad

Dad and I sat in the front room of his little bungalow, looking out over the pristine patch of lawn and rose bushes which he'd tended every day since moving back to Blackpool. It was a desperate shame he could only get out there for ten minutes at a time by 1997. But his breathing was so poor that anything more was too much for him. Mum was out down the town and it was peaceful, just me and Dad reminiscing about the old times. When I spoke he still had that ability to pay complete attention and make it feel like I was the only person in the world.

'Do you remember the time the fella said he wasn't going to pay us the full rate at that working men's club so you pulled us up through the changing-room window and we did a runner,' I laughed.

'I certainly do,' smiled Dad. 'They were great days, weren't they, Linda.'

We loved to chat about the amazing times we'd had as kids. Of course there had been plenty of times which weren't amazing too. But we didn't talk about those.

Dad had cut right back on his drinking after he and Mum moved to London in the mid-seventies.

Twenty years on from then and he barely touched a drop.

Mum and Dad were happy back in Blackpool. It was always 'home' for all of us and they'd found a beautiful little bunga- low. But Dad looked like an old man now. It was sad to see. He'd been such a handsome fella in his youth but time was stealing him from us.

He had smoked all his life, sixty a day at one point. And for years he smoked cigarettes without a filter – Players, then Senior Service. They'd clearly wrecked his lungs and at the start of the 1990s the doctors told him he had a serious lung disease.

'I'm afraid this is very serious, Mr Nolan,' the doctor had said. 'You will have to stop smoking immediately.'

And incredibly, he did. Just like that. Well, with a little help from our GP. Despite the prognosis being bleak he battled on through the 1990s, although each year was more of a strug- gle. When I was still doing *Maggie May* and *Rosie O'Grady*, Mum and Dad would sometimes come down to watch the show. I loved that. At the end Mum would get up and sing 'Danny Boy' or 'Bless This House'. Then Dad would get up and sing 'My Way'. Lots of folk who'd been coming to Black- pool for years still remembered them from their heyday. And even though they were nearing their seventies they still had the most fabulous voices.

As Dad's condition deteriorated he needed an oxygen tank at home to help him breathe and a wheelchair (which he hated) to get around. It meant he didn't like leaving the house, even for family parties at one of his children's houses. He was a very proud man and I think he couldn't bear the idea of people seeing him being pushed in a wheelchair. The only time I ever knew him leave the house in the chair was when my Brian got tickets for him to see the singer Tony Bennett perform in Liverpool. That was how much he loved Tony Bennett! Our brother Brian and a family friend took him, and he had a brilliant time.

Dad's garden was his pride and joy and most of the time he was happy just pottering out there for a few minutes then going back in to sit in the chair. And he loved his children and grandchildren visiting.

Mum was so good with him. He certainly wasn't an easy patient to look after. In fact he could be a real pain in the neck.

'Maureen,' he'd call in the morning. 'Can you pop out and get me some lunch. Now I want that nice bread I like from the baker's in town, then the ham needs to be the good stuff from the butcher in South Shore and pop in at the shop down the road for some beetroot.'

Poor Mum couldn't drive so it meant she was dashing about all over town on the bus just to get him exactly what he wanted. But as ever, Mum never complained. More often than not there'd be something wrong with whatever she bought. He was a difficult man to please. But although they may not always have had the happiest of marriages, they were happy then.

In the years since they'd moved back to Blackpool Mum had built up a good life of her own. She adored my dad, always had done. But it was great she finally had time for friends and interests of her own. Her life revolved around the church. She went to mass every day and took part in productions in the Music Hall Tavern summer show. And each year she went on a pilgrimage to Lourdes in the south of France. Dad hated it when Mum went away. He missed her terribly and she'd tell us that when she got back she'd find he'd cooked something ready for when she got in.

In their own way they really did love each other.

When Mum was away my brothers and sisters would set up a rota to care for Dad as he was finding moving around increasingly difficult. He wasn't any easier with us, except we took less of his nonsense than Mum! He did once, though, have my Brian driving all over Blackpool searching for tinned pears in their own juice, NOT in syrup, under any circumstances.

'Oh, this is beautiful beetroot you've found, Linda,' he said one day when I was looking after him. 'Your mum never gets me beetroot like this – did you go to that lovely little greengrocer's in town?'

'No, Dad,' I snapped. 'I got it from a jar in the shop across the road.'

One morning when Mum was away Dad called up.

'Can you come over, Linda?' he asked. 'And bring some TCP, I seem to have grazed myself.'

When we were kids Mum and Dad's solution for everything was a quick swab of TCP. There was no ailment on earth they didn't think could be remedied with the stuff. It certainly smelt sufficiently medical and stung like hell, whatever it actually did. That day when I turned up at the bungalow with a bottle in my hand, I couldn't believe the state of Dad. He had got up to use the toilet during the night and fallen. He looked like he had been beaten up, he was covered in bruises and there was dried blood all over him.

It was clear our Dad was becoming a lot weaker. I was working in Blackpool and it was nice to have time to spend with him during the day. My brothers were at work then and the other girls were off touring or doing shows. They all helped out when they were around but I liked having that time with Dad when it was clear he was moving towards the end of his life.

One morning Brian and I took him to the hospital for a blood test. The nurse asked Dad's date of birth.

'Second of September 1926,' he replied.

'That's BC' Brian joked.

They got on great by then. All the problems of the past when we'd worked together were long gone.

Then, one morning in September 1998, my brothers Tommy and Brian called to say Mum had rung them to take Dad to hospital. His breathing was bad and he was very weak. He was seventy-two years old. Brian and I went straight to the hospital and met them there. When the consultant gathered us all into a room we knew what was coming.

'We all know Tommy is coming to the end of his illness,' he said. 'We intend to make it as comfortable for him as possible.'

Mum looked so sad. 'And he's been an amazing patient,' she said.

It was such a terrible moment, but at the same time it was so funny, the way she said that. Tommy, Brian and I couldn't help looking at her in shock. Amazing? He'd run her ragged over the past few years! But there, Mum loved him. She'd put him on a pedestal since she was a teenager and that wasn't ending now.

Coleen was still living down south and the other girls were away working so we rang round them all.

'Dad's not great,' I said. 'You'd probably better come back as soon as you can.'

I went to see him lying in the ward and he seemed so calm. He wasn't moaning or complaining or anything. On my way out I chatted to the man in the bed opposite. 'He was calling for your mum all night last night,' he said. That broke my heart.

Dad stayed in hospital for several days. Every morning Mum would go to mass and then go and sit with him all day. His two sisters, Auntie Doreen and Auntie Sheila, and my cousin Eithna came over from Ireland to see him.

After a couple of days the nurses said they had moved Dad into a private room off the ward because it would be more comfortable for him. My brothers Tommy and Brian and I weren't convinced.

'I think that may be God's waiting room,' Tommy said sadly.

Each day I'd ask if there was anything I could do for him or if he was in pain, and each day he just smiled, saying, 'No, I'm fine, Linda.'

Then one day the pain was obviously too much, even for him.

'Do you think the nurses might give me something?' he asked.

They put him on diamorphine, which eased the pain but made him very sleepy.

Each morning his first question to any of us kids who were there would be: 'When's your mum coming in?' From never being very demonstrative during their marriage, all he wanted in his final days was to lie there holding her hand. And that's what she did, hour after hour.

Coleen and I were sat with him quite early that last morning when the nurses came in and asked us to step outside while they turned him over in the bed. A couple of moments later they came back out of the room.

'I'm so sorry,' the nurse said. 'I'm afraid your dad has just passed away.'

Tears rose in my eyes and I turned away, looking up the corridor. And there, bustling down towards us, was Mum.

'Oh, I'm so sorry I'm late, girls,' she said. 'How is he? I bumped into Mr Fleck on the street and he wanted to chat and then I missed the bus, but I'm here now.'

'Oh Mum,' I said. 'I'm so sorry. He's gone.'

Her face fell. She was devastated and felt awful she hadn't been with him for his last moments. But he hadn't been conscious so wouldn't have known. The last time he was awake he'd known Mum was holding his hand. 'That's what counts, Mum,' I said.

Coleen and I called our brothers and sisters and everyone got there as quickly as they could.

We all gathered round the bed with Mum and Auntie Theresa. The nurses had put flowers in vases and a priest had appeared from somewhere to say prayers. You probably have to be a Catholic to get this, but there is a prayer for the dead where you say with the priest: 'St Anthony, pray for us. St Thomas, pray for us. St Paul, pray for us. St Jude, pray for us . . .' And so it goes on. And on. And on. Bear in mind there are more than ten thousand saints!

After about five minutes I could see Coleen's shoulders starting to shake with giggles. And then my brothers joined in. I think we were all on the verge of hysterically laughing or crying. Or both.

When the priest finally finished, Coleen whispered to me: 'Phew, thank goodness that's over. I've got a gig in February!'

It was one of the saddest days of all our lives but that's Nolan humour for you – our way of coping.

Bernie was working up in Glasgow but got home late that night. We sat round at Mum and Dad's – except Dad would never be there again – and talked and laughed about the old times. Then there was the funeral to arrange. We held it at St Kentigern's Catholic Church, right next to the infant school I'd started at weeks after we arrived off the boat from Dublin.

When we arrived for the service it was already teeming with people. Hundreds had turned out to pay their respects and to support the family and it made the whole day much more bearable to see how many people had thought so much of Dad. Family had come over from Ireland and there was also a representative from the Irish branch of Equity, the actors' union. My Brian even got Blackpool Tower to fly its flag at half mast. Lots of the clubs in the town did the same. Dad had been a big character in the Blackpool scene for years and his life had touched so many people. Bernie gave a eulogy and was as brilliant and funny as ever.

'For those of you who knew our father,' she began, 'you'll know this is the first time he has ever been on time for something.'

The grandchildren did readings and then Maureen spoke the words from the Celine Dion song, 'Because You Loved Me'. There really couldn't be better words to describe what our dad had done for all of us. 'You gave me wings and made me fly,' that song says. And that's what Dad did. Yes, he did other bad stuff too. And at that time there was still a lot of stuff we knew nothing about.

But he had made us what we were. And he was my dad and I loved him.

It was so sad for Mum afterwards. Since us kids had left home they'd spent so much more time together on their own, and she felt lost without him.

'Oh I do miss your dad,' she would say to me each time I popped round.

'I know, Mum,' I said. 'We all do.'

Maybe it was the shock. Maybe it was loneliness. Maybe it was just one of those things. But in the weeks and months after Dad's death we could tell Mum was changing. It seemed at first like grief but there were other things too which were worrying. She'd always had a sharp mind in the past but now she kept forgetting things, silly things at first. She threw herself into church life even more. She became a minister of the eucharist and gave out communion to parishioners who couldn't get out of the house. So she kept herself busy. But something was different. We didn't realize then that it was the early stages of Alzheimer's disease, which would blight the last ten years of her life. We just hoped that as she came to terms with Dad's death she'd feel a bit better.

I popped round to see her whenever I could. To be honest it gave me something to do. The work situation was still bleak. And Brian's mood hadn't lifted. He seemed so low all the time and we were squabbling over silly things.

At the start of 1999 a call came in to Brian asking if I would do a twenty-week summer season at the Layton Institute Working Men's Club in Blackpool.

'I can't do it, Brian,' I said, shaking my head. It was the same club where I'd sung 'Big Spender' when I was six years old. Now thirty-four years later to go back there felt like my life was going in reverse. I wasn't being snooty about the work – well, maybe I was – but I was disappointed things had worked out like this. It really wasn't what I'd dreamed of.

'It's a good opportunity, Linda,' Brian said.

Walking back into the club on the first night was terrible. The tables were laid out in exactly the same order, the bar was decorated the same, even the carpet looked the same as nearly four decades earlier. I walked into my dressing room and cried.

'Oh God,' I whispered to myself. 'Back to the beginning.'

Every night I cried after the show. It wasn't just the idea of going back; I didn't enjoy performing there either. The club committee were totally controlling. There was no joy in any of it. And deep down I felt a failure.

I took my anger and frustration out on Brian. We were niggling at each other over everything and anything.

'Just leave if it's making you that unhappy,' Brian said. He was trying to put me first again but even him saying that annoyed me. I couldn't just flounce off with no other work to go to. One of us had to be earning. I rang Bernie at my wits' end.

'What am I going to do, Bernie?' I asked.

'Suck the cheque,' she said. Bernie was right. There were worse things I could be doing and we needed this money. So I got my head down and got on with it.

But it didn't stop me and Brian bickering. One night on the way home from the show I was on at him again. He pulled the car to the side of the road and turned off the ignition. 'Linda, I love you more than anything on earth. But if you carry on like this it's going to tear us apart.'

He was right. I had to let my frustrations and anger go. It wasn't easy though.

By then there was never going to be the patter of tiny feet in our house. Well, that was what we thought. Until one day Coleen turned up with a gorgeous little puppy for us.

A couple of days earlier I'd fallen down the stairs at home. Linda 'Lucky' Hudson had struck again! I think I must have tripped on my jeans and then toppled all the way down. What with everything else that had been going on I felt thoroughly sorry for myself. Until the doorbell rang. I opened the door to see Coleen standing there, a massive grin across her face and a tiny little Bichon Frise puppy in her arms.

'I thought he might cheer you up,' Coleen said, lifting him into my arms.

'Oh Col,' I gasped. 'He's gorgeous.'

And he was. He was just a few weeks old and not much more than a ball of fluff but he was utterly adorable. Brian and I fell in love with him instantly.

We decided to call him Hudson. There was never any doubt he was going to be part of our family, and should have the family name as well.

We were supposed to be going to Marbella on a working holiday a few weeks later – two shows and a free holiday.

'We can't go now,' said Brian, holding Hudson on his lap.

'Why not?' I asked.

'We can't leave Hudson,' he replied. And we couldn't. He was too gorgeous to leave.

At first we had strict rules that he had to sleep downstairs. But when he gave us a look with those chestnut eyes we agreed to let him into our bedroom at night – so long as he slept on the floor. Well, that lasted about twenty minutes! He wanted to be lying between us in the middle of the bed and so he did.

Brian used to call him Captain Condom! The first time we were trying to have a bit of 'romance' after Hudson arrived Brian had to suddenly stop.

'Sorry, Linda, but I really can't do this with a dog lying on the pillow staring at me!'

After that Hudson got used to knowing that sometimes even he wasn't allowed in our bedroom.

And then, at the end of 1999, more good news . . . It was just before New Year's Eve that I landed the role of Mrs Johnstone, the lead in the hugely popular *Blood Brothers* national tour. Bernie had had the role before she gave birth to her gorgeous daughter Erin. And just weeks after the baby she'd landed a fantastic job in *Brookside*. Now they needed a new Mrs Johnstone and wanted me. It was going to be a long-running tour and the money was amazing. Rehearsals were due to start in February 2000. What a great way to start the new millennium.

Me, Bernie and Brian about
to perform in Blackpool.

Nine years old and belting
out my solo 'Big Spender'.

Dad singing 'Thank Heaven for Little Girls' at Cliffs Hotel in Blackpool.
From left to right: Dad, Mum, Coleen, Bernie, me, Maureen and Denise.

Me, Bernie and Coleen with Mum and Dad in 1970.

Top The Nolan Sisters. Living in London and about to fly to Paris to support Frank Sinatra, May 1975. From left to right: Bernie, Denise, me, Anne and Maureen.

Bottom Our image in the 1970s was glamorous, but sweet.

Left Messing around with thirteen-year-old Coleen in 1978. One year later, she officially joined the group.

Bottom Anne married her Brian in June 1978.

OPPOSITE PAGE
Top Photographed in 1980.

Bottom Getting ready to go on the Russell Harty show in 1981, with our brothers Tommy and Brian.

On my way to the church to get married, 28 August 1981.
Dad is wearing his emergency set of teeth.

All my sisters were bridesmaids.

Marrying Brian was one of the happiest days of my life.

Above Now called The
Nolans, my relationship
with my sisters was
becoming fraught.

Left My first solo photo
shoot in 1984. 'The
Naughty Nolan' was
the newspaper headline.

OPPOSITE PAGE
Top left Brian with
his son Lloyd; *top
right* Brian and me in
Maggie May, Blackpool;
bottom I played Maggie
May on the Central Pier
between 1986 and 1996.

Nine

Brian Falls Ill

Brian had been feeling off colour for days.

'It's just this flu bug that's going round,' he said, lying on the sofa, 'I'll be fine by tomorrow.'

I made him another cup of tea and felt his forehead. He was incredibly hot and hadn't eaten a thing for the entire previous day. And there was a flu bug going round. It had even been on the news.

We were staying with Denise and her partner Tom in West Drayton, Middlesex. They had a beautiful home and always made us welcome if I was touring down south in *Blood Brothers*.

I'd done the tour for two years now and loved it. Hilariously, Denise had been playing Mrs Johnstone in the West End at the same time. Then in 2002 we swapped. Denise did the tour and I did the West End. And that's why we'd ended up living at their house for a while. It was fabulous because it meant Brian and I could spend all day together before he drove me to work in the evening. That had been the pattern of my life for so many years that I couldn't imagine it any other way.

'Why don't you stay here this evening and I'll get a cab to work,' I said that night, thinking Brian looked decidedly peaky. 'No, I'll come with you,' he replied. Like I've said, Brian regarded looking after me as his job. In fact it was more like a mission – and the idea of me going into work on my own was a definite no-no.

It had been hard for him since I'd gone into *Blood Brothers*. It was a big established show and I think he felt a little redundant. The moods where he was withdrawn had become more frequent. I think we both knew he had become depressed. But we rarely spoke about it because the conversation never ended well.

'Why don't you go to the GP and see if he could give you tablets or something to help?' I'd ask.

'No, I'm not doing that,' he'd reply. 'I'll be fine.'

Unless you've lived with someone with depression it is hard to explain how powerless you are to change things. Onlookers might think: 'Well, why didn't you just give him a shake and sort him out?' But the reality is much, much more complicated. It was as if very, very slowly Brian was drifting away from me. That spark which he'd always seemed to have was dying inside him, and nothing I said or did seemed to get it going again. We'd always been so close that it was horrific to think I couldn't make him feel better, but I couldn't. I tried date nights or cooking nice meals and he'd be perfectly polite and kind. But it all seemed such a terrible effort for him. It was like he was swamped with sadness and I couldn't pull him free. And we both knew he was still drinking too much, which was only making everything worse. Since he'd had more spare time on his hands he was turning to his whisky and Coke earlier in the day. And returning to the bottle more and more frequently.

By that stage Brian was a functioning alcoholic. It's only in the last year that I've actually been able to say those words, actually been able to admit it to myself and other people. Back then I was still stuck with the idea that alcoholics were blokes huddled in doorways on the street, slurping cider from bottles in paper bags. Brian wasn't like that at all. He was always clean, tidy, funny, and never aggressive or violent. But more and more often he was drinking all day.

One morning a few months earlier I'd come down at about ten in my dressing gown after a late night at work. Brian was sat at the table, nursing a large mug of Coke in his hands. Something niggled at me.

'What's that you're drinking?' I asked.

'Just a Coke,' he replied defensively.

'Got any whisky in it?' I shot back.

He didn't need to answer. I could see it in his eyes.

Other days I would walk into the kitchen and see him quickly finishing a glass before slipping it into the sink. I'd sniff the glass, smell the whisky. 'That's just a glass from last night,' was his usual excuse. But I knew. He knew. We both knew. What we didn't know was how to get away from the grip alcohol had on him.

'Why don't you just drink after the show with me?' I'd suggest sometimes. And Brian would agree. But then I'd find the telltale glasses around the house again.

Once or twice he resolved to turn over a new leaf. One morning he strode into the kitchen, a look of determination across his face. 'Right, that's it, from now on I'm only drinking water.' It might last a day. Maybe two.

Once I found a whisky bottle hidden at the bottom of a cupboard in the kitchen and held it up accusingly. 'Have you put this in the wrong cupboard by accident?'

Hiding booze from me was clearly a bad sign but beyond nagging him to go to the doctor I didn't know what to do. And it wasn't as if his behaviour towards me had changed. He was still loving and attentive.

Perhaps I should have been tougher. 'It's me or the booze,' I could have said. But I didn't. Why? Because at that point I really wasn't confident he would have chosen me. And why would I push away the man I adored? So much of this stuff I wasn't even thinking about consciously. It was subconsciously running through my mind while we muddled through each day much the way we had always done.

It's strange to think I ended up in that situation having grown up with a father who was alcoholic. But my sisters have been attracted to heavy drinkers. Maybe it's the showbiz life that creates temptation. Maybe we were all looking for someone a bit like our dad.

So that morning in Denise's house, despite Brian's claims that he was suffering from the flu, I couldn't get rid of a nagging concern it was more than that. And that it had something to do with his drinking.

As he drove me home after the show he looked dreadful. Back at Denise's he went straight to bed. It was the middle of the night when I became aware of Brian moving around the bedroom.

'What's up?' I said.

'I've been throwing up,' he replied. 'And there is blood coming out.'

'Oh God, Brian,' I said. I got him downstairs and gave him a glass of water then ran back up to Denise and Tom's room. They were on a break from the tour.

'Quick,' I said. 'It's Brian, he's really not well. Can you take him to the hospital?'

Tom jumped out of bed and together the three of us helped Brian walk ever so slowly to the car parked outside. He was in terrible pain and even getting him into the front seat was making him gasp in agony. I opened the rear door of the car to get in behind him.

'No, Linda,' Brian winced from the front. 'You're not coming. It's my job to look after you, remember, and if you come with me I'll just be worrying about you. Stay here and then I'll know you are OK.'

'But, Brian?' I said.

'No, wait here.'

So I did. I know that might sound strange to a lot of people – and perhaps it was unusual, but that was how our relationship worked. I spent the next hour walking up and down Denise's kitchen waiting for news about what was going on.

Tom had hared towards the nearest hospital, in Hillingdon, jumping every red light along the route.

'You can't park here, mate,' someone yelled as he screeched up outside Accident and Emergency.

'Oh yes I can,' he replied. Tom knew Brian was in a very bad way.

At A&E a nurse took one look at Brian, then barely able to walk, and helped him onto a bed.

Within minutes a doctor had diagnosed a perforated ulcer and internal bleeding. 'Just in time,' the doctor told Tom. 'Another forty minutes and he wouldn't have made it.'

Back at Denise's, not knowing what the hell was going on, I found myself thinking about what life would be like without Brian. It was impossible to imagine. Too alien to consider.

After an hour had gone by I called the hospital.

'And you are Mrs Hudson?' a nurse asked.

'Yes,' I said. 'And I'm really, really worried about my husband.'

'Yes, I'm afraid it is serious. They are going to operate immediately. You should come now.'

Tom returned to pick me up and then raced his car back to the hospital again. At the reception desk I asked if anyone knew where my husband was. 'Yes, he's currently in Resus,' a nurse said.

Resus? That meant resuscitation. Was Brian dying?

'Where is he? I said. 'I've got to see him.'

It's hard to explain how I felt in that moment. I'd been scared at different points in my life – going on stage, being made bankrupt, losing Dad. But this was more than that. It was sheer, utter terror, like the ground was cracking under my feet and there was nothing I could do to prevent it.

A nurse guided me to the ward where Brian was lying on a bed. He was so pale and looked dreadful.

'Told you not to come,' he said, smiling and reaching out for my hand. 'Now I'll be worried about you.'

'Don't be daft,' I said. 'It's my turn to be worried about you.'

Oh and I was worried. It was all such a shock because I hadn't realized he even had an ulcer. He'd hardly been a picture of health recently but there had been no symptoms of an ulcer.

They put him on morphine for the pain but it sent him completely doolally, which despite the trauma of the situation was really funny.

'Don't look over your shoulder,' he said, as I sat next to his bed. 'There's a huge great lizard climbing up the wall.'

And when his best friend John Parker came to visit and offered to get me dinner after visiting time, Brian became convinced we were having an affair. It was bonkers but hilarious.

Denise was off on tour by then so I went to stay with Coleen for company. Except her boys really had come down with the flu virus – and I caught it from them. That meant visiting Brian was out of the question so Coleen went instead. On her return she flung me a box of chocolates.

'When I got there Brian was hobbling down the ward with the drip still in his arm,' huffed Coleen jokingly. 'He was on his way to the hospital shop, determined to get you these as a Get Well present. Honestly, you two!'

By the end of the week Brian was allowed home.

'When you arrived here you had forty minutes to live,' the consultant said. 'But you've done everything we've asked and you're going to be OK. Now go home and look after yourself properly.'

That of course was the tricky bit. The ulcer had given Brian a shock and for a few weeks he did try to cut back on the booze and swapped whisky for beer. And he tried to eat more healthily and lose some of the weight he'd put on. But although physically he was on the mend, his spirits were still low. Things soon slipped back to the way they had been before.

The drinking continued. It had just become Brian's way of life. And so the damage he was inflicting on his body continued. It felt like there was nothing I could do to stop it by that point – it was Brian. And so I didn't even try after a while.

Challenging Brian about his drinking would only make him retreat into himself more and so it didn't seem worth it. He was never violent or aggressive when he drank and so day after day slipped by and his drinking was a constant in our lives.

A couple of years later he collapsed again. We were living with our best friends Sue and Graham that time, in between doing the *Blood Brothers* national tour. The four of us had been out for a lovely Sunday lunch. Brian wasn't drinking and really didn't seem like his usual self. The following day he refused to even come out for a walk when I went to the park with the nieces and nephews.

He had an early night while I sat downstairs watching the television. Suddenly I heard the most almighty crash from upstairs. It was so loud that at first I thought a wardrobe must have toppled over. We went running upstairs and there was Brian collapsed on the floor. And he was literally frothing at the mouth. I was convinced he was having a stroke. I put him into the recovery position like I'd seen people do on television, then told Sue to ring 999.

'Hurry, please hurry,' she begged the operator, 'his lips are turning blue.'

At the hospital Coleen turned up and stood watching as the doctors checked Brian out. A minute later she came over to me, looking serious.

'They've asked him if he drinks,' Coleen said. 'He told them, "Not a lot." Linda, he's got to start owning up to what's really going on.'

It turned out that because he'd suddenly stopped boozing his blood sugar levels had plummeted and he'd had a fit. It was another serious warning that all wasn't well, but still not serious enough to stop Brian drinking permanently. It felt as if nothing could lift him out of the rut he'd got himself in. I certainly couldn't – he wouldn't even discuss his drinking with me. When we were young Brian and I could sit and giggle about any kind of nonsense for hours on end. But the laughs were few and far between now.

About six months after that scare, when I was back in *Blood Brothers* in the West End, we were lying in bed at Tom and Denise's. 'Hey, Lin, feel this,' Brian said. 'I've got a lump in my chest.'

I leant over and ran my hand firmly across his chest. There it was, a hard pea-size lump just by his breastbone. At first I thought it was a spot but I couldn't see anything on the surface.

'It's probably nothing,' I said. But even then I didn't really believe that. There's something about finding a lump that makes everyone panic. We all know exactly how bad something quite minor can turn out to be. Brian didn't say any more about it but I could tell he was worried too.

The next morning I was really happy to hear him on the phone to the local GP, booking himself in for an appointment but again he wouldn't let me go with him. I'd long since given up being annoyed by things like that.

'How did it go?' I asked when he stepped back in the door.

'All right, I think,' he replied. 'But they've referred me to the hospital for tests and a biopsy. Just to be on the safe side.'

'Oh, OK,' I replied. My fear was growing. But despite us being the closest married couple imaginable in many ways, this then became just another topic we couldn't discuss – it was too frightening.

It was about a week later that I came downstairs in my

dressing gown mid-morning, after a late night on stage, made myself a cup of tea and went to drink it outside in Denise's lovely garden. Brian wasn't around but it wasn't long before I heard his car draw up and the front door open and close. Looking up I saw my still gorgeous Brian walking through the house towards me. Then, totally bizarrely, he started skipping out into the garden, round and round in a circle.

'What are you doing, you idiot?' I giggled. Brian hadn't acted the fool like this in years.

'I've got cancer, I've got cancer,' he started singing.

'What?' I said, laughing at his odd behaviour and a bit uncertain what the words were. 'I can't hear you properly.'

He carried on chanting the same words like a kid singing a nursery rhyme in the playground and gradually I heard exactly what he was saying. It was horrific. I thought he might be going mad.

'Stop it, Brian,' I shouted. 'Just tell me what the hell is going on?'

I think I stunned him out of the weird trance he was in and he turned and looked me straight in the eye and said in a deadpan tone: 'I've got skin cancer. It's a malignant melanoma.'

There was a pause that possibly lasted a second but at the time seemed to go on for ever and ever as my entire world was smashed into tiny pieces in the front of my mind.

I could feel the inside of my mouth start to fill with saliva as though I was about to vomit. My head was spinning. Brian looked horrified by the fear on my face. He leant forward and held my hand.

'Sorry about the skipping, Lin,' he said. 'Just wasn't sure how to tell you.'

There was never ever going to be a good way.

We sat on the swing chair in Denise's garden and held each other.

'Oh Brian, I love you so much,' I said.

'I know, Lin,' he replied. 'I'm scared this time. Really scared.'

It was such a tiny lump I couldn't believe it could be *that* dangerous. But cancer is such a terrifying word. The doctors told Brian that all his years of sunbathing on our holidays in Turkey or Spain – or even in our garden – had taken their toll on his skin. Brian had been a real sun worshipper and back in the seventies and eighties no one even thought of putting on suntan lotion. We thought a tan made us look and feel healthy.

As ever the Nolan cavalry rallied round. 'Stay here as long as you want,' Denise said.

Brian was sent to the Royal Marsden Hospital in London which has an incredible reputation for cancer care and I thought that he couldn't be in better hands. The consultant told him that rather than surgery they would begin by blasting him with a strong dose of chemotherapy. That would reduce the lump and then they could consider all the other treatment options available.

We just went along with what we were told.

But in show business, even when your world is falling apart, you have to work or you don't get paid. And the *Blood Brothers* tour was still moving up and down the country most weeks.

'You should stay with Denise while you're having the weekly chemo and I'll do the tour on my own,' I said to Brian.

'Absolutely not, Lin,' he replied. 'My job is to look after you and that's what I'm going to do. Cancer or no cancer.'

Brian was a proud man and the thought that he could no longer look after me was something he'd find hard to deal with. So I had no choice but to agree.

Off we went to Glasgow. And then Manchester, Nottingham, Sunderland. Wherever I needed to be, Brian was there too. They even arranged to have his chemo done while we were touring. We arrived in Glasgow late one evening and Brian spent hours decorating my dressing room with the flowers and the make-up, cards and keepsakes, just the way he always did. As soon as he'd finished, he was in the city hospital having chemotherapy drugs pumped into his arm.

Initially the chemo didn't affect him too badly although he was very tired. And he was still feeling very low. His legs had swollen up and he found walking difficult. Even taking Hudson for a walk seemed too much for him. And he refused, totally refused, to discuss how he felt about any of it. Although we were together all the time in some ways, in others we were further apart than we'd ever been.

He spent his days sat in hotel rooms watching television, rarely even looking up to talk to me. He seemed to have lost himself.

'It'll be OK,' I'd say as we sat in our hotel room in near-silence, watching the telly.

'I know, Lin,' he replied. But I wasn't so sure he believed it any more.

Other times I'd say: 'I want to help you, Brian.'

'Nothing you can do – unless you can cure cancer of course.'

He was becoming bitter and frustrated. I knew he was struggling – both physically and emotionally – to come to terms with what was happening. But the harder I tried to help, the more he pushed me away. Days would go by when he would barely look at me, let alone properly talk to me.

There were brighter moments when he would lift himself. Like when we renewed our wedding vows on a Turkish wooden gulet boat in the summer of 2005. We'd been on holiday lots of times to Olu Deniz in Turkey, which has to be one of the most beautiful bays on earth. Coleen and her partner Ray were coming with us that year along with her sons Shane Jnr and Jake and her and Ray's new daughter Ciara. Our niece Alex and her friend and some of our friends from *Blood Brothers* were joining us too.

Brian thought renewing the vows would be a way of putting the last few years behind us and would enable us to look forward to a time when he would be totally better again. I think we both hoped it would be a turning point.

That day was magical. We set sail from the beach in the morning and spent the day swimming off the side of the boat, catching fish for lunch and lounging in the sun. Then, just as the sun was beginning to set we prepared for the ceremony, which was to be carried out by the manager of the hotel where we'd been staying.

One of my best friends, Drew, washed my hair on the boat and my niece Alex tied it into a French plait and then I changed into a beautiful peach dress I'd bought specially for the day. It was a floaty chiffon material with spaghetti straps. Over the top I wore a wrap on which my friend Sue had embroidered our initials. It was beautiful.

When I was ready I stepped onto the main deck of the boat and was stunned. Brian had had pictures from our wedding day blown up and then everything had been decorated with fairy lights and rose petals.

We read our vows to each other and afterwards Ray played guitar while Coleen sang 'Looks Like We've Made It'. Everyone was crying. It was amazing.

After the ceremony we drank champagne and ate the beautiful cake the hotel owners had made us. We partied for hours then as it got dark we all lay on sun loungers under thick blankets, looking at the stars. It was utterly beautiful.

And it reminded me how wonderful my husband could be.

But back home things soon returned to the rut we'd found ourselves in over the past few years. It was strange that Brian had done so much to make me happy on that holiday but back home he was completely unable to make himself happy.

Day after day he returned to watching television, barely talking and drinking too much.

'I'm going out for a walk with Hudson,' I said one day. 'Fancy coming?'

'No,' he grunted back. I felt I was losing my husband into a dark abyss of sadness and self-pity and nothing I could do would pull him out of it.

'Well I'm going,' I snapped back. 'I love you, Brian, and you know that but I can't sit here and let you drag us both down.' Then I put Hudson on his lead and strode round the park, crying to myself.

I'd tried everything but he refused to accept he needed help.

The side effects of Brian's chemotherapy had become terrible. His legs swelled up so that walking even a short distance was difficult for him and he hadn't the energy for anything. At the time I put all that down to the chemo but in hindsight I wonder if more of it was due to the toll alcohol had had on his body. But as he never let me go to any of his hospital appointments there was a lot about his treatment that I never understood.

Each time Brian went in for more chemo he seemed more battered. Two days after each session he'd be too weak to even get out of bed.

'We can't give you any more,' the doctor told him one day. 'We just don't think your body will take it. We're hopeful we've done enough to stabilize you.'

No one sounded very certain, however. And now I wonder whether they had to stop the chemo because his liver was too wrecked to take any more. I'd hoped that with the chemotherapy over, Brian's depression might lift. But it didn't.

I looked back on the early days of our marriage as such a golden, happy time. And then we'd had that magical holiday when we renewed our vows. But everyday life had lost its sparkle.

Ten

This Isn't Us

I knew it was there. I'd known it was there for months. But maybe it would be gone tomorrow. Or maybe if I didn't think about it, then it might not really be happening. But it was.

The hard lump I'd first felt in my left breast at the beginning of 2005 was growing. I could feel it when I put my bra on every morning. But Brian had been so poorly, and then I was touring with *Blood Brothers*. Then there was our holiday to Turkey, and then a booking for panto at the end of the year. I needed to work or we'd be going bust again. Now was just not a good time for me to have, well . . . whatever.

And it could be anything, anyway.

When I was nineteen, I went to the doctor utterly convinced there was something seriously wrong with me because I'd found a lump in my breast. But that had turned out to be a blocked milk duct.

Chances were this would be the same, I thought. Although deep down, further down than I even let my consciousness go, there was a feeling it might be something more. Now I'm ashamed it took me so long to own up to anyone – including myself – about the lump in my breast. And I'd always advise other women to go straight to the doctor the very moment they spot or feel something unusual. But back then? Well, who knows what I was thinking?

For months I didn't tell Brian what I'd found in my breast. He had enough to worry about after his cancer diagnosis. And like I said, there were so many things we couldn't talk about by then.

The first person I finally confided in was Coleen while we were chatting on the phone one day.

'I've got a bit of a small lump in my left boob,' I said as casually as I could manage.

'What?' said Coleen, her usual laid-back tone instantly changing.

'Do you think I should go to the doctor?' I asked, knowing all too well what a totally ridiculous question that was.

'Of course you must,' she replied. 'Today.'

But still I didn't. I was on the road every week with *Blood Brothers* and I never seemed to get round to making the call. Every couple of days Coleen was on the phone nagging me. 'Have you made that appointment yet?' she would say.

'I'll do it tomorrow,' I'd reply.

Next day: 'Made the appointment, Linda?'

'I'm on it. I really am.'

Next day: 'Have you made that bloody appointment or am I going to have to do it for you then drag you there myself?'

After a fortnight I was all out of excuses.

'Linda, what are you playing at?' Coleen said one evening. 'I've tried persuading you, I've tried getting mad at you – now I am just begging. Please will you go to the doctor. This may well be nothing but you really have to get it checked out so that you can know for certain.'

That's when I told Brian, and of course he begged me to get

it checked out too. Finally, in September 2005, when I got back from a stint of *Blood Brothers* in Darlington, I had a week off work so made an appointment for a check-up. I lay on the consulting table in the surgery as the doctor ran his hands over my left breast. A frown was forming over his face as he asked me: 'And how long do you think the lump has been there?'

'Er, four months, maybe five,' I replied. I was mortified that I'd left it so long.

'OK,' he said slowly. 'I fear this isn't going to be great news but we need to send you for a mammogram and see what happens. There is definitely something there – we just need to know exactly what it is.'

I felt sick when I left the clinic. But I also knew I had to finish the *Blood Brothers* tour and do the pantomime booking in Belfast to get a bit of money in the bank if I was going to need a couple of months off. Without a bit of cash in the bank there would be even more pressure on Brian, and the way he was feeling, I couldn't face that. And so I finished the last few weeks of *Blood Brothers* and caught the plane to Belfast – and still I hadn't been for the mammogram.

'You're mad,' Coleen said flatly, furious at how much more time had drifted by.

'I will. Soon. I promise,' I replied.

'Well if you don't, I'm telling all our brothers and sisters you've got a lump and then you'll have them all on your case too.'

I was playing the Wicked Queen in *Snow White* that Christmas and we had a great time in Belfast. But the fear of what this lump could be was hanging heavy on me. Over the New Year I gave myself a bit of a talking-to. I had to make sorting it out a priority for 2006. So I was one of Belfast Infirmary's first appointments of the New Year.

The doctor examined me, did a biopsy and sent me straight through for a mammogram.

I'd expected him to do a load of tests then come back to me with some results in a few months' time. So I was totally stunned when he turned to me and said: 'Right, I'll send those off for testing, but I have to tell you now that I do think you probably have breast cancer.'

I felt nauseous but still didn't allow it to sink in. There was no time to think about it, even if I wanted to. I had two more performances of *Snow White* that day. As ever, the show had to go on.

'Oh no,' Brian said when I told him. 'Oh God, no.'

He had a great relationship with his cancer care specialist at the Royal Marsden Hospital and that evening he rang her to discuss what it all meant.

'Don't panic,' she said. 'They can't know anything for certain until they've got the results back. And they wouldn't break news like that to a woman unless there was a specialist Macmillan nurse in the room. So try to keep calm.'

Which is exactly what we did. Although it wasn't easy. I was due back at the hospital on the Friday that week. They'd been so helpful and squeezed me in for an appointment at 5 p.m. – sandwiched between the matinee and evening performances of the panto. It all felt rather surreal, sitting there in the hospital reception area with some of my stage make-up still plastered on my face and the chorus of 'Oh yes he does, Oh no he doesn't' ringing in my ears, while waiting to find out if I had cancer.

We'd only been there a few moments when a kind-looking

lady walked up to us and said: 'Hi, Linda Hudson? I'm Karen and I'm your Macmillan nurse.'

My stomach crashed to the floor. So this was it then. I had cancer. And here was my specialist nurse, just as Brian's counsellor had predicted. Brian and I looked at each other, unable to speak.

Karen led us into an office where my consultant, Mr Whitaker, was waiting. I think I had already gone into a state of shock and barely took in anything he was saying but I heard enough to realize it was bad. Very bad.

'I'm afraid, Mrs Hudson, your cancer is very aggressive and already at stage three,' Mr Whitaker said.

'What does that mean?' I asked. 'How many stages are there?'

'Four,' he replied quietly.

I started to shake. Oh God, was this it? Was I going to die?

The lump was already about four inches long – the size of a small courgette – and needed to be removed immediately. Mr Whitaker explained I would need a full mastectomy.

'Will I have to have chemotherapy?' I asked, thinking of all the horrific treatment Brian had been through.

'Yes, you will,' said Mr Whitaker.

'Will I lose my hair?' was my only other question.

'Probably,' he said. 'You have to understand your cancer is very aggressive – we are going to have to throw everything we have at it.'

It sounded a shallow question to ask about my hair but in all the confusion it was the thing which was dominating my mind.

Brian barely spoke an entire word the whole time we were in the office. When we stood up to leave, his face was grey and he looked like he was going to be sick. I guess he knew better than anyone what I was about to go through. Later he admitted that in those moments he simply felt absolute terror at the idea of losing me.

We gripped each other's hands and took the lift downstairs in silence. As soon as we got out of the main entrance Brian looked at me and said: 'It's OK, you can cry.' I fell into his arms and sobbed and sobbed and sobbed. Brian put those strong arms around my shoulders and pulled me to his chest.

'This isn't what we are about,' he whispered into the side of my head. 'Cancer isn't us.'

I knew what he meant. Brian and I were about showbiz, after-parties, whisky and Coke, holidays in the sun, laughing, singing. We weren't about hospital wards and pills and sickness. Except, that was what the future seemed to be.

We drove back to the apartment where we'd been staying and I rang Coleen.

'Hey, Coleen,' I said. 'It's cancer.'

There was a moment's silence on the phone and I could tell she was trying to collect herself. 'Oh Linda, I'm so sorry,' she said. We cried together. There wasn't much more to say.

Coleen offered to call the rest of the family as I couldn't face breaking it to them individually – I knew how devastated they would all be. And I didn't have much time either – I had to be back on stage as the Wicked Queen in two hours.

'Take the night off, love,' Brian begged me. But I couldn't.

'You're the one who always says the show must go on,' I said, trying to raise a laugh. 'And what does it matter? Whether I go to work or not, I've still got cancer. But for once, Brian, please don't come to the theatre tonight. If I get there and can pretend it's just a normal night I'll be absolutely fine. But if I see you at the side of the stage I'll never be able to hold it together.'

So for the first time in twenty-five years Brian wasn't in my dressing room when I went out on stage. I blanked out everything that night and just concentrated on being the Wicked Queen.

The following day there were the final two shows to be done and after that the last-night party. The last thing on earth I felt like doing was partying but they were such a great cast that I didn't want to put a dampener on things by telling them what was happening. Instead I put on my slap and got out there one more time. On Monday morning Brian and I were on the ferry back home.

Two days later I was at Blackpool Hospital meeting my lovely breast cancer nurse, Sarah Middleton, for the first time. I put on a hospital gown and lay down on the bed. But looking down at my chest as I lay there it was evident something was badly wrong. My right boob slipped down to the side as most women's do (unless they're a supermodel). But my left boob just stayed completely upright. Clearly the lump must have been so big it was just holding it up.

Deep down I'd still been hoping there might have been some terrible mistake in the tests they'd done in Belfast – but it was looking pretty unlikely. And yet my total refusal to cope with the reality unfolding around me continued.

A couple of days later I called Sarah, who'd said I could ring her any time with any concern.

'I think I might get a second opinion on all this,' I said.

'By all means, Linda,' Sarah replied. 'But you will be wasting your time. You have got cancer. And rather than wasting any more time you've just got to put all your energy into fighting it.'

She was, of course, right.

The surgeon wanted to carry out a mastectomy the following week but still I ummed and aahed. I felt I needed time to process everything that was going on. And I was scared. When I'd been in The Nolans I'd been the blonde one with the big boobs. And now both of these were going. I felt the things which identified me as a woman were being taken away and that was scary.

'I'm just not ready for the op. Not yet,' I said to Sarah.

Oh, and I still had two more weeks of *Blood Brothers* to do in Coventry and Nottingham. I know that might sound crazy but my entire world was falling apart and work was the only certainty I could hang on to.

'Well at this stage another two weeks before the operation won't make too much difference,' Sarah replied.

Finally it was agreed I'd go in for the mastectomy on 21 February – two days before my forty-seventh birthday. The next few weeks were spent trying to come to terms with what was happening. My sister Anne was an enormous support. She'd had breast cancer six years earlier and had to have a lumpectomy, chemotherapy and radiotherapy.

'I'm scared, Anne,' I said.

'You'll be fine,' she assured me. 'Everyone reacts differently to the treatment. But you'll get through this.'

Beyond the family I was a bit embarrassed to discuss what was happening. It felt so private, particularly as it was my breast. And I imagined people would think I was stupid for having ignored the lump for so long. We were staying with Sue and Graham at that time, but I couldn't even bring myself to tell them. Finally, one night over dinner, Brian just said it. I felt so awkward and embarrassed that I stood up and left the room. In fact, everyone who knew was brilliantly supportive and I felt bad for being so secretive.

On one of my last nights in *Blood Brothers* in Coventry I asked all the cast to come to my dressing room after the vocal warm up. 'Oh, Mam's having a party,' they were laughing. (Everyone called me Mam because I played Mrs Johnstone.) We'd been touring together for months and we felt like family. I knew the story about my cancer was about to come out in the press and I wanted to tell them myself first. When they turned up in my dressing room I made sure they all had some wine in one of those plastic cups, then cleared my throat and nervously began to speak.

'I just wanted to invite you all round because I'm going to have to take a bit of time out of the tour,' I said. 'I'm afraid they've found a lump in my breast. It's, er, cancer. I'm going to have to have it removed.'

Saying the word was still incredibly difficult. But gradually I was accepting it. There was a terrible silence in the room for a moment and then everyone gathered round, hugging and kissing me.

'Thanks so much, guys,' I said. 'But please don't be nice to me. I can cope with anything apart from people being nice to me!'

So they treated me just like normal and that kept my spirits up in the last few days of the tour.

We even had a laugh about it. 'Woman with breast cancer coming through,' I'd yell as I squeezed through the cast and crew huddled backstage before the show started. It was heartbreaking the day I had to leave them all. I had no idea how long I'd be gone for – or if I'd ever be back. It was one of the scariest days of my life.

My brothers and sisters were on the phone every day in the run-up to the operation and after the story appeared in a newspaper I received beautiful flowers, cards and letters from people across the country. But the strangest message came one day when I was in the car with Brian and his phone rang.

'Can you answer it – I'm driving,' Brian said.

'You answer it on hands free,' I said, 'I hate the phone!'

'Answer it,' he shouted, 'it might be important.'

Reluctantly, I picked it up and accepted the call.

'Hello,' I said.

'Hi, is that Linda?' an American voice said at the other end.

'Yeah.'

'Hi, it's Donny Osmond here – I just wanted to wish you good luck with everything you're going through.'

I could barely squeak 'thank you' back down the receiver as my mind instantly went back to the Donny Osmond wall posters, pillowcase and calendars which had decorated my teenage bedroom.

I discovered later that Brian had fixed up the call, knowing how much it would mean to me. And it absolutely did.

Brian was great through that period. He'd been low for a long while but when I needed him he seemed to grow in strength again. He was there for me every step. I was due to arrive at the hospital on a Monday afternoon, ready for the op first thing Tuesday morning. But Brian and I hated the thought of spending even a night apart so he asked the consultant if I could arrive very early on the Tuesday morning. He agreed just so long as I went the previous day and had myself all marked up to show where the surgeon would have to cut. Which is why the day before my surgery I was sitting with Brian, Coleen and Ray in a Harvester restaurant tucking into fish and chips while underneath my shirt I had big black arrows felt-tipped on my boob.

The next morning Brian stayed with me until the very last moment before I went into the operating theatre. And when I woke up again afterwards he was there by my side. The operation had taken longer than the surgeon had anticipated because the cancer was even worse than feared – it had spread to my lymph nodes so fourteen of them had to be cut out from under my armpit.

When I opened my eyes I looked from Brian down to the sheet resting across my chest, to the place where my boob used to be. I'd always had quite big boobs – a 36D – so the difference between my right boob still in position and the totally flat left side of my chest was shocking. 'Well that's that then,' I thought entirely matter-of-factly. I think I was numb – my emotions had just been turned off.

My brothers, sisters and their families were next in to visit me. As Brian always said, whenever there was a crisis the Nolan cavalry always came out in force, armed with grapes and boxes of chocolates. Brian had totally Brian-ed my hospital room, so there were cards, flowers and balloons all over the place.

Denise was performing on a cruise at the time and was all the way out in Vietnam, but she phoned on my forty-seventh birthday. That morning Brian rang the ward, singing 'Happy Birthday' in his mock Pavarotti voice. But hearing his voice on the phone just did for me. I'd been so brave up until then but I collapsed into a heap of tears. Twenty minutes later he was sprinting through the door, clutching more balloons, chocolates, cards and presents. He'd bought me a beautiful loose cardigan to wear for going home because it was still very painful to have anything heavy on my chest.

And my sisters had been to Marks and Spencer and bought me some mastectomy bras. My breast-care nurse, Sarah, showed me how to fit the sponge prosthesis into the space where my breast had once been. I knew it would be several months before I'd be ready to have reconstruction. Nowadays they tend to do reconstruction on the same day as the mastectomy but at that time you had to wait.

For the first few days when the nurse came to change my dressing each morning I couldn't bear to look down and see what was under the bandages but then one morning as she was gently removing the padding, I said: 'OK, I think I'm all right to see it now.'

I looked down and it was so neat. It was a tiny row of stitches where my breast had been. It wasn't horrific or scary, just very neat.

I recovered quite quickly and after five days I was able to go home to Graham and Sue who cooked a beautiful Beef Wellington as a celebratory dinner. It was such a relief to be out of hospital and to get into bed next to Brian that night. Nothing was too much trouble for him when I was poorly. I had to return to hospital every other day to have the wound drained, as it filled with fluid, but all in all I made good progress.

After about a week all the bandaging was removed. I got used to wearing the prosthesis in my bra during the day and fully clothed I looked perfectly normal. But naked I felt very different. After years of getting into bed next to Brian with only perfume on, I would insist on covering myself up in one of his old T-shirts. Of course Brian told me over and over again that he didn't care what I looked like. But that wasn't the point. I cared what I looked like in front of him. He'd always loved my big boobs. I wasn't scared he might love me less, because I knew he wasn't that kind of man. I just thought he would be sad. Disappointed. Like me.

It was a couple of months later when I was sitting at the end of the bed taking off my bra that he saw the scar for the first time. I'd totally forgotten about my missing boob – I must have been getting better.

'Amazing,' Brian said. 'You're not hiding any more.'

'I wasn't hiding, Brian,' I smiled. 'I just wasn't ready.'

Chemotherapy was due to begin six weeks after the operation and I was truly terrified about it because I knew how sick it could make people. And I was horrified about the thought of losing my thick blonde hair. It had been my pride and joy. Obviously, I know staying alive is way more important than having nice hair. But when you're in the middle of an experience like cancer, it is the strangest things that can get to you. Sometimes I'd wake in the middle of the night struggling for breath and sobbing. Brian would sit up next to me, put his big arms around me and I'd cling on to his chest until I'd cried it all out.

Brian was determined to come with me for my first session of chemo but I put a ban on that. I had to do this myself. I'd be braver on my own. Although as soon as I met Sarah, my breast-care nurse, I was sobbing again.

'Try to explain to me exactly which bit of it all is most worrying you,' she said gently.

'Everything,' I said.

But as we talked it was pretty obvious that my major worry

was still losing my hair. Sarah recommended wearing this new 'cold cap' device while having the treatment, which was supposed to reduce the risk of your hair falling out afterwards. It was like a swimming cap which freezes your hair follicles during the treatment and makes them less likely to fall out. I put it on and felt completely daft, but the way I looked right then was the least of my worries.

After that first day of chemo I went home to bed feeling rotten. A couple of hours later I woke and was immediately violently sick. All night it went on – and twenty-two times I was sick.

'Oh Brian,' I said. 'If this is chemo I don't think I can do it.'

Brian phoned the hospital for advice.

'This isn't the chemo,' a doctor said. 'You've picked up a bug.'

What a relief that was. I still felt rotten but at least I knew I wasn't going to be suffering like this for months on end. And after one anti-sickness tablet I felt fine.

After that the chemotherapy didn't affect me too bad physically at all. But emotionally it was causing havoc. All my life I've been fairly laid-back but now I started acting like a crazy woman. I could feel this bubbling anger inside me a lot of the time. Maybe I was angry about losing my health, my breast, my hair, my career. Brian was still quite low and drinking too much too, so maybe I was angry about that as well. With hindsight I think the early onset of the menopause due to the chemotherapy may have been a cause of it. At the time, though, I had no idea what was going on – my emotions were out of control. I was constantly ratty and picking rows with Brian. Whatever the reason, I must have been terrible to live with. I'd start rows with Brian just for the hell of it then lash out, saying terrible things to him.

It was a very difficult time. Maybe it was good in some ways when I had to go back to work in *Blood Brothers* in May 2006, about three months after the operation and while I was still only halfway through the chemo. It got us both out of the house, because of course Brian always came with me when we were touring. But those first few weeks back on stage I felt as though every single member of the audience was just sat there looking at my boobs, trying to work out which one was fake. And if one more person had told me I'd been 'incredibly brave' I'd have throttled them. I didn't feel brave at all. I felt scared, angry and depressed. This was not some kind of white-water-rafting expedition I'd chosen to do. That's brave. No, this was just staying alive, which isn't brave at all. It's human flipping nature.

As the weeks went by my hair started to fall out regardless of the cold cap. I'd see it on the pillow in the mornings and there would be clumps of it in the hairbrush whenever I dried my hair. The treatment meant I couldn't dye my hair either, so the roots coming through were grey and wiry. With that and the scar still running across my chest I felt like a freak.

I started wearing a wig on stage. Coleen's Ray had a friend in Leeds, a hairdresser who had won awards for making wigs, and they fitted me out with a fabulous one. On stage no one had a clue it was a wig but I didn't wear it at home, it was too uncomfortable, so I got used to my friends and family seeing my thinning grey hair.

At the time everyone was talking about the new miracle breast cancer drug Herceptin, and that summer my doctors put me on that. Among the side effects it caused were terrible blisters on the soles of my feet. Standing on stage every night for a few hours was agony. The drug also accelerated the menopause which had begun fairly soon after my chemo. And so in addition the mood swings I was getting violent hot flushes. Sleeping was difficult and being on stage under the lights was excruciating. To make matters worse it was the hottest summer there had been in years. As for my moods? I felt like I was losing my senses.

One day I was standing looking at the flowers Brian had just planted in our garden and suddenly became furious they were all different colours and didn't match. I was overtaken by this urge to grab the kitchen scissors then go outside and cut all the heads off them. 'Where is this coming from?' I asked myself as I picked up the scissors. After a minute or so I was able to calm down, put the scissors back in the drawer and take myself back to bed. I lay with the duvet pulled over my head, wondering what on earth was happening to me.

Another day, when the *Blood Brothers* tour had arrived on the island of Jersey and we were staying in a rented apartment, I totally lost it again. It was a day off and Brian went to buy food for Sunday lunch.

'Get Aunt Bessie's Yorkshire Puds,' I yelled as he went out, 'and some jelly.'

He reappeared an hour or so later with Yorkshire pudding mixture instead of actual frozen Yorkshires, and orange jelly.

'Orange jelly?' I screamed. 'Who buys bloody orange jelly? And how the hell am I going to make Yorkshire puddings from scratch in this rubbish oven?'

I was like a crazy woman. Brian quietly turned around.

'I'm walking away from this, Lin,' he said.

But that made me even madder. He'd barely made it halfway

across the kitchen when I lobbed the bag of batter straight at him. Fortunately it missed him by a whisker but hit the kitchen wall and burst open. It was snowing batter mixture all over the wallpaper and carpet. I calmly walked right past Brian and into our bedroom where I slept for six hours without stirring. When I woke I was mortified about what I'd done. But I was scared too – why was I turning demented? I realized I needed help. My breast-care nurse put me in touch with a clinical psychologist, who diagnosed that the menopause combined with the stress of everything I'd been through was making me act irrationally. I began counselling sessions, which helped enormously in dealing with the anger and sense of loss I felt.

But poor Brian. I must have been a monster to live with. And he was still struggling himself too. He was finding it harder and harder to walk and was really quite unwell. But he always remained patient with me. No matter what I did or how I behaved I knew his love for me was unshakeable. It was the ultimate sense of safety.

Eleven

Love You, See You Later

Brian and I stood at the window of our hotel room and looked out over the Eiffel Tower. His arm was slung round my shoulder and he kissed my still-thinning hair.

'I love you just as much as twenty-five years ago, Lin,' he said.

'Me too,' I replied.

It seemed extraordinary that we were back in Paris for the first time since our honeymoon to celebrate our silver wedding anniversary. And it felt incredible too that the time seemed to have passed so quickly – but that so much had happened in those years.

We hadn't been sure we'd make it to Paris. I still hadn't completed my chemo and Brian was in a lot of pain when he walked. The first couple of days weren't great as I felt rotten from my last bout of chemo and stayed in the hotel room. Brian kept popping in and out trying to occupy himself while I slept.

'Oh, Paris is so romantic on your own,' he laughed, coming back into the room.

'You bastard,' I grunted back, laughing and trying to lift my head off the pillow.

That evening we stayed in and had room service. By the following day I was feeling much brighter.

I put on 'Paddy' as I called my hairpiece (Irish jig, wig), and we set off to see the sights, just as we'd done together a quarter of a century before. We went to the Lido and the Moulin Rouge and ate in the same restaurant on the Champs-Élysées that we'd visited on our honeymoon. Then towards the end of the week our friend John Parker, who'd been Brian's best man, and his wife came over to surprise us. We had the most fabulous few days.

We still weren't in great health but I was at least coming to the end of my treatment and was hoping the doctors would soon feel I was ready for breast reconstruction surgery. On top of that Brian and I had just moved into a lovely little semi in Blackpool which we were renting from Coleen and Ray.

That was a golden week in my memory.

Less than a year later, though, Brian and I were far from the romance of the Champs-Élysées and River Seine. We were by the North Sea in Skegness on the next leg of the *Blood Brothers* tour. It was mid-September 2007 and the leaves were starting to turn on the tree outside our hotel window. It was getting darker. And I knew, just knew, Brian really wasn't well at all.

He had an ulcer on one leg and both legs were so painful to walk on that when he moved around he hobbled like an old man. So different from the strong, fit, thirty-two-year-old I'd first fallen in love with. I'd kept on at him about going to hospital in Skegness but he wasn't having any of it. He was so poorly that – on Saturday, 15 September 2007 – I insisted I'd get myself home from the theatre. I came off stage and

into the dressing room which Brian had fully Brian-ed for me
at the start of the week. Between shows, I packed the cards
and gifts away and now it was empty. I couldn't smell his
aftershave, couldn't see his reassuring smile.

'This is what it would be like without Brian,' I thought to
myself. 'Empty.'

Earlier that day Brian had still insisted he'd be there to pick
me up from work but when I put my foot down and said he
really should stay indoors, he almost seemed relieved. He was
trying so hard to pretend to me that he was OK. But clearly
he wasn't.

It was only a couple of months earlier that we'd been at my
brother Brian's wedding to his partner Annie and everyone
had said how fit and tanned my Brian was looking. We didn't
know it then but his skin colouring was probably due to liver
disease rather than the sun. It had been a lovely day. Brian
and Annie had been together years but finally decided to tie
the knot and they did it in the church where my Brian and I
had married. It brought back so many happy memories.

But now, in Skegness, Brian was a shadow of the man he'd
been back then. Thank goodness it was our last night at that
venue before the tour moved to Manchester. It meant finally
we'd get a night back home in Blackpool. The next day Brian
insisted he was fine to drive us home but he really didn't seem
well enough. His speech was rambling and I found it hard to
understand what he was talking about for most of the journey. I stared out the window, fretting, as every now and again
I saw him wince in pain. I tried not to nag at him about going
to the doctor because that only ever ended in a row.

First thing on Monday morning I was due at the hospital
for my Herceptin treatment. 'When I drop you off at the

hospital I might pop in to get myself checked out at A&E,' Brian suddenly said as we drove.

'Good idea,' I replied. I was so relieved he was finally admitting there was a problem. But by the time we were back in Blackpool that evening he was even worse. I helped him into a chair and lifted his legs up to relieve the pressure, then made him a cold drink.

Our friends Sue and Graham popped round for a cup of tea to welcome us home. Sue took one look at Brian and came straight into the kitchen where I was putting the kettle on.

'He needs to go to hospital straight away, Lin,' she said. Graham didn't listen to any of Brian's protests, and persuaded him he really needed medical attention. At the hospital I saw panic in the face of the nurse who took his blood pressure and knew we were in trouble. His blood pressure had dropped through the floor. He had to be admitted immediately for observation.

I went home with Sue and Graham but was back at the hospital next morning at the crack of dawn for my Herceptin so as soon as it was done I could scoot up to Brian's ward to see him. He looked shattered but I knew he was now in the best place.

'How you doing, love?' I asked.

'Don't you worry about me, Lin,' he replied. 'What about tonight? How are you going to manage getting to Manchester for the show?'

'I'll be just fine,' I said, trying to stop him worrying about me for just one day. My nephew Danny – Maureen's son – had offered to drive me to the theatre and home again afterwards.

The first night of the show in a new venue is always exciting but that night I wasn't really up for it. I kept thinking about Brian lying in that hospital bed all on his own. The doctors said they were awaiting test results but it seemed they thought it was an infection – a couple of days' rest and some antibiotics and he'd soon be absolutely fine.

When Danny dropped me home I still didn't feel right. 'Must be missing Brian,' I told myself. Two hours later I woke in bed with a terrible urge to be sick. I rushed to the bathroom and chucked up everything I'd eaten all day. I felt shocking. Shivering, achy and my head was pounding.

I was backwards and forwards to the bathroom all night. Brian was in the hospital and I felt totally alone. At 6 a.m. I thought it was just about late enough to call Maureen. She was round within minutes, bundled me into the front seat of her car and took me to the on-call GP. I was dressed in a vest top, leggings and slippers and was wrapped in Brian's big outdoor coat. I lay on the doctor's bench moaning in agony – goodness knows what people must have thought.

The doctor checked me out and found a rash across my chest and my temperature spiking. He looked serious as he opened a book.

'Looking it up in a book doesn't feel too reassuring,' I managed to just about joke to Maureen.

Turned out I had cellulitis, which is a bacterial skin infection which often affects women who've had lymphoedema (which was caused by having my lymph nodes removed). The doctor sent me home with a truckload of antibiotics and strict instructions to stay in bed. But that was entirely out of the question with Brian in hospital. As soon as I got back I was calling the ward to check about visiting times. But when the nurse discovered I'd got an infection she said there was no way I'd be allowed in to visit.

'If Mr Hudson were to catch an infection it could be very serious,' she said.

All day Tuesday and Wednesday I had to lie in bed at home thinking of Brian lying in hospital. I spoke to him on the phone but he didn't seem to have much energy to chat for long. I called the nurses' station time and again. 'He's stable,' they told me. 'You can come in Wednesday evening if you're not sick again.'

Of course my family all rallied round and were in and out to see him during visiting times but I missed him dreadfully. It was only two days but it was one of the longest periods of time we'd ever been apart. Coleen went to see him on the Tuesday and called in on her way home. She was holding a box of chocolates and a copy of the *Daily Mirror* which Brian had asked her to bring me.

'What did he say, Col?' I asked.

'He said, "You couldn't even let me be ill on my own,"' she laughed.

Even then, Brian could still make me laugh.

The following day Sue and Graham came round straight from the hospital. I could instantly tell from their faces that something was seriously wrong.

'The hospital have asked for you to speak to the consultant as soon as possible, Linda,' Sue said. 'He is very poorly.'

'What's happening?' I said. 'I've been ringing up and they keep telling me he's stable, and had a good night. What's happened?'

I was furious and immediately rang my breast-care nurse,

Sarah, who worked at the hospital. By then I was sobbing. 'Please find out for me what's going on,' I begged.

"I'll call you back in half an hour," she said. When the phone rang thirty minutes later I was almost too scared to answer it.

'Come up to the hospital now, Lin, and you can see Brian,' she said. 'But come to my office first and bring someone with you.'

'Oh God, oh God,' I thought. I called Coleen who was round within minutes to drive me there. All the way I kept wondering what it meant. Were they going to tell me . . . No, no. That couldn't be happening.

Coleen and I trooped into a small room and sat, side by side, facing Sarah. She wasn't smiling. There was little hope to be found in her eyes.

'Linda,' she said slowly. 'Do you know how sick Brian is?'

My heart started to pound. It really was everything I had feared. I knew exactly what she was saying.

'Is he going to die?' I said, barely above a whisper.

'Yes, I'm afraid so,' she replied.

I remember hearing a voice screaming: 'No. Don't say that. Don't say that.' But I didn't realize for several seconds it was my voice. It was just a dreadful wail filling the room. I was screaming. Desperate. Hopeless.

I fell forward in the chair and remember Coleen on her knees in front of me, trying to hold me up. It was like someone had just smashed me over the back with a baseball bat. I couldn't move. Couldn't breathe. Couldn't think. This could not be happening. Not to Brian. My Brian.

Slowly Coleen and Sarah got me sitting back up in the chair and my screaming subsided into long agonized sobs.

'I'm afraid Brian has suffered liver failure,' Sarah explained. 'His other organs are now beginning to fail too.'

I felt shocked to my core. I'd known he was poorly and had expected him to be in hospital for a couple of weeks but then I'd thought he'd be coming home. Then I'd thought everything would be back to normal. But this? Coleen called Brian's children Lloyd and Sarah straight away. They got on so well with their dad and I knew they'd be desperate to see him. They jumped on a train from London.

'If I don't make it in time, tell him that I love him,' said Sarah.

'Of course I will,' I replied. 'Of course I will.'

Then I called Brian's best friend, John Parker, who had been driving down south. He turned the car round and headed straight to Blackpool too. And, as ever, the Nolans all turned up for support.

I went into the hospital loos to try to tidy myself up before going up to Brian's bed. I didn't want him to see me with mascara all down my face and my hair bedraggled. That would just make him worry about how I was going to cope. But my God it was so hard not to cry as I walked up to the bed. There he was, the love of my life, and he was leaving me.

I gave him a kiss then sat on the chair next to the bed and held his hand. He was still conscious but he was groggy and confused. I talked about Hudson and what had been happening at home – anything to make him feel safe, secure.

When Lloyd and Sarah arrived that evening they spent time with their dad and then the nurses told us we might as well go home for some rest. We'd only been back an hour or so when the phone rang.

'You ought to come straight back in,' the nurse said. 'We are struggling to stabilize your husband.'

Brian's liver had now completely packed up. It was a horrific experience. Six nurses were trying to find a vein to inject him but it was impossible. I was holding one of those paper trays for him to be sick in and could see he was vomiting blood. Then blood started coming out of the pores of his skin. 'Sorry about this, Lin,' he mumbled as we sat around the bed while the nurses tried to clean him up.

'Don't you be sorry about anything,' I smiled. 'You've been my hero.'

It was incredibly distressing and after a while my brother Tommy came in. 'Come with me, Linda,' he said, 'you don't need to be seeing this.'

A doctor told me they could perform a small operation to put a stitch in Brian's oesophagus to stop the bleeding. But it was dangerous. I knew Brian hated having tubes down his throat and would hate the op. I didn't know what to say.

'What do you think?' I said desperately to Lloyd and Sarah.

'Whatever you think is best for Dad is fine by us,' Sarah replied as Lloyd nodded.

'Well actually it is up to me,' the doctor snapped at all of us. Fortunately there was a wonderful nurse there too who took me to one side.

'Mrs Hudson, I'm afraid if Brian doesn't have this operation he is going to bleed to death and that is a terrible thing. This will be kinder to him.'

And so of course I agreed. As the nurses prepared him for theatre I bent down and kissed him again on his forehead. 'Love you, I'll see you later,' I said.

'Love you too, Lin,' he mumbled as they pushed him away. Took my love away.

Me, Lloyd, Sarah, John Parker and my brothers and sisters hung around the hospital. We went to the cafe but it was the middle of the night and all closed up. In the end we finished up crowded inside my sister-in-law Annie's office as she worked at the hospital as a medical secretary. None of us could really talk. We were all wrapped up in our own memories. I felt like I was hyperventilating. My heart was pumping and I was sweating. Everything was a blur. Finally, an hour later, the doctors called to say he'd pulled through OK.

'Quarter of an hour and you'll be able to see him,' they said.

But just a couple of minutes later my mobile phone rang again.

'I'm sorry but we're finding it hard to stabilize Mr Hudson's blood pressure,' the nurse said. 'You need to come immediately.'

All of us ran through the hospital back to the ward where Brian had been. Just as we got to the curtain which surrounded his bed a nurse came out of the cubicle. She looked up at me. 'I am so sorry,' she said. 'Mr Hudson has just stopped breathing.'

It was like an out-of-body experience. I didn't think it could be happening to me as I pushed the curtain aside and saw my Brian lying there motionless on the bed. I threw my arms around him and kissed his cheeks as tears poured down my face onto his. It looked as if he'd just dropped off to sleep. He still looked so handsome. He was still the man I'd fallen so entirely in love with twenty-six years ago. But he was gone.

Lloyd and Sarah kissed him and I held his hand. But I

wanted more, I wanted to be closer. I needed those strong arms to be wrapped all the way round me just one more time. After a while I lay on the bed next to him and stroked his face the way I used to when we lay in bed together late at night, chatting about what we'd done that day.

'Oh Brian,' I said. 'Oh Brian, please.'

Brian and I hadn't been regular churchgoers but I guess at that moment my upbringing kicked in and I asked the nurse to get us a priest. This little man scurried in, glasses perched on the end of his nose. He whispered in Brian's ear, giving him the last rites, and then knelt to say a prayer with us all around the bed. Then he stood up, looked at me and said: 'Oh, I loved you in *The Bill*.'

Even at that very worst moment of my life there was still humour. I didn't have the heart to tell him he had the wrong Nolan sister – it was Bernie in *The Bill*!

It was 21 September 2007. My life felt over. I had loved Brian completely for all those years. And he'd made me feel so loved too. Yes, I had my family and my friends. But Brian loved me in a way no one else had ever done. Only he made me feel special.

I can't remember much about what happened afterwards. I think we went back to my brother Brian and Annie's house. Then that night Lloyd and Sarah came back to ours. Except it wasn't 'ours' any more because Brian wasn't coming back. It was so hard to understand because his clothes were still hanging in the wardrobe where he'd left them. His toothbrush was in the mug in the bathroom. His copy of the *Sun* with a half-finished crossword was on the coffee table. But he wasn't there and he wasn't going to be ever again.

When my brother Brian was young he'd married a lovely

woman called Linzi and they'd been so happy. But she died suddenly from a rare heart disorder, leaving him devastated. Afterwards he never once went back to their house. Our older sisters went in, cleared it out and sold it and he never stepped foot in it again. Too painful. It was different for me. Because every mug, every tea bag, the television, the chair, the bed – they all reminded me of my Brian. And I wanted to be where I felt close to him.

That first night Lloyd and Sarah heard me crying through the bedroom walls and came in to me. In the end we all lay next to each other on our double bed, telling stories about their dad, laughing and crying in turns. Sarah had a little girl by then, Lucy, who was eight. Brian adored his little Lucy Lastick. And she adored her Granddad Sherbet (she named him that because he loved those Flying Saucers). I was so pleased Lucy and Brian had had those special times together. And so pleased he had such good relationships with his children by the time he died.

We woke the next morning all hunched up together on the bed. For a moment you can forget what has happened. And then the loss hits you all over again. It was like that every morning for months and months.

Friends and family were wonderful. I had more than three hundred condolence cards and my front room was full of lilies. And then there was the funeral to organize. Sarah, Lloyd and I all wanted it to be a celebration of his life. And because his life was dedicated to entertainment and touring – that's what it had to be. We hadn't been a maudlin couple but we had talked about how we'd like our funerals. And it had been Brian's idea to have a send-off which was like his last big tour. I'd just come up with some of the details, which I knew he'd have loved. All the guests were sent laminated cards bearing the words 'Brian Hudson Farewell Gig '07'. The order of service was designed to look like a concert programme. The pall-bearers wore T-shirts like a production crew and the coffin was black with what looked like gaffer tape on it and a sign saying 'This Way Up' so it looked like one of the flight cases he used for moving our gear around on the road.

As we walked into the church where we had married twenty-six years earlier, Faith Hill's song 'There You'll Be' was playing. I remembered the day we'd been listening to that in the car and Brian had said he wanted it played at his funeral.

'No, I want it at mine,' I'd joked.

'OK, whoever goes first gets it,' Brian had replied, laughing.

And now we were here and the lyrics were echoing around the church: 'In my dreams I'll always see you soaring by the sky . . . And everywhere I am, there you'll be.'

John Parker and I had written Brian a couple of 'fan letters'. Jake read out one from me, and Coleen helped John finish his when he choked with emotion. Then Bernie sang 'Wind Beneath My Wings'. That had always been my and Brian's song and Bernie did us proud when she sang it. The only hymn was 'Abide with Me', which always made Brian cry when it was played at the FA Cup, and we left the church to a song by one of the bands Brian had been in as a young man, Harmony Grass.

From there the family went on to the crematorium where my brother Brian gave a beautiful eulogy. Then they played 'Always Look on the Bright Side of Life'. Everyone was singing along and it was hard to know whether I was laughing or crying or both. And then the curtains closed around my lovely boy's coffin.

'Ladies and Gentlemen,' my brother Brian said in his American presenter's voice, 'Please put your hands together for the fabulous Brian Hudson.'

Everyone did just that – it was a standing ovation. And then it was done.

The next few days were among the hardest. After a funeral everything goes quiet. After a week the condolence cards stop arriving each morning. Other people's lives went back to normal. Mine never could. We'd been together 24/7 and now I was entirely alone.

Of course I wasn't physically alone because my brothers and sisters would never have allowed that. They were amazing and barely left me for a moment, even taking it in turns to stay over. But if they even popped to the shops for half an hour I'd be on the phone after five minutes saying: 'I can't do this. I'm scared.' I was having panic attacks and felt utterly lost.

My brothers and sisters all invited me to stay with them but I couldn't leave our home. I felt closer to Brian there. And I could sit out in our little back garden with Hudson, the way me and Brian used to do.

I didn't wash the sheets on our bed for five weeks because I couldn't bear washing the smell of Brian away. And his clothes were to stay hanging in the wardrobe for two years. Some days I'd take them out and just breathe in the smell of him which still lingered on. Other times I'd get them all out with the plan of taking them to the charity shop. But then it just all felt too final, so I'd put them all back in again. I'd spray the Fahrenheit by Dior aftershave Brian always wore into the air and close my eyes. For a moment I could believe he was back with me. But when I opened my eyes the reality hit all over again.

Some days I did nothing but lie on the couch with a blanket over me. My sisters would be on the phone, constantly checking up. My counsellor had told them that one day lying on the couch was OK. But two days was the limit – then they wanted me up and about.

'I'll be coming to drag you out for a walk if I have to break in and do it,' Maureen would say.

I was struggling practically too, because all the finances and planning had been done by Brian. I didn't have a clue. I couldn't write a cheque, didn't know what was in the bank, who our insurance was with . . . nothing at all. I had been completely and utterly spoilt. Shielded from the real world. But now I had bills and letters pouring through the door and not the first clue how to deal with them. That just made my panic attacks more frequent. Each time they'd start with me struggling to catch my breath. When I couldn't breathe the panic got worse and worse until I was convinced I was going to die.

Coleen's Ray and another friend of ours, Mark Styles, came round to help me out with all the paperwork you have to trawl through after a bereavement.

'Right, where did Brian keep all the bank details and insurance policies?' Ray asked.

I looked at him blankly. I really didn't have a clue. Ray and Mark were so patient but it took weeks to get through and I couldn't concentrate on any of it.

My sisters and Annie were amazing. They'd plan girlie nights in front of *X-Factor*. Denise would turn up with a bagful of DVDs so there had to be something I wanted to watch. Other times they'd lie on the bed and hold me while I cried. 'I don't know what to do,' I kept saying. 'I can't do this.'

'You can, Linda,' they always replied. 'You will.'

If I could avoid leaving the house I would. The outside world just seemed too much to cope with without Brian. And going out was always awful because I knew when I came back and opened the door to an empty house it would be agony all over again.

Two weeks after his death I had another Herceptin session. Brian had always taken me to my appointments and walking in without him I could feel myself starting to crack. As the nurse got me ready for treatment I sobbed and sobbed and sobbed.

I rarely went out in the months that followed. But on the couple of occasions I did I couldn't wear most of my dresses or my favourite bracelet because I couldn't do them up without Brian to help me. Another time I stood weeping in my bedroom with half my wardrobe discarded on the floor around me. Without Brian I had no idea what looked fine and what looked terrible. And then there was all the stuff I had to remember without Brian. Before, I'd never even carried cash or a set of keys – my sisters joked I was like the Queen!

I was living in constant torture. All I wanted night and day was to be with Brian again. Many, many times I thought about ending it all. The only thing that stopped me was my brothers and sisters. They'd looked after me so well and I couldn't put them through the pain I was now going through.

Three times I rang the Samaritans in the early hours of the morning. I had gone as far as lining up the tablets. I needed someone to explain to me why it wasn't the best idea for me to be with Brian.

About the only thing that kept me going back then was that Coleen was due to marry Ray that autumn. Before Brian had died they'd asked us to be witnesses at the register office and I was to be maid of honour at the church ceremony afterwards. We were delighted. Brian and Ray had been great mates and made each other laugh. But now it would be just me as the witness. I couldn't do anything terrible that would upset Coleen's wedding so I just clung on.

I know Coleen had considered cancelling her wedding but I wouldn't entertain the idea.

'Lin, I totally understand if you don't feel up to being maid of honour,' Coleen said. 'You really don't have to do it.'

'No, I'll do it, Col,' I said. 'It'll give me something else to think about.'

So I threw myself into shopping for gifts for the bridesmaids, going with Coleen for her final dress fittings and choosing suits for the groom and ushers. Then there was the hen night to sort too. I was like a crazy woman, dashing around trying to organize everything. Anything, so long as I could stop myself thinking about Brian.

It was a fabulous wedding. The only time I broke down was in the morning before the ceremony when I was rehearsing a song for the service with Maureen, Bernie, and our nieces Alex, Amy and Laura. Ray had chosen 'Let It Be Me' because he used to sing it with Brian. Suddenly I collapsed in tears. The girls all gave me a huge hug and I was fine. And I knew I wouldn't cry when Coleen was there – I wouldn't do anything to upset her big day.

My other job of the day was to look after Coleen and Ray's daughter, Ciara, which again kept me busy – and meant I had a great excuse to disappear off and put her to bed when she started feeling tired. I still wasn't ready for a big night of partying.

After the excitement of the wedding I slumped quite badly.

Dr Jean Briggs, a consultant clinical psychologist who I'd been referred to during my cancer treatment, was a life saver. Looking back she probably did save my life. The first time I went in to see her after Brian had died I sobbed in her arms for twenty minutes. I did pretty much the same thing every fortnight for the next couple of months. Then gradually I was able to talk to her about how I was feeling. How utterly alone I felt.

She helped me see I wasn't going mad – and had practical advice too. One thing that was really upsetting me was waking in the night and not being able to remember what Brian looked like. She suggested putting a picture of him by the side of the bed and that helped loads. And when I was panicking that I couldn't remember the sound of his voice she suggested I should play old home videos. It was too painful at first. But gradually the pain was preferable to the panic of feeling Brian's memory drifting away from me.

I'd watch the videos and remember the amazing life we'd had together. The life that was now gone for ever.

Twelve

Miss You, Mum

That terrible autumn Mum was getting weaker too.

Over the past few years her Alzheimer's disease had become worse and worse. What had started out as general confusion, constantly asking where her handbag was or repeatedly asking the same question, had deteriorated quickly.

It had been terrible to watch. Mum used to devour magazines but now when I bought her one she'd toss it aside, saying it was too hard to read. And in her younger years she'd loved bingo. She could have six of her own cards on the go and keep an eye on everyone else's on the table too. But as the months went by she'd be missing more and more numbers.

We had a phone call one day from the church bazaar saying Mum had left her purse there with £600 cash inside. Another time we got a call from the Queens Hotel in Blackpool saying: 'There's nothing to worry about but we've got your mum here. She's been here since six this morning. We've given her some breakfast and she's welcome to stay as long as she likes.'

People were wonderful with her but it was so distressing to think of her waking up in the morning with no concept of time and wandering down to the hotel where we had performed so many times as kids.

She still loved to sing and would go to the places where they had singalongs in the afternoon for the old folks. But as time went by she found it harder to remember the words. Denise would go with her and sit behind, prompting her when she forgot the words.

After a few years she moved into a sheltered accommodation flat but then she put the kettle on the electric hob and nearly caused a fire. Fortunately someone spotted the smoke and Mum wasn't affected at all because she was safe in another room. But it could have been terrible. It was clear she could no longer live on her own.

Increasingly she had to stay with one of us kids. But even that was a worry. I was in London or touring with *Blood Brothers* during this time, so much of the responsibility fell to my older sisters. They were wonderful with Mum. I'd come back as often as I could to visit at weekends but even in the space of a week or so it was possible to see how quickly she was going downhill.

One day when Coleen's Ciara was a toddler she showed her mum three tablets in her hand.

'Gran gave me these saying they are sweets but I don't think they are, Mummy,' Ciara said.

Thank goodness she didn't eat them. But it was another sign Mum was slipping fast.

The whole family were trying to look after her. Brian and his wife Annie were fabulous and the other girls were amazing with her. They would bath her and take her to the toilet and cared for her the way she had cared for us when we were children. But by then Mum needed care 24/7 and all of us were either working during the day or off touring in stage shows. In the end it was Mum's GP who sat us all down together.

'Look, I understand you all want to look after your mum and feel that's what you ought to do but I think you have to consider residential care. I've seen what caring for someone with such severe Alzheimer's can do. It destroys families.'

And so reluctantly we agreed to find Mum a nursing home. Our brother Brian, Denise and Maureen took her to see lots and she chose the one she liked. The nurses there were wonderful, caring for her as she became frailer and frailer. But as can often happen with Alzheimer's, she began to get a little aggressive with people.

Once we got a call saying: 'We wondered if one of you could come down and persuade your mother to let go of the carer's hair.' When we got there she was convinced this lovely carer called Margaret had stolen one of her shoes. But within a couple of minutes we'd found it under the bed. Sometimes she would lash out at the carers for no reason other than, I guess, she felt confused and frightened. It was incredible to think that our mum, who'd always been so warm and friendly to others, was now like this.

It was heartbreaking. Once Maureen caught her talking to herself in the mirror as though the reflection were a total stranger. Another time I was visiting and helping her get ready when she saw my reflection in the mirror.

'Look, Linda, there's a woman over there who's the image of you,' Mum said.

'Oh, isn't she?' I replied. 'What a beautiful woman,' I joked.

A lot of the time we felt it was easier to joke along with Mum than keep pointing out how she'd got things wrong. She was never getting better so there was no point in giving her anything more to worry about.

Even though one of us would go in most days she'd always be complaining that no one had been to see her for months. And then, as more time passed, she forgot entirely who we all were. All those years she'd dedicated her life to us and now we were like strangers. Other times she'd become very distressed and be screaming: 'My babies, my babies, let me see my babies.'

For the last eighteen months she had no memory at all. But still she had the heart of an ox. She just kept on going. Soon after Brian died I went up to the home and sat with her.

'My Brian has gone,' I said quietly.

I so desperately wanted her to put her arms around me and make it all better like she did with a bottle of TCP when I was a kid. But she was barely conscious by then and had no idea who either me or Brian were. It was so sad because she'd loved him so much and he adored her.

Mum was very weak by this stage and soon afterwards I got a call from the carers saying she had now forgotten how to swallow. I called my brothers and sisters and went to the home where we talked about getting a priest to give Mum the last rites. But still she battled on and a couple of days later I had another call from the carers saying she'd just eaten an entire yoghurt. She wasn't giving up without a fight!

We knew that the sense of hearing is one of the last things to go when someone is very ill so when us girls went up to visit we'd sing to Mum. Once me, Coleen, Bernie and Maureen stood round the bed singing all the old songs like 'Danny Boy' and tunes from *The Sound of Music* that she'd loved when we were kids. Sure enough it wasn't long before we started bickering about the harmonies (it really was like old times!). Once we'd got it sorted we went back to singing and it did sound lovely. When we turned round there was a big crowd of nurses and other patients at the door listening to us.

It was December 2007 when Tommy, Brian, my sisters and I went up to the home and sang carols to Mum for what we knew would be her last Christmas. She looked so at peace although she barely opened her eyes. Then, when we finished and were preparing to leave, she moved her head. 'I think she wants an encore,' Bernie laughed. So we carried on singing.

That first Christmas without Brian was very tough. Coleen invited me to go and stay at hers from the middle of December as she knew how difficult it would be. The previous Christmas there had been thirty-three presents for me from Brian all wrapped and laid out underneath our tree. This year there would be none. And every Christmas morning Brian would make me smoked salmon and scrambled eggs. This year it was Coleen who cooked it.

'I'm not quite sure I've made it right,' Coleen said, looking dubiously at the pile of egg she served up that Christmas morning.

'It's fabulous, Col,' I replied.

It was just fabulous that she'd tried so hard to remind me of Brian. I managed to hold it together all day until one of our friends called in the evening to say how much he was missing Brian. That set me off and I collapsed into tears – the pain was still all too real.

After Christmas Coleen had to go back to work and my other sisters were all in pantomime so it was desperately quiet in Blackpool. Then, on 30 December, there was a call from the home saying Mum was now very poorly. Once again we all gathered around her bedside.

I'd seen her the previous day and she'd eaten some yoghurt and seemed a bit stronger. But now her body was giving up. She was tiny with barely an ounce of fat on her and looked so frail in the bed as we stood and chatted about the old times when we were kids and sang her some of the songs she had taught us.

Gradually her breathing became slower until we knew she had taken her final breath. At last, after all those years of confusion and pain, she looked at peace. It was a terribly sad moment. But the reality was we had lost our mum years before.

We sat with her for a short while before going downstairs to the day room while the nurses washed Mum and made her look nice. All of us kids sat round in a big circle in the high-back chairs of the nursing home staring at each other.

'Oh my God, I guess this'll be what it's like when we're old and all sitting here together,' I said. Everyone laughed despite the awfulness of the moment. That Nolan humour again!

After a few minutes we went back up and sat round Mum's bed and all said our final farewells. The carers had put flowers around the bed and it was lovely. As the others got up to leave I said, 'I'm just going to have another quick moment with Mum on my own.'

'You don't need to,' Tommy said. I think he was worried about me, with it all still being so soon after losing Brian.

'She'll be fine,' Brian said. My brothers were so protective of me.

I sat with Mum for another twenty minutes, holding her hand.

'I'm going to miss you so much, Mum,' I whispered to her.

'But it's OK – you are going to be with Dad.' Then I kissed her on the forehead. 'And give Brian a kiss from me, won't you, Mum,' I said.

Tommy came in and said the funeral director had arrived. When the undertaker walked in the room he took one look at me, recognized me from Brian's funeral just seven weeks earlier, and looked so sympathetic. 'Oh, I'm so sorry, Mrs Hudson,' he said. 'I didn't realize it was you. Please don't tell me you've lost your mother as well?'

I just nodded.

A couple of days later it was New Year's Day. I found that one of the hardest days I'd had to contend with yet. 'I just can't believe it,' I kept saying to myself. 'I can't believe it is 2008 and Brian will never be part of it.'

We still had to wait almost a fortnight for Mum's funeral, which was difficult. I spent a lot of time thinking about my childhood and everything that had happened. What seemed to hang over all those memories by then was my sister Anne's shocking revelation which had emerged a couple of years earlier.

When Anne had invited me and Brian round for dinner that evening it had seemed a perfectly ordinary night. We got on great with Anne and her husband Brian and always had a lovely time round at theirs. But I could tell Anne seemed a bit on edge that evening. And then she just said it.

'There's something I need to tell you, Linda,' she'd said, looking me direct in the eye. 'Dad abused me when I was a kid.'

I felt my stomach lurch exactly the way they say it does in books. I felt stunned, horrified.

'What?' I croaked. 'When?'

177

'It went on for years,' she said. 'I just don't want to have to keep that secret any more.'

And that was it. I was stunned, floored by what she'd said. But I instantly believed her. There was not a shred of doubt in my mind she was telling the truth. Maybe some folk might find that odd, given that I'd never seen or experienced sexual abuse from my dad. But Anne had always been the straight, eldest, sensible one. If she was saying that's what happened, that is what happened. I was horrified for her. Both that it had happened and that now she was having to summon the strength to tell people. I could see even talking to me and Brian about it was very stressful.

There was no long conversation about it and I didn't ask a single further question. After a couple of minutes I said quietly: 'I think I'll pop up to use the loo.'

Upstairs I went into the bathroom and burst into tears. I think it was shock and confusion. But there was also, and this really sounds a horrific thing to say, almost a sense that this confirmed everything I'd always feared . . . Dad didn't love me as much. I'm ashamed to say that but I know Coleen felt something similar. Apparently in this situation siblings often do feel a sense of not being loved as much, not that they would wish to be abused of course. We always knew Dad had his favourites and this, however sick it was, proved it.

Our dad was an amazing, charismatic man and we were all desperate for his approval. It's only now, looking back, I can see we were all caught up in something really quite warped. But even then, even believing everything Anne told me, I still loved my dad.

Anne then went on to write about her experiences and her life in a book which sent shock waves through the family. She told how the abuse started when she was eleven, soon after we moved to Blackpool. It had continued for years and Dad obviously became fixated on her. At one point when she was in her teens he suggested they should run away together as if they were lovers, not father and daughter.

Such a shocking admission from one of the original Nolan Sisters got loads of attention in the press. Anne had waited until Mum was so poorly she couldn't have understood anything that was going on but it was distressing for Dad's sisters, who were still alive. It was Anne's story, though, and I'll always defend her right to tell it. For years afterwards I'd be asked about it in almost every newspaper interview I did, but I always said the same thing: 'That's Anne's story and I feel terrible for her that she went through that. But nothing like that happened to me, and the man who abused my sister is not the man I knew as my dad.'

Maybe that sounds weird, but separating the two men is really the only way I can get my head around it. Anne and Dad were always very close. She even worked as his secretary when she left school but no one ever imagined anything like that. I've never asked Anne about any of the abuse and I've never read her book. I have deliberately shielded myself from all that. I don't want to know where it happened or when. Even now us sisters don't talk about what happened. I don't think there is anything to be gained from bringing it all back up again although I'll always support Anne's decision to talk publicly about her experiences when she did.

People have asked if I think Mum knew. I cannot believe that. I have to believe that in my heart. If Mum had known, that would destroy me. I honestly don't think she did. I think there were many things which Dad did during his life which

Mum never knew anything about. She put up with so much during her time with him: the affairs, the drinking, the violence. When we were young women in relationships of our own we'd sometimes ask Mum: 'Why did you never leave him?'

She'd just shake her head and say: 'Leave to go where?' And really how could she have done that with all us kids? And by the time we'd left home and she finally had a little independence Dad had stopped drinking and things had calmed down. And beyond all that, she loved him.

So all that was there in our minds that day we walked through the lashing rain into Sacred Heart Church in Blackpool on 11 January 2008 for Mum's funeral.

Inside it was packed with Mum's friends from church and people she'd met back in her youth singing in Blackpool. It showed just how loved she had been.

Anne sang 'Ave Maria', which was the song Mum had always sung at family weddings and events and it was beautiful. And then the grandchildren got up and read poems. It was a really lovely service.

Afterwards I felt exhausted. I'd lost my husband and my mum in less than two months of each other. But two days after Mum's funeral I was due to go back into *Blood Brothers* in the West End. I was dreading it. The thought of living in a hotel room in London without Brian terrified me.

'Maybe it'll do you good,' Maureen said.

I knew deep down she was probably right. What's more, I needed the money. No work, no money. I told myself I just had to get on and do it.

Maureen was brilliant and came down to London with me on the train and then Bernie offered for me to stay at her and her husband Steve's house in Surrey. The girls in the show were so kind to me too and every night when we'd finished they walked me to the tube for my trip back to Bernie's.

But it was a horrible time. I remember once sitting on the tube late at night and it was pitch-black outside. I could see my reflection in front of me. All I saw was a desperately sad woman.

'This isn't how it was supposed to be,' I thought. I was still only forty-seven years old – I was a young woman. But it felt like my life was over.

From London, *Blood Brothers* went back on the road again, up to Nottingham then Cardiff, Malvern and Wolverhampton. Staying in hotel rooms without Brian was devastating. And at every new theatre, when I went to my dressing room and there were no flowers, no keepsakes or cards left out, the way he always did for me, I felt the pain all over again.

Then at the beginning of June 2008 in Wolverhampton I started being violently sick. The cellulitis was back. I had to get a cab on my own to hospital, where they hooked me up on antibiotics and kept me in for the rest of the week.

I'd have felt sick and poorly that night even if Brian had been there. But without Brian I felt sick, poorly and lost. Maureen and Bernie were performing at a theatre in Lichfield and for the rest of the week they scooted back and forth between the show and my hospital bed. They were incredible.

When I was finally discharged, my brothers Tommy and Brian turned up in a car with pillows and duvets all laid out on the back seat. They lay me down in it and drove me back to Denise's where I stayed for the next few weeks.

My family had saved me again.

But as I recuperated I became increasingly anxious about

going back into the *Blood Brothers* tour. I spoke to my counsellor who suggested I needed a bit of time out to come to terms emotionally with everything that had happened. My chemotherapy and Herceptin treatments had finished but I still felt exhausted from it all as well as grieving for Brian and Mum. In the back of my mind, though, I could hear Brian saying: 'The show must go on, Linda.'

I was desperate and rang my brother Brian for advice.

'What would you say if I said I wasn't going back into *Blood Brothers*?' I asked him.

'Oh Linda,' he said. 'We would all be totally delighted.'

Turns out the whole family had been worried about me putting myself under too much pressure. As soon as Brian said that, I felt a million times lighter. I felt it was OK for me to go home now.

Go back to 'our home' and stay there with my memories of Brian.

Thirteen

Surviving

I felt safer at home. Closer to Brian. I would sit around the house all day in one of his old T-shirts. Inside me there was a terrible emptiness. And all that stuff about time being a great healer? Rubbish. If people said that to me I'd look at them utterly bewildered. 'What do you mean?' I thought. This can never be healed. I firmly believed I would never get over Brian. I didn't want to get over Brian. I wanted to immerse myself in every memory I had of him. But I was angry too. I still wouldn't really admit it to myself or anyone else but deep down I sort of knew that in the end it was Brian's liver which killed him – not the cancer. I was angry he'd deserted me and could have stayed with me so much longer if he'd just stopped drinking.

As the months slid by I felt worse and worse. Some days I couldn't stop myself from crying.

'I hate this life,' I'd say over and over. My brothers and sisters were all incredible. They were patient and kind. But none of them could take the pain away.

I was still seeing Dr Briggs, my psychologist, and could talk to her about anything, but counselling alone wasn't enough and so when my GP suggested antidepressants, I agreed. Up until then I'd avoided pills as I had been simply experiencing profound grief. Pills weren't going to bring Brian back. But now it seemed to be developing into a full-blown depression where everything seemed hopeless. Pointless.

There were money worries too. Brian and I had been living a pretty hand-to-mouth existence for several years and now I wasn't working there was nothing to fall back on. We had no savings and Brian's life insurance was refusing to pay out because he'd missed a couple of payments. My brothers and sisters were amazing, leaving cash on the side when they popped round or getting me a week's worth of shopping in. But the bills continued to pour in – a mountain of paperwork on the front-room table which I couldn't even bring myself to open. The more it piled up, the more anxious I became.

'Why don't you try claiming benefits?' Dr Briggs suggested.

'Oh I couldn't,' I replied. 'I've been working since I was three years old.'

'Precisely,' she replied. 'And that's why they're there – to help people like you who've always worked but who've hit a bad patch.'

A few days later an accountant who Brian had found us years earlier rang to check how I was getting on. He could see the scale of my problems and he suggested I should enquire about benefits too.

'If you don't claim housing benefit and some income support while you're not working you're just going to sink further and further into debt,' he said.

'Oh, I couldn't,' I replied. 'No. I'd be too ashamed.'

But over the next few weeks I kept thinking about it and talked to my brothers and sisters about whether I should.

'There's nothing to be ashamed about,' my sister-in-law Annie said. 'Benefits are there for people going through a tough time – and that's what you are. You've paid your tax when you've been working all these years so it's only right that you get a bit of help when you need it.'

So, finally, I agreed. But the thought of all those claims forms was terrifying. I'd never had to fill in a form all the time Brian and I were married – he looked after everything like that.

'I'll sit down with you and we'll do it together,' Annie said. But it wasn't easy. One of the questions was: 'List all your previous employers.'

'But I've had hundreds,' I gasped to Annie. Those forms clearly weren't designed for people who've spent their lives working in showbiz, where one year you could earn £80,000 and the next £10,000.

After weeks of working our way through the forms I then had a meeting at the benefits office in Blackpool. Again Annie was by my side. I was terrified of even walking through the door but Annie gripped my arm and we marched in together. We were ushered into a little room by a lady from the benefits team. She pulled out a file of documents and looked up at me intently. 'Here we go,' I thought to myself. 'Here comes all the suspicion and tut-tutting about what a hash I've made of my life.' But I couldn't have been more wrong. The lady was lovely and totally understanding.

'Well, Mrs Hudson, if there was ever someone who needed benefits I would say it is you,' she said.

That made me feel so much better. It lifted a lot of the shame from my shoulders.

But late at night I'd still worry that going on benefits meant the end of my career in show business. Sometimes I felt I was mourning my husband, my mother and my career.

Within a couple of weeks of the meeting I started receiving

disability living allowance for my depression and housing benefit, which enabled me to pay the rent on my house and my bills.

I didn't like it. I could accept now that there was nothing to be ashamed about, but somehow I felt I'd let Brian down by not being able to support myself.

There wasn't a ray of hope anywhere on the horizon. Even going back to hospital for breast reconstruction didn't help. I'd been due to have it in the January after Brian and Mum died, but when I went for an assessment the surgeon and my breast-care nurse both agreed I wasn't ready.

'I'm sorry, Mrs Hudson,' the surgeon said. 'Of course you have to be physically fit to undergo such a big operation. But you have to be mentally fit too and it seems this may be just a bit too early for you.'

I looked across at my breast-care nurse, Sarah, and she nodded in agreement.

By the end of that year they agreed I was ready for the op. I still hated the thought of going back to hospital without Brian by my side, but I had to have it done. Maureen came with me for the operation at Wythenshawe Hospital in Manchester and was fantastic throughout. When they put me in the hospital gown and took me down for surgery Maureen and I hugged and then I started to cry. I had such a wonderful family who would do anything for me but I missed Brian more than ever.

The operation was going to be a long one because the surgeons had to take muscle from my back and move it under my skin, then put the implant behind it. Then afterwards it would be pumped up with saline to make it match the size of my right breast.

When I was about to go under the anaesthetic I cried out for Brian.

'He'll be here when you come round,' the nurse said. Then she looked across the bed over to Maureen, mouthing: 'Who's Brian?'

'Her dead husband,' Maureen mouthed back.

'Oh.'

It was hilarious and awful all at the same time.

Maureen was by my side again when I came round after the operation.

'How's it look?' I mumbled as I opened my eyes.

'Amazing!' laughed Maureen. Although all either of us could see at that point was a mound of bandages.

They don't call me Linda 'Lucky' Hudson for nothing in my family. And sure enough, just when I should have been ready to come out of hospital I came down with an infection. At one point it looked like I was going to have to spend the entire Christmas in hospital but in the end I was allowed out to recuperate at Maureen's.

Maureen had a terrible bad back at the time and one night was in such pain she took a Tramadol painkiller. It immediately disagreed with her and she started throwing up. She could barely move, and I couldn't either because my reconstruction and back scars were so painful. We decided to call Denise.

Denise is fabulous at everything . . . except she can't cope with seeing other people in pain. So when she turned up and saw the state I was in she went all woozy and fainted on the sofa. When a cab turned up to take Maureen to hospital with us two limping along behind her, we looked like the Three Stooges. The cab driver was utterly confused.

'I'm not being rude, but which one of you is the ill one?' he said.

And of course my breast reconstruction wasn't without a hitch either. When the doctors tried to pump in the saline to make the breasts the same size it wouldn't work. Apparently my skin had lost all its elasticity during radiotherapy which meant it couldn't stretch. So instead I had to carry on wearing a half prosthesis until I could have the other breast reduced in size to make my figure more balanced.

But then came one small light on the horizon. It was a call from Coleen's agent Mel who I'd got to know over the years.

'Now, Linda,' she said. 'How do you like this idea – a Nolan reunion tour?'

'Wow, that would be incredible,' I said. 'More than incredible, it'd be amazing.'

I hadn't worked for more than a year and had begun to think I'd never work again. The thought of being back on stage with my sisters beside me was incredible. Over the years when we'd got up and sung at family parties we'd often talk about how wonderful a reunion tour would be. But to actually be on stage in front of thousands of people? And going back into the recording studio?

Truthfully, I wasn't sure whether I was mentally strong enough for it. But the old fluttering of excitement I used to get in my stomach whenever I was offered a new job was back. What's more the money would help clear my overdraft and credit card debts which had been mounting up.

'I'm in,' I said.

But then that's when things started getting complicated. We were told that the record company, Universal, only wanted to use four of us – Maureen, me, Bernie and Coleen. That meant

Denise and Anne wouldn't be part of the line-up so at first we flatly rejected the idea. Denise had left the band quite early on but Anne had been a part of it for years when we were working in London.

'If there's going to be a reunion Anne has to be part of it,' we said.

'Sorry, Universal and the promoters Live Nation say "No",' our agent said. 'They say it will only work with four of you. It's this deal or no deal.'

In the aftermath I think Anne and Denise felt we gave in immediately to the idea of them being left out, but we really didn't. The negotiations went on for weeks and we tried everything we could to persuade them to include the others but nothing made a difference. If we didn't agree with everything they suggested they'd drop the entire plan. And the amount of money they were offering was so huge I couldn't afford that.

We knew Anne was going to be really upset and angry and were dreading telling her what had happened.

'I'll talk to her,' said Maureen. 'I'll explain we haven't got a choice.'

Maureen had always been closer to Denise and Anne as they were closer in age. And Maureen is the family mediator – she always has been. But not even Maureen's easy-going nature could calm Anne down when she told her what was happening. Anne was furious and felt we had all betrayed her. Denise immediately took Anne's side and within days we found ourselves stuck in the worst fall-out that us sisters have ever had.

Anne and Denise had already fallen out with Coleen a couple of years earlier after a row with her husband Ray. Me,

Maureen, Bernie and our brothers had managed to keep out of that. I loved all my siblings and was devastated they'd fallen out so badly. But this time I was firmly in the middle of the feud.

I can see it from both sides now. Anne was hurt and angry that she hadn't been invited for the reunion and Denise was angry on Anne's behalf. They both felt we should have refused to take part unless Anne was included in the line-up. And maybe we should have done. But back then I just thought the tour was something to feel hopeful about for the first time in a long time. And, like I said, I desperately needed the money. I'd been getting by on benefits since Brian died and I needed to work.

Some terrible text messages were hurtling backwards and forwards between us and we all said things we shouldn't have done. I received one message saying: 'Enjoy your thirty pieces of silver' as if I'd sold my soul for the tour. But then in another I wrote: 'If you can pay me what they're offering to pay me for this job, I won't do it.' I knew they couldn't.

And then Denise said something about my Brian and it just lit the fuse paper in my mind. Stuff was raked up from the dim and distant past and none of us handled that well.

It was awful. I decided the only way I could cope was to take a big step backwards and not respond to any more text messages. All contact ended between me and Maureen on one side and Denise and Anne on the other. Denise lived at the bottom of my road and we weren't speaking. It was soul-destroying. All our lives we'd been so close. We'd shared everything and now they had gone from my life. It was a major shock to the system.

Sometimes we'd all still go to bingo on a Sunday night but

then would sit at different tables. It was so embarrassing because everyone could see what was happening. I guess the only good thing was Mum and Dad weren't alive to see it – it would have broken their hearts.

It was with a heavy heart that me and the other three girls started rehearsing, recording and doing all the promotional photo shoots and interviews we were going to need to launch the tour. Returning to work was tough enough for me as it was but the feud just made it all the more stressful.

'Are you OK with all this?' Maureen asked me one day.

'I think so,' I replied. I really couldn't be much more certain than that. For months I'd barely left the house and so it was tough having to get myself out there every day and face the world.

We rehearsed for six weeks in London and stayed in a beautiful hotel in Kensington. There was a huge amount to learn because we had a team of dancers and some quite complicated choreography. We also had to learn all the harmonies and record an album.

The news of our reunion was on the front page of the newspapers and we got invited on endless TV shows – it was incredibly exciting. The only dampener was that Anne and Denise were so angry about it. And there were difficult days.

We were due to rehearse on 21 September, the anniversary of Brian's death. I phoned the girls in the morning saying I couldn't face it. Maureen came round and hugged me, saying: 'What will you do if you don't come in today? You'll just sit here feeling worse and worse. Come in for a bit and see how it goes.' So I did.

We were going to finish the concert with the amazing Christina Aguilera ballad 'The Voice Within', which has the words: 'No one ever wants or bothers to explain, Of the heart-ache life can bring and what it means.'

'Right,' our producer said, 'let's rehearse "The Voice Within" now.'

'No,' screamed Maureen, Bernie and Coleen all at the same time. 'Not today.'

They knew it would push me over the edge. Instead we focused on our upbeat encore song.

But other days were better. And for the first in a long time I had a reason to get out of bed in the morning. And I had my sisters next to me 24/7. There's no way I could have done it without them.

It was October 2009 – just over two years since Brian died – that I stood on stage for the opening night of the Nolans tour. We were in Nottingham in front of thousands of fans and it was incredibly exciting. We'd seen coachloads of them turning up at the venue. They were mainly women and by their age we could tell that they'd been Nolans fans the first time around. And here they were again but this time they were with their kids and even grandkids.

'You're going to be great,' the producer had been telling us over and over again in rehearsals.

'But what if we're not?' I said frantically to Bernie, Maureen and Coleen one night. 'What if we're a complete disaster?'

I was only saying what the others were thinking. We all knew we could still sing – but what if we weren't what the audiences were expecting after all these years? There was only one way we were going to find out.

For our entrance we stood behind a Nolan's sign with our backs to the audience and started singing as the sign parted to reveal us standing there. My heart was pounding with nerves but within seconds the screaming and whistling had started. It was an electric atmosphere. Before we'd even finished the first verse of our first song 'Holding Out for a Hero', we knew the crowd really did love us. We were wearing black and white trouser suits with black leather gloves and shades and we felt amazing. By the time we got to 'I'm in the Mood for Dancing' as our finale, dressed in black sequinned catsuits, the entire auditorium was going crazy. It was the most incredible sensation you can imagine.

Still, for most of that first performance I was fighting back tears as I thought about doing all this, this incredible tour, without Brian. He had always joked that The Nolans were his favourite band, and he was missing the comeback. Even walking into my dressing room had been tough. If he'd been here it would have been totally 'Brian-ed' with flowers, mementos and photographs. But without him it seemed sparse. Empty. A bit like me. And waiting in the wings that first night without Brian had been terrifying.

Night after night we had the same response and as the tour went on, it lifted me enormously. And we had some fabulous nights out after the shows too. In Brighton we all went out with our make-up artist Sally O'Neill and some of the other crew. We all got on so well that after the show it was like being on holiday. That night we went for dinner and ended up in a gay club. When four Nolans walked into the club I think some of the regulars thought they'd died and gone to heaven! By the end of the night Coleen was up on stage poledancing with four women. The next thing I knew I was outside singing 'I'm in the Mood for Dancing' with a group of girls we'd met. I was so drunk, I was screeching: 'You're getting the f***ing words wrong!' before collapsing into helpless laughter. What I didn't realize was that someone had filmed it and put it up online. It went viral and is utterly hilarious.

I crept into bed at about 6 a.m. – and had to be up at 8 a.m. to get on the tour coach. I was up and packing the next morning when I realized that somehow during the night I'd managed to lose my prosthetic breast. Maureen and I searched high and low but we couldn't find it. I bounded onto the tour bus shouting: 'Right, I don't want anyone to panic but I've lost my breast. Wardrobe have a spare so I'll be okay for the show.'

Everyone cracked up laughing.

I was unpacking at the next hotel on the tour in Bourne-mouth when I found it at the bottom of my suitcase. I ran into the theatre where my sisters and the crew were getting ready for a sound-check.

'I've found it,' I said. 'I've found my breast.'

The theatre sound guys looked at me like I was completely insane.

The last night of the tour was in Belfast. When the curtain came down for the last time we all felt desolate. We'd had the best of times. It had been a massive adrenalin rush and a real reminder of how wonderful performing could be. But what now?

Returning to Blackpool was tough. Going back to an empty house was a brutal reminder that Brian had gone. It almost felt like losing him all over again.

At home life was quieter than ever. I went to Coleen's house for Christmas which was lovely but it felt so strange to go through the entire day, Boxing Day and New Year without once speaking to Anne and Denise.

Denise only lived five doors up the road from me and I would have to walk past her front door most days. I remember walking past her house one day that Christmas and thinking to myself: 'This just isn't right.' But I didn't know what to do about it. It felt like such terrible things had been said that I couldn't imagine how we would ever get through it.

And that was really sad because I knew how good Denise had been to me, so many times. When Brian died she brought round a big bag of DVDs and we sat and watched them together for hours, just being together. It was terrible I'd lost her but I was so hurt by what had gone on that I didn't know how to rebuild the relationship.

My mood sank even lower at the beginning of 2010 and it was then that my psychologist said she felt my grief and loss had developed into complex clinical depression. She prescribed me antidepressants but at first it didn't feel like they were doing anything to help.

Some days I wouldn't get out of bed at all. Hudson, my little dog, slept next to me. In the mornings he'd sometimes lift his head from the pillow and give me an enquiring look as if to say: 'Are we getting up today?' I'd stroke the top of his head and reply: 'Not yet, Hudson. Maybe later.' Other days I'd wake to Hudson licking the tears from my cheeks. I would cry in my sleep then wake and cry over again.

If I did get up, I'd only make it as far as the sofa. The outside world all seemed like too much effort. Unless you've had depression it's hard to understand the utter hopelessness of it. Others might think: 'Why doesn't she just give herself a shake'. But I couldn't. I really couldn't help myself.

I didn't have the energy to eat and some days I made it

through to the evening before realizing I hadn't even drunk so much as a glass of water. I could go days on end without showering. My sisters and friends were amazing, inviting me over for dinner, turning up unannounced with pots of food, anything to lift me out of this pit of despair. But there was nothing anyone could do.

I was constantly cancelling plans at the last moment when I couldn't face leaving the house and I booked and paid for three holidays with different members of my family – then couldn't bring myself to go on any of them. It was always so disappointing, knowing I had to cancel, but there was also this incredible sense of relief that I wouldn't have to leave my home and spend a week pretending I felt better than I did.

Brian had been dead for almost three years but my sense of loss only seemed to be growing.

I visited psychics in the desperate hope of making contact with him again. It was difficult knowing who to trust because of course if people wanted to take advantage of me they could read about my life in newspapers or on the internet. But still I went along, frantic for information, asking for help reaching Brian.

One spiritualist said to me: 'There is a man here and he won't look at me. He seems quite old. Was he very thin?'

And then I realized that it wasn't Brian she was talking about, it was Dad.

'He's holding a book,' the psychic said, 'and he's saying he is sorry. He says he knows you are going to write a book too and he knows you'll let people know that you loved him.'

That felt incredibly real – and is one of the reasons I wanted to write this book.

There was another psychic I went to and I'm sure she made

contact with Brian. For years when close friends had rung up and said 'How's it going?' my answer was always, 'It's a fucking nightmare.' It was part joke, part absolute honesty. But this day, when I sat with the psychic she said: 'He's talking to me. He says he knows it's a fucking nightmare but you're doing a great job and he is proud of you.' I am convinced that was from Brian. It was a wonderful feeling.

Another lady I visited told me Mum was up there holding a little girl who was exactly the right age by then for Bernie's little girl Kate, who'd tragically been stillborn.

'Brian is there too,' the lady said. 'He will be waiting for you when it is your time but right now he wants you to be happy.'

That left me feeling very peaceful – it was a real comfort. But the feeling didn't last. At other times I just wanted to be with Brian immediately. I desperately needed to be with him wherever he was, and if that meant I'd have to be dead, then so be it.

One day I sat with my psychologist Dr Briggs, tears once again running down my face. 'There's no point in going on without Brian,' I said. 'My life will never get any better because Brian will never be here.'

I'd only been back home an hour or so when the phone rang. It was my GP, Dr Murphy. Apparently Dr Briggs had been straight on to her saying she thought I should be referred to the local mental health team. Amid my tears I was furious. I felt Dr Briggs had betrayed my trust – and said so. I wasn't mentally ill, I was just sad.

'You know that as a strong Irish woman I won't be taking no for an answer,' Dr Murphy said. 'You need help from this mental health team and that's what they will give you.'

Less than twenty-four hours later a woman psychiatrist and two burly male nurses were standing on my front doorstep. Even in the thick of my depression I knew what this meant. 'If this doesn't end well you're going to be leaving here with them to get locked up,' I said to myself.

But they came in, I made a cup of tea, and they were lovely.

'Look, Mrs Hudson,' the psychiatrist said. 'If you really want to commit suicide there is nothing anybody can do to stop you. That's why people take their own lives. But I think I can help you. So all I'm asking is for you to give us a chance. Just give us a chance to help you.'

I looked at her and thought hard. I felt so tired. But she was right, what did I have to lose? I had to give her a chance.

After that day the team would turn up unannounced several times a week. I think a few years earlier I would have been sent straight to a special unit because I was in such a bad way, but this was a new method of working with people like me in our own homes.

The mental health team encouraged me to keep a diary of my moods and each time they came round we'd discuss how I'd been feeling. Or I could call them at any time. I never drank alcohol at home but if I ever went out with a friend or my sisters I would drink way too much. Then I'd get home and feel terrible and phone the crisis team. They must have known sometimes I was just drunk and so they'd tell me to make a cup of tea and get into bed, and then they'd call back in twenty minutes to check on me. By then I'd be fast asleep.

As for work? I was just too scared. I was offered a role in a touring production called *Grumpy Old Women*. The money was good and the script looked great. How could I turn it down? But I was terrified by the thought of being away from home for six weeks.

As ever I turned to my sisters for advice.

'You can do this, Linda,' said Coleen. 'You'll be amazing.'

Maureen and Bernie were more cautious.

'Don't do it, if you don't feel up to it,' said Maureen.

'But what do you really want?' asked Bernie, with her usual wisdom.

'I don't want to do it,' I replied flatly.

'Well don't do it then,' she said. 'Simple.'

It was such a relief having someone telling me that I didn't have to do it. And so I didn't.

Looking back, dealing with my depression was hard for my whole family. I know often Coleen wanted to shake me. She really believed the longer I stayed at home the worse I would get. Maureen and Bernie were anxious I could make myself even more ill, while Tommy and Brian just worried themselves sick.

There were some bright spots during that time, though. Maureen's son Danny and his girlfriend Maddison had their baby, Sienna. Maddison became a great friend to me and we spent loads of time together because I wasn't working and she was on maternity leave.

Sienna was just six weeks old the first time I looked after her on my own. Maureen was away touring and I was more than happy to stand in as surrogate nanny. Never having had children of my own it was a challenge but I loved it. From the beginning there was something very special about the relationship between me and Sienna. She was so tiny and gorgeous and perfect. And she gave me hope when there wasn't a lot of hope around.

From then on if there were family parties I would always be happy to nip off home with Sienna while the others carried on partying. As she got older I would sing to her, play games or we'd snuggle up on the sofa and watch our favourite Disney films.

Another bright point during that period was when Maureen asked me to be chief bridesmaid at her long-, long-awaited marriage to Ritchie. The whole family was a bit stunned that they were finally getting round to marrying almost twenty years after they first met. But we were delighted too. Maureen and Ritchie were such a laid-back couple and seemed a perfect match. I threw myself into my chief bridesmaid duties, organizing a hen-do garden party round at a friend's house and helping Maureen choose a lovely traditional white wedding dress.

The wedding was beautiful. They took their vows by a pool in Spain just as the sun was setting. Maureen looked gorgeous and Ritchie was so handsome. I was so pleased for both of them. The only sadness that day was that Denise and Anne weren't there as the rift still hadn't been healed. And of course I missed Brian. But then, I always missed Brian.

With Mum and Dad at Lord Delfont's lunch in Blackpool.

In my dressing room with Denise, when we were both
playing Mrs Johnstone in *Blood Brothers*, March 2000.

With Bernie on her fortieth birthday, October 2000.

Brian and I renewed our wedding vows on a gulet boat in Turkey, summer 2005.

Top Me and Brian at my brother Brian's wedding in August 2007. Five weeks later, my Brian died; *above right* With Brian's daughter Sarah on her wedding day; *above left* My granddaughter Lucy was a beautiful bridesmaid at her mum's wedding.

I was Coleen's maid of
honour at her wedding to
Ray, November 2007.

The Nolans reunion tour in 2009 gave me something to live for.
Once I got over my nerves, I loved it.

Me, Bernie and Maureen in Spain for Maureen's wedding in 2010.
Bernie's cancer had come back.

Above left My great-nieces Sienna and Roma; *above right* With Maureen's son (and my godson) Danny; *below* With my friend Sue at the Pink Ribbon Ball in London.

My friend Liz Emmet bought me these Louboutin shoes as a
present when the cancer came back. Wearing them is a sign that
I am living, not dying, with cancer.

Fourteen

Bernie Comes Out Fighting

Maureen was driving me back from town when she told me.

'Linda, I've got some bad news,' she said, pulling the car up outside my house. 'It's Bernie. She's got breast cancer.'

My stomach flipped over. 'Oh no, not Bernie,' I said.

'Yes, we didn't want to tell you until we knew for certain because of how low you've been recently.'

'Thanks, Maureen,' I said. I tried to smile. 'But she'll be OK – Bernie is the toughest of all of us.'

'Definitely,' replied Maureen. 'She's going to have all the treatment and be fine. You know what Bernie's like – she won't let anything get the better of her.'

We smiled at each other as if to show a reassurance we didn't really feel. Then I gave Maureen a kiss, picked up my bag and walked up the path to my front door. The moment I closed the door behind me I crumpled to the floor. Any pretence at bravery had disappeared.

'No, not again. Not Bernie,' I whimpered.

My darling little sister. Now she was going to have to endure the curse of cancer. I didn't for one moment doubt that she'd get through it – you had to know Bernie to understand what a fighter she was by nature. I just felt heartbroken for her that she was going to have to endure all that treatment – and I knew exactly how awful that was. Although we could fight like cat and dog at times, we were desperately close.

I had to screw up all my energy for that first phone call to Bernie.

'Hiya, Bernie,' I said, pausing to find the right words. 'I'm just so sorry.'

'It's OK, Lin,' she replied. 'I'm going to beat this bastard.'

'Of course you will – if I can get through it, you definitely can.'

Bernie had been appearing in the TV show *Popstar to Operastar* when she first noticed her left boob had changed shape and that her skin had the texture of orange peel. Her GP referred her for a mammogram and ultrasound which had shown cancer in the breast. She would need a mastectomy and chemotherapy. Her gorgeous daughter, Erin, was just about to turn eleven. How could this be happening to full-of-life Bernie?

Over the next few days I spoke to Bernie regularly on the phone. Being the trooper she was she was still turning up for work on a tour of the stage show *Mum's the Word*. But when she started chemotherapy she gave that up and threw every ounce of her being into fighting the disease.

I rang or texted Bernie every single evening. She'd been there for me every moment when I was poorly and then depressed and I vowed I'd be just as supportive now she needed me.

Bernie was super-focused on getting well and spent hours reading up on all the different types of treatment and drugs available.

'So did you have Herceptin or Carboplatin or Pertuzumab or Docetaxel?' she'd ask.

'Oh, I haven't got a clue, they just shoved it in my arm,' I'd say.

Honestly, we couldn't have been more different in our attitudes. Bernie was forensic in keeping on top of what was happening to her. She didn't just know what the drugs were – she could spell them too! I meanwhile had just put myself in the hands of the doctors and hoped for the best. Of course our older sister Anne had also been through the ordeal and it was great she and Bernie were able to put their differences behind them and talk about it. Anne was a great support to Bernie, as she had been to me when I was ill.

News had started to leak out about Bernie's illness so she decided to do an interview with the *News of the World* about her diagnosis. It was typical Bernie: 'Cancer's a scary word,' she said, 'but it can bugger off.' The story made front-page news and she was inundated with support from all over the country. Her ballsy approach to cancer became a national talking point. I was so proud of my little sister being so strong when faced with something so awful. I hadn't a shred of doubt that the cancer would do just as it was told and bugger right off!

Bernie did well all through her chemotherapy sessions in that summer of 2010. She knew how sick I'd been every seven days after chemo and I think that was a worry for her but she was different from me.

'Chemo is our friend,' she'd say, because to her it was her ally in winning the war on cancer. Which of course it was.

It was still a shock for her when her hair started to fall out. And she suffered terrible mouth ulcers as a side effect, which made it too painful to eat for weeks on end. As the chemo progressed it made her sicker and sicker but she put on an incredible mask when she was suffering. She was determined her illness would have the minimum impact on Erin.

During that time Bernie and I also had lots of long conversations about mastectomy. I'd asked for a double mastectomy but the surgeons had recommended a single one. Bernie was in the same situation – she too wanted a double but it was decided again a single would be better, followed by immediate reconstruction.

'How you feeling about it all?' I asked her during one of our late night phone calls.

'I'm actually quite excited,' she said. 'I want to get on with it. Get it over and done with and then move on with life.'

Bernie's operation was booked for the start of October and I went down to her house to help look after Erin while she was in hospital so Steve could spend as much time at the hospital as he needed. Then when Bernie got home I stayed to help out with nursing duties. Steve was a wonderful carer for Bernie – there was nothing he wouldn't do. But when he could be persuaded to take a rest, I'd step in. It was wonderful having that time with Bernie and feeling, after everything she'd done for me, I was there to help her.

A few days after the operation, Bernie turned fifty. Maureen and Ritchie, my brother Brian and Annie all turned up at the house and had a wonderful dinner cooked by Steve. Bernie was still too ill for a party but we all sang 'Happy Birthday' and there was a lot of laughter that day. Bernie was still poorly but she was on the road to recovery.

By the following January Bernie was in remission and was feeling strong enough for a proper party. She held a fiftieth-birthday 'I've Kicked Cancer's Butt' party at a hotel near her home in Weybridge, Surrey. There was an eighteen-piece orchestra and loads of people got up to sing. Everyone was dancing and it was a fabulous night.

Even though I was still struggling with my depression, Bernie's illness had given me something to focus on. The work the mental health team had done with me was brilliant and very slowly I was beginning to feel stronger. Relations were even getting better with Denise and Anne.

For months, when Maureen and I went to bingo on a Sunday evening we'd ignore Denise and Anne at the other end of the room and they'd ignore us. Maureen started chatting to them first as she found the rupture with them utterly agonizing. But for me, it ran deeper because of the things which had been said in anger about Brian. Then one evening at bingo I noticed Denise was sitting on her own.

'Why don't you ask her if she'd like to come and join us,' I said to Maureen.

'Really?' she replied. I think Maureen had given up all hope of us ever being reconciled.

She went over with the message and Denise was really pleased. 'Oh, I've got all my cards sorted here now,' she said. 'But thank Linda for me, that's a really nice thought.'

And after that we started talking more and more every week. And slowly but surely things improved with both Denise and Anne. Within a few months we were even all sitting together at bingo again. The feud was over. And I was more relieved than I would ever have thought possible.

I had occasional bits of work too. I was asked to film a slot for *The One Show* on genetic testing for breast cancer which was interesting. The idea was to discover whether Anne,

Bernie and I were carrying the BRCA gene that makes women more susceptible to breast cancer. As it turned out we weren't, but the geneticist I met during filming was pretty certain that it was no coincidence all three of us had got the disease while we were still under fifty.

That autumn I also felt well enough to give panto another go, even though the thought of being away from home for a couple of months was terrifying. 'But you can't stay locked in here for ever,' I told myself. Filled with apprehension I agreed to take the part of the Wicked Queen in *Snow White* in Worthing, on the south coast – about as far from Blackpool as it is possible to go.

In hindsight it was probably too far from home. As soon as I arrived for rehearsals I felt anxious and down. Being so far from home with no one I knew nearby made my depression more intense than ever. One day during rehearsals I couldn't even make it in to the theatre. I told the producer I had a bug, then sat in the apartment I'd rented in Worthing panicking I couldn't go on. It all seemed so pointless without Brian.

I was slumped on the sofa feeling utterly hopeless when the intercom went. It was Bernie. 'Open the door, I've got stew.' And in she bounded, carrying all the ingredients she needed to make one of the stews our Mum always made for Saturday tea. She'd even brought a bag of the little banana sweets we'd loved as kids. As soon as I saw Bernie I sobbed. I just needed someone to put their arms around me which is exactly what she did.

Bernie was amazing. She was still recovering herself but she'd driven down from her home in Surrey because she was worried about me. During that whole terrible time she called or texted twice a day, every day, just to check in on me. It was that and all my sisters' support which kept me alive.

That day Bernie and I just chatted, watched a movie, went for a walk in the fresh air and hung around together. It was all I needed and the next day I was able to face rehearsals again.

The cast I was working with were lovely but at the end of every show I'd go home and sit slumped in front of a DVD. I couldn't sleep and was tearful a lot of the time. One night I was walking round the apartment like a mad woman, crying and feeling utterly hopeless. I went into the kitchen, opened the kitchen drawer and pulled out a knife. I'm not really sure what I was thinking, I just seemed to be on autopilot.

I wanted to take the knife and slice through my skin. Not to kill myself but somehow to hurt myself so badly that it might take the pain away inside.

Something stopped me. Cowardice, perhaps. I threw the knife back in the drawer and slammed it shut.

But I had begun hurting myself. Self-harming is what it was, although at that time I'd never have admitted it to myself. Sometimes I would dig my fingernails so deep into my hands that I'd draw blood. Other times I would bite my hand until I broke the skin.

It began when I was having panic attacks but the panic attacks were becoming more frequent and so was the self-harming. I'd never had a panic attack until the night in the hospital before Brian died. But in the months and years that followed they'd kept coming back every time I felt something else was overwhelming me. Once I'd gone into town with Maureen and checked my bank balance at a cashpoint machine. When I saw I had hardly anything left in my bank account the panic attack started almost immediately. Each attack was the same. It would start with me struggling for breath, but when I couldn't catch my breath I'd become more and more convinced I was going to suffocate. Then the gasping for air would get worse and worse. Sometimes it could take me an hour to calm myself and get my breathing back to normal.

Then one evening I bit so deeply into my hand that it bled. It hurt, really hurt. But somehow, for a split second, the pain was in my hand and not in my heart.

It became a habit. The deeper I bit, the more it hurt and the more it seemed to ease something inside me. I admitted what I'd been doing to Dr Briggs, my psychologist.

'OK, Linda,' she said. 'I can understand why you feel that helps, but you really mustn't injure yourself. It could be dangerous.'

She suggested I put an elastic band around my wrist and snap it against my skin. Or hold an ice cube against myself until it hurt. I did it with a hair bobble and it seemed to work. A bit. It was certainly painful. But there was something brutal about biting and digging my fingernails into myself, until they drew blood, which seemed to bring a deeper sense of relief.

Somehow I made it to the end of the run of the pantomime. The snow was really bad that year and I was terrified I'd get stuck in Worthing all on my own. Maureen phoned me and said: 'Don't you worry, if we have to get a tractor to get you back home, we will.'

I was desperate to be back in Blackpool. But the strange thing was that after my friend picked me up from the station for the drive home, I started crying all over again. It was the thought of returning to 'our house' again – but with no Brian there to meet me.

I'd learned my fight back to health from depression was going to be a long journey but that I really shouldn't rush it or I'd only end up going backwards. And gradually, very gradually, with the right medication and continued counselling I began to feel a little better again.

For a while I'd been thinking that I wanted a way to do some kind of voluntary work to give something back to the town which had given me so much. And I knew I loved spending time with kids. But I wasn't sure how to go about doing it. I was discussing it one evening on the phone with Suzanne, my old friend from next door.

'I'll see if I can find something suitable,' Suzanne said. She's always great at solving problems like that. By the next day she was back on the phone.

'I've found the perfect thing,' she said. 'There's a charity in Blackpool called The Tramshed. It's an inclusive theatre company within Blackpool, Wyre and the Flyde.'

'That sounds perfect,' I said. 'But I might not be the kind of person they're looking for,' I went on, the doubts starting to re-emerge in my mind.

'Look, I'm sure they'll be delighted to have a Nolan. Promise me you'll try.'

So I did. I asked Annie if she'd come with me for moral support, then I plucked up all my courage and rang the Tramshed number that Suzanne had found on the internet.

'Oh hi,' I said, my voice quivering. 'My sister-in-law Annie and I were wondering if we might be of any use if we were to volunteer.'

'Oh, I'm sure you could,' the man on the end of the phone said. 'Do you have any showbiz experience at all?' he asked.

'Oh, only about fifty years,' I laughed. When I explained who I was and that Annie had previously worked as a dancer he was delighted.

Annie and I started volunteering once a week. The kids were amazing. They were utterly inspiring. Some of the children had learning difficulties of some sort. One of the boys I had to help played the lead in the show they were putting on. He was a fabulous performer but he was also autistic and found it very hard to communicate. I became incredibly fond of him. At the end of the first show when I saw his parents run up to hug him and I realized how proud he was of what he'd achieved, I felt utterly overwhelmed.

What I was doing was helping people – and that felt amazing. It was wonderful to feel useful for the first time in a long time. And after a while the charity asked me to become one of their patrons. I felt very proud to be asked.

I talked to my psychologist frequently about the youth theatre work and the great times I'd have when I was looking after my great-nieces and -nephews.

'You know, Linda,' Dr Briggs said one day, 'sometimes, when you're talking about the theatre kids or when you're telling stories about Sienna and Ava there's a light in your eyes which I never see at any other time.'

'It's because I love them I suppose,' I replied. 'And I love the person I am when I'm with them too. The sadness seems to fade away when I'm with the kids. It's like I'm back to the fun-loving Linda that I used to be.'

'Well it's wonderful,' said Dr Briggs. 'You should have a

think about what else you could do to bring back that light in your eyes.'

I went home and over the next few weeks I did just that. And it was then that the idea of fostering children began to take hold in my mind. It seemed daunting at first but quite quickly I became convinced it was what I wanted. I've always loved children and they usually seem to like me too. But of course being approved to foster takes a very long time. There was a whole year of meetings with social services and discussion about whether I would be suitable. It was certainly a whole lot more complicated than the question of whether I could provide a loving and stable home for a child in need.

Some people thought I was mad to be considering it and that I might have to deal with kids who had all sorts of emotional or physical problems. That didn't bother me at all. I knew I had a lot to offer a child who'd had a tough start in life. But I was terrified my depression might rule me out from being chosen. I was brutally honest throughout it all and told the social workers all about my depression and suicidal thoughts.

I so wanted to be accepted that I was feeling sick with nerves the day I stood before a panel of eight experts in the fostering department of the council offices just outside Blackpool. In front of the panel members was a huge pile of all the paperwork I'd had to fill out and the social workers had had to complete over recent months.

I knew the only thing that might stand against me was my history of depression. I had the most enormous smile plastered to my face in the hope that would convince the panel I wasn't remotely depressed any more. I was so desperate to be selected. All the reports from social workers, my mental health team and counsellors said they thought I was suitable for fostering. But there was still a big risk they might say no.

Waiting for the verdict was terrifying and when I got the call saying I'd been approved I was whooping around the kitchen in delight.

To start me off it was decided I would do respite foster care, so basically I'd have children for weekends and holidays to give their usual carers a break. A few weeks later I received another call from a social worker.

'Hi Linda,' she said, 'are you free this weekend?'

'Yes, of course,' I replied.

'OK, in that case we have a child who we hope you can look after. He's only a baby – four weeks old.'

'Oh, wow,' I replied. Four weeks seemed incredibly tiny. But I wasn't worried by that. I'd looked after my great-nieces Sienna and Ava when they were tiny. I just felt terribly sad that a little baby had no stable home at such a young age.

He was a fabulous baby. He was still so little that really all he did was eat and sleep. I held him in my arms for hours, knowing he'd already come through a tough time. For the two days he was staying with me I just wanted him to know he was loved.

Meeting the social workers and undergoing foster training had opened my eyes to the lives some children have to lead. The social workers had told me there were children living in Blackpool who'd never been to the beach – or seen a Christmas tree. It seemed too unlikely to be true. But it was. And while my family may have had its troubles over the years I always knew how it felt to be loved. It seems terribly sad how many children are growing up without knowing what that is like.

A few weeks after having the baby, I looked after another little boy who was about two and a half. He arrived at my front gate with a social worker, looking really bewildered. It must have been confusing for him being told he was going to be looked after for the weekend by another total stranger. And at first he was a bit volatile – but in that situation, I would have been too!

I'd been told in advance that he loved cars so I'd made sure I had some for him to play with. When he was finally coaxed inside we sat on the floor and played car games together for ages, having a great old time. Then I made him some tea and afterwards gave him an ice cream cone. But he'd clearly never had ice cream before because the coldness panicked him. It was heartbreaking to watch. How can a kiddie grow up without ice cream? After a while he got used to it and started to suck it up as though drinking a bottle of pop. Then he looked up and smiled at me. It was an utterly heart-warming moment. He was brilliant.

To give a child that had come from a very upsetting background a sense of love and normality, even for just a weekend, was a wonderful feeling.

Fifteen

Losing Bernie

Life settled into a routine back in Blackpool. It felt that week by week I was getting better and my depression was definitely subsiding. Maureen even suggested I should give it a go without the antidepressants but I was too nervous. I was frightened of falling ill again. Then, at the end of 2011, Maureen and I went into pantomime together in London. It was *Jack and the Beanstalk* and Maureen was the Good Fairy (obviously!) while I was the Bad Fairy (obviously again!). We were staying in a beautiful hotel and it was wonderful us doing it together. But once again I found myself starting to panic. Even though I knew my lines well in advance, whenever we started rehearsing I couldn't remember a thing. Some mornings, after Maureen had left, I'd just pull the duvet over my head and hope it would all go away. The panic attacks became more frequent as the weeks went on and on the day of the dress rehearsal I broke down in tears in front of all the cast and crew. Everyone was lovely but I was so embarrassed I hadn't been able to hold it together.

The director came up with the idea of pasting my script into the Bad Fairy's spell book to prevent me from panicking for the first few performances. I didn't actually need to check it at all but it was a safety net.

Maureen was so patient with me. We spent that Christmas at my brother Brian and sister-in-law Annie's house. Under the tree I'd wrapped a fabulous coat for Maureen as a big thank you for getting me through the past few months.

'You deserve that, having to put up with me,' I joked when I gave it to her.

'Is it a million-dollar mink?' she laughed back.

The pantomime finished at the start of January and once again I had that trip home which I dreaded – knowing I was returning to an empty house with no Brian and no work on the horizon. The previous year I'd really thought I was coming through the depression but my sense of hopelessness seemed to be back and worse than ever. What was terrifying me by then was the fear that I would never truly be rid of it. If every time I had a disruption to my routine I plunged back into this dreadful sense of darkness then maybe I'd never be fixed. That was horrible, as I really could see no hope.

I don't think my depression actually hit its absolute rock bottom until 2012 – which was five years after Brian had died. That's why now when people talk to me about grief and depression I never tell them they'll be over it soon. Hopefully they'll get over it one day. But it is a long, hard road. And the longer it goes on, of course, the greater the fear becomes that it will never go away. And that is terrifying.

By the beginning of 2012 I was feeling utterly hopeless. One night I found every tablet I could in the house and lined them up on the kitchen worktop. I don't think there was any-thing specific to cause me to hit rock bottom that day – it was just extreme depression. It was then I wrote a letter to my brothers and sisters. In it I said I knew they'd understand why I was doing this and thanked them for being so amazing. I begged them not to feel guilty because it was what I wanted. And then I asked them to look after Hudson.

When I wrote those words I really did think my brothers and sisters would understand and that they'd be better off without me. Of course in hindsight I can see they would have been devastated, but when you're so low you think you have no worth to anyone, you just can't imagine that.

I sat there for hours crying and feeling completely hopeless. I didn't really want to die – but I didn't want to live either. I just wanted someone to take the pain away. It was then I googled a number for the Samaritans on my phone. Tears were pouring down my face as I dialled the number.

A woman answered. 'Hi, this is the Samaritans,' she said. 'How can we help you?'

At first I couldn't even speak. I just snivelled, gasping for breath between the sobs. The woman was so patient it was incredible. She didn't bombard me with questions, she just waited until I was ready. Even just hearing her breathing on the phone seemed a comfort. Bit by bit I told her everything about Brian and my depression and the sense there was nothing left to live for.

'I just miss him,' I said. 'There's no point carrying on without him.'

The lady didn't say anything like 'of course there's a point' or any of that stuff. She just listened.

After an hour of talking and crying I said I was tired and wanted to go to sleep. I put the phone down, closed my eyes and didn't wake up until morning.

Of course in the morning I still felt low and my head ached from crying. But I was still alive. That wonderful woman had got me through the night.

The next day I was able to talk to my sisters about how low I'd been and I had the strength to make an appointment with my GP. From there the local mental health care team got involved again. They came to visit me and talked about how I was feeling and took away any additional tablets I had lying around the house – they clearly didn't want to take the risk that I might feel suicidal again. And neither, in all honesty, did I.

People say that suicide is a selfish act but I think that misses the point. Because when you are feeling that low you genuinely think that all you are doing is being a drain on everyone else's lives and the best thing you can possibly do is to disappear.

One of the many sadnesses of my relapse was that I had to put more fostering on hold. I just didn't feel well enough to be taking responsibility for a child who would already have enough problems of their own.

The horrible irony of this whole time was that while I was contemplating throwing my own life away, something terrible was on the horizon threatening to steal the life of my wonderful sister Bernie.

It was back.

Bernie's bastard cancer was back. When the news came the entire family were heartbroken. We'd always believed that if anyone could beat this cursed disease it was Bernie but we all knew that secondary cancer is bad, bad news. And just when she'd been doing so well. Since going into remission more than a year earlier she'd seemed full of life and had been working like a Trojan.

She was touring in a stage show of *Chicago* when one evening she felt a new lump in her chest. While I tend to be someone who sticks their head in the sand, Bernie couldn't be more different. Within a couple of days she had been examined at the hospital and undergone a biopsy.

Less than a week later the doctors told Bernie the worst – the lump was cancerous. Bernie was raging with anger. After everything she'd been through – and after how hard she'd fought – this was so unfair. But her surgeon remained optimistic that with an operation and radiotherapy it could all be fine.

Bernie underwent a couple of scans and was booked in for an operation. But before that she and Steve were off to Monte Carlo where she was performing in *Chicago*. I was staying at theirs for a few days to look after Erin while they were away so I answered the phone when a surgeon from the hospital rang for Bernie.

'I'm afraid she's away until Sunday,' I said.

'OK, well can you ask her to call me as soon as she gets back,' he replied. I had a horrible feeling about the urgency in his voice. Doctors rarely want a patient to call them on their mobile phone on a Sunday night unless it is serious. Very serious.

'Oh God, please let Bernie be OK,' I said to myself. But the sense that something terrible was waiting for her wouldn't leave me for the next few days.

That Sunday evening Bernie had barely been in the house for an hour when the surgeon rang again. Bernie thought it was to confirm details of her op which was scheduled for the Tuesday. It wasn't.

'I'm so sorry, Bernie,' the surgeon said, 'but the scans we did before you went away have shown that the cancer has spread.'

'Where to?' Bernie asked.

The specialist wouldn't tell her over the phone – she had to go into the hospital the next day to find out face to face. It didn't sound good at all. Bernie, Steve and I sat that night terrified about what the next day might bring. We had a drink and let Bernie talk.

'What if it's spread all over?' she said.

'Oh, it won't have done, Bernie,' I said. Of course I had no idea. But what could I say? 'Maybe they can't tell you over the phone because they've got to talk to you about chemotherapy rather than radiotherapy.'

'Maybe,' she said. But Bernie was worried this time. 'What if it's spread to my brain, Lin?' she said.

"Don't be daft,' I replied. 'You've just got to get some rest and we'll know tomorrow.'

By then the only thing any of us could do was hope, pray and put all our faith in the doctors.

I stayed at home when Bernie and Steve went in for the appointment. I became obsessed with the clock, working out when they should have been out by, when they should be back in the car, when they should have called by. The times came and went and there was silence.

Finally the telephone rang. It was Bernie.

'Hi, Lin, it's me,' she said. 'It's not good news.'

'Oh Bernie,' I replied. There was nothing more to be said.

She explained that the cancer had spread to her lung and her liver. 'OK,' I said, barely trusting myself to speak.

'And . . .' she paused, 'there's a little bit in my brain.'

'Oh,' I said. 'But we can do this. You can fight this again. Look what you did last time – it's a bugger but you can do it again.'

'It's not curable, Lin,' she said. 'Treatable but not curable. That's what they say. Do me a favour – can you tell the others, I can't face upsetting them all over again.'

'Of course – anything you need Bernie,' I replied. 'Come home and I'll be here.'

I put the phone down and sank to the kitchen floor sobbing. Why Bernie? Why did she, who'd always been so full of life, deserve this?

I had tears pouring down my face as I rang our brothers and sisters to tell them our little sister's cancer was incurable. It was one of the hardest things I've ever had to do. Maureen was distraught and dropped the phone. She was with her daughter-in-law Maddison, who picked it up, saying: 'What's happened? Maureen is in pieces.' Then I had to call Anne at work who went straight round to comfort Maureen.

Then I rang our brother Brian. It went through to his answering machine so I left a message asking him to call me. When I saw his number pop up on my phone a few minutes later I felt frantic. I knew he'd be devastated. He works in sales and is often out and about driving. Later he told me he stopped in a Sainsbury's car park and cried and cried. It broke my heart. Then I phoned our eldest brother Tommy. After that I dialled Coleen's number. Even now we all still think of Coleen as the baby and so breaking bad news to her always seems particularly tough. She, like all of us, was desolate.

Bernie had decided she wanted to get up to Blackpool as soon as possible to be with us all, so she, Steve, Erin and I drove up a few days later. We all met at Annie and Brian's. It was strange because Bernie still looked great. She seemed a bit shocked, but beyond that very well. Steve was devastated – you could see it in his eyes. I don't know whether they had thought about how long Bernie might have left but we all knew it was very, very serious.

Yet she still wanted to carry on as normally as possible – mainly to prevent Erin from feeling scared. So the first thing she insisted on doing after the trip to Blackpool was going straight back on tour.

'Will you come with me, Lin?' she asked.

'On tour?' I said. 'I'd love to.'

Steve had to stay at home looking after Erin while she was at school and Bernie couldn't face the thought of living in hotel rooms on her own as the tour continued.

It's hard to explain but we had a fabulous few weeks. What a laugh! Even in this most awful of circumstances we dealt with it with humour – it's always been like that in our family.

None of the other cast in the show knew Bernie's cancer was back and I guess they thought I was just hanging out with my sister because I wasn't working at the time. The good thing about no one knowing was we could almost forget ourselves what was really happening.

In Cardiff we stayed near the marina where there were lovely restaurants. We'd go for something to eat before the show, then afterwards go back to our room and chat about the old days when we were kids, playing out in the street in Blackpool. Bernie and I could talk about anything and everything.

But she was starting to feel tired and drained. The doctors had put her on medication for the cancer and it made her feel rubbish. Sometimes she looked shattered but then I'd go along to the show an hour later and she'd be singing and dancing and looked a million dollars. She was just amazing.

I was astonished she could carry on performing with such passion when she kind of knew what lay ahead.

One evening she decided to tell the rest of the cast – they'd all become great mates and she didn't like keeping such a big secret from them. It was an incredibly tough thing to reveal publicly but still she kept up her determined front. The cast were all so supportive – but devastated too. And no one knew how much longer Bernie would be able to continue in the show.

The tour was in Belfast by the night of Bernie's fifty-second birthday in October 2012. She arranged a meal and every single member of the cast and the band came along – that's how popular she was. Then just as we were about to start eating Steve and Erin walked in the door. And half an hour later Maureen arrived too. It was a brilliant night.

Deep down I knew Bernie might not have many more birthdays like this but I pushed that thought out of my head.

I was devastated about what Bernie was facing. But worrying about her and doing whatever I could to help Steve and Erin had given me a purpose. And I think it was that – and keeping on with my medication – which meant my depression felt more manageable. I would still often cry for Bernie and what she was going through but I was crying for myself a lot less. I liked being useful to people and feeling I could help.

It was half term soon after her birthday so Steve and Erin were able to join Bernie on the tour and I went home to Blackpool. I still texted or spoke to her every day.

'I've got a stupid cough I just can't shift,' Bernie said on the phone one day. 'And my voice seems to have got a lot higher when I'm singing.'

The tour was in Plymouth by that point and she was able

to get an appointment at the hospital down there. After tests, the news came that she'd been dreading – it was the cancer causing her cough.

'I'm not going to be able to go on stage with this cough – it'd drive everyone mad. And my voice isn't right. I think my performing days are over. But I'm still going to finish the tour.'

'You really don't have to do that, you know, Bernie,' I said. 'No one's going to think you're swinging the lead.'

But she did it. There was another three weeks of the tour left to run and Bernie stayed with it right to the end even though she was unable to go on stage and had to be covered by an understudy. But that was Bernie through and through. Even when she was sick she felt she couldn't let the rest of the cast down by going home. She had such a showbiz mentality. By then she'd talked about it publicly too, doing an interview in the *Sunday Mirror*. She didn't want the story leaking out like gossip – she wanted to tell it just the way it was.

As the weeks went on Bernie was becoming more tired and frail. The drugs they'd put her on to slow down the advance of the cancer were taking a terrible toll on her body. She developed dreadful mouth ulcers again and blisters on the bottom of her feet. She was shattered. I think too she was starting to realize that she really was *that* ill.

Me, Maureen and Ritchie, Brian and Annie, all spent Christmas with Bernie, Steve and Erin. None of us said it but I think we all had it in our heads by then that this could be Bernie's last and we wanted to be together. Some of our cousins from Ireland flew over too. Steve is a fabulous cook and we all had a wonderful meal on Christmas Day. Bernie had really gone to town and had made every detail perfect; there were bows on the backs of chairs and boxes of chocolates on our beds when we arrived. Bernie loved Christmas and she did herself proud that year. But it was clear it was tiring her out.

Then in February 2013 it was Steve's birthday. Bernie had rung me a few weeks earlier to ask if I could help her make it extra special. We booked a restaurant in Blackpool as it would be easier for Steve's family from the north-east to travel there than to go all the way down south.

I made sure everything was 'just so' – exactly the way Bernie would normally have done. She was so excited, but when she arrived at the restaurant and was getting out of the car her legs gave way from under her.

'I'm fine, I'm fine,' she laughed.

'Do you want a glass of water?' I asked, all worried.

'No, Linda,' she shook her head, 'I'll have a glass of vodka!' And she remained determinedly upbeat all night long. But that had given us all a shock. She was becoming weaker.

The following day, Saturday, was my birthday and we were all going out for a family meal again. But Bernie was having trouble breathing and was out of sorts that day and left early. And Bernie never left a party early! When I popped in the next morning to see her at Brian and Annie's, where they were staying, she was lying on the couch looking very frail. She started coughing again and began to panic, calling for Steve. When she was worried Steve was the only person she ever wanted.

He took her straight to hospital where they kept her in for a couple of nights. Erin stayed at mine. She was just thirteen and worried about her mum. It was very tough on her. On the second morning Steve asked if I could bring Erin up to the hospital to see her mum.

'Could you let Erin come in on her own for a bit first?' he asked.

'Sure,' I replied and we got ourselves ready and rang for a cab. I was worried about Steve asking to see Erin first alone. What could that be about?

After Erin went into Bernie's hospital room, I wandered up and down the corridor becoming more and more anxious. After about ten minutes I knocked gently on the door and stepped into the room. Steve and Erin were sitting on either side of the bed, their arms wrapped around Bernie. They were all crying.

'Hi, Lin,' said Bernie, looking up at me. 'More bad news I'm afraid. I'm not going to make it. They've given me two weeks.'

I was stunned. I looked desperately towards a nurse who was standing at the side of the room. She shook her head and whispered: 'I'm sorry.'

Outside, it was just starting to feel like spring but I couldn't imagine summer coming and Bernie not being here. How could I think of her birthday passing without her here to celebrate it? And how could I possibly imagine Christmas without her infectious excitement?

But at that moment there was nothing I could say. All I could do was hug her and hug her and hug her.

'Look, Bernie,' I said, trying to smile through our tears. 'It's not over till the fat lady sings. And I haven't sung yet!' Bernie laughed and we hugged each other again.

After a while I left Bernie, Steve and Erin to be alone. I walked out into the corridor and collapsed onto one of the hospital plastic chairs. Then I started ringing round the family with yet more bad news. And, as my Brian used to joke, the

Nolan cavalry turned up from all corners of the country. In times of crisis it's an incredible support to have a family who are there for you whatever.

It was suggested to Bernie she might want to move to the nearby Trinity hospice in Blackpool. Hospitals are there to make you better but that wasn't going to happen for Bernie so a hospice was thought to be the best place. She agreed, but it was a big step for all of us emotionally.

The hospice staff were incredible. They managed to get rid of the 'stupid cough' which had been really irritating Bernie and within a couple of days of being there she was sitting up in bed and appeared much brighter.

She had so many brilliant friends who travelled from all over the country. Not to mention Nolan relatives pouring in from Britain and Ireland. 'It's like My Big Fat Gypsy Hospice in here,' Steve joked one day.

On Mother's Day we brought in food and drink for a little party and Erin was able to give her mum a card and presents. We had what we'd call a Jacob's Join with everyone bringing in a different dish so in the end it was like a proper Nolan family knees-up. We were even allowed to have a little drink at the hospice – everything is about making the family feel as comfortable and happy as they can be.

Erin was still staying at mine and it was hard to see her trying to cope with everything that was going on around her, knowing how scared she must have been deep down. Steve slept next to Bernie at the hospice every night – she wanted her family around her. It was what made her feel safe.

Bernie seemed peaceful but increasingly she wanted to be back in her own home in Weybridge to see it one more time. Then while she was still in the hospice her house was burgled.

It was horrendous that someone must have known that the family were away because Bernie was so sick, and broke in anyway. Everything was taken and they even rifled through a little box that Bernie kept by her bed with keepsakes of Kate, her daughter who had died. I think maybe that made Bernie want to go home even more.

All of us brothers and sisters gathered at the hospice on the day Bernie left. It was a really difficult goodbye as they carried her out to the ambulance which would take her home. We all had plans to go down and visit as soon as we could, but we also knew that it was possible we were saying goodbye for ever. No one mentioned it – the thought of this last goodbye remained a huge elephant in the room.

'See ya' next weekend,' I said cheerily as I hugged Bernie goodbye. I could only pray that I would.

As the ambulance pulled away down the drive of the hospice I felt a terrible sense of loss. I think that was a reality check for all us brothers and sisters because this was what it would be like. This is what life would be like without Bernie.

But back home Bernie kept battling on and we took it in turns to go and spend time with her. It was tricky because we wanted to give her space with Steve and Erin – but we desperately wanted to see her too. And Bernie, being Bernie, she just kept on arranging things even though she was so weak, giving us some happy moments amid the sadness. She had a Stanna stairlift put in to get her up to bed and I remember one day watching her going up and down the stairs while me, Maureen and Brian stood at the bottom singing: 'So long, farewell, auf Wiedersehen, goodbye,' from *The Sound Of Music*. It was hilarious.

There were a couple of days when Steve had to go away

for work so I stayed at the house looking after her and Erin. I would get Erin up and give her breakfast, then make Bernie some toast and administer her oral morphine. I'm not the best nurse and one night the liquid had stuck to the side of the pot and I almost ended up choking her.

'Are you trying to kill me?' Bernie said, laughing.

After I'd got Erin off to school I came back and lay on the bed next to Bernie. We chatted and then dozed off holding hands. It was such a special moment.

I went down to visit again for Erin's fourteenth birthday in April 2013. Normally Bernie would have been running around blowing up balloons and wrapping presents so Steve and I did it instead. We wanted it to be special for Erin. She had a huge cake and we all sang 'Happy Birthday'. Bernie's voice was pretty wrecked by then and as she started croaking along to the music even she was laughing at how bad it was. It was so funny but so sad. Bernie's voice had been so powerful and it seemed particularly cruel that cancer had even taken that away from her.

In July I was down again with Maureen, Brian and Annie. Bernie was fading by then and she could no longer even get out of bed by herself. Steve was doing absolutely everything for her. He was amazing. Still she tried to be brave in front of us but sometimes we'd hear Steve comforting her at night. She was in terrible pain.

We didn't know then that she had already organized her own funeral – the venue, cars, readings, music, the lot. She had never spoken to us about dying until that weekend. I was in the house with her for a while as the others chatted in the garden.

'I've done OK, haven't I, Lin?' she said, smiling. 'They gave me two weeks to live in February, and now it's July.'

'You've done more than OK,' I replied. 'You've been amazing, Bernie.'

It felt like she was asking permission to stop fighting.

Then she talked about the jewellery that she wanted Erin to have. 'Of course, we'll sort it,' I said. There was no point in pretending any more.

Later that Saturday the cast from *Chicago* turned up to sing to Bernie. At first I thought it was a terrible idea. How would Bernie feel seeing all these people singing the way she'd been doing on stage herself just a year earlier, when now she could barely move?

Bernie was dozing when the cast turned up. They walked in single file into her room and one by one started singing so softly. After a while she woke up. She was thrilled and there were tears all round. Then later Erin sang by the piano – it was truly lovely.

On the Sunday night we had to say goodbye again as Brian had to be back for work in Blackpool. We'd only been home a couple of hours when Steve called. Bernie had been taken poorly during the night and they'd had to get the doctor out.

'It's highly unlikely she'll make the week,' he said.

Maureen and I set off back down south again and over the next couple of days family turned up from all over. Bernie had a big house but there were so many Nolans dotted around the place that a load of us still ended up sleeping on blow-up beds on the lounge floor. Bernie had told Steve she never wanted to be on her own when she died – and there was no danger of that.

It was Wimbledon week, the year Andy Murray got to the

final. The television was on in Bernie's bedroom so we all sat around her bed watching. Bernie was drowsy, in and out of a very deep sleep, but Coleen sat beside her like her personal commentator for the entire match.

'Fifteen love to Murray,' Coleen said.

'Thirty love to Murray.'

'Thirty–fifteen.'

And so it went on. All against the background hum of the oxygen machine feeding the oxygen mask Bernie now needed all the time.

We watched the tennis, chatted and laughed. There were stories from when we were children or when we were touring with The Nolans and funny memories of Mum and Dad. At times like that you can be treading a very fine line between hysterical laughter and hysterical crying. One second we'd be giggling in unison and the next we were sobbing. We couldn't know whether Bernie heard what we talked about or not, but she knew that we were there. And that she was loved.

At mealtimes a couple of us would stay with her while the others trooped downstairs to eat. And at night Steve stayed in her room. We knew we were in the final days and it was tough. We all went through times when we needed to get out the house for some fresh air but I was almost too frightened to leave as it was clearly so close to the end.

One evening Steve went out and bought champagne and poured us all a glass. Then he made a toast to his wonderful wife, our gorgeous sister.

'To Bernie,' we chorused, lifting our glasses.

And we didn't leave her out – Steve poured her a glass and placed it on her bedside table.

On the Wednesday night Bernie was calling out for Maureen.

Maureen was convinced she was actually calling for our mum – who of course was also called Maureen.

We knew this was it and it was time to go in individually and say goodbye. When I went into the bedroom I couldn't stop the tears however hard I tried. I sat on the chair next to Bernie's bed and laid my head gently on her stomach.

'Oh Bernie,' I said. 'You've been so brilliant. I love you so much and I'm going to miss you so much. You've been an amazing little sister . . . But it's OK, we're going to look after Erin.' And Bernie's hand lifted and rested on my head. I was amazed she had heard me, but she had.

Then Erin, Steve and all us brothers and sisters sat around the bed until Bernie took her final breath. There was no doubt, she had gone.

The house fell utterly silent and all you could hear was Erin sobbing. It was 4 July – Independence Day. Bernie was free from her pain at last.

However much you think you are prepared for the worst happening, you never are. I felt lost. And I had this guilt growing inside me too.

'It should have been me,' I said to my sister-in-law Annie. 'There was a time when I wanted to die and I don't have a fourteen-year-old daughter. Bernie had so much life she wanted to live with Steve and Erin – this is just so unfair.'

But what could Annie say? None of it made sense. None of it ever will.

After the nurses had been and prepared Bernie's body the family went in to see her one final time. Then we all stood in the kitchen, not quite sure what to do next. A lovely neighbour came to walk the dog. Then the funeral director brought Bernie down the stairs and out the door. They'd suggested we might find that distressing to watch but I didn't want Bernie to leave the house alone. I stood in the downstairs corridor as they carried her out. 'Goodbye, Bernie,' I whispered.

The next few days we swung into organizational mode. Steve explained that Bernie had planned everything and written a letter with explicit instructions as to what must happen – we just needed to carry them out. The funeral was set for 17 July so we had almost a fortnight of waiting before we could lay her to rest. It was a strange time waiting for the funeral as we all felt in a kind of limbo, devastated Bernie was gone and unable to focus on anything until she had been buried.

Bernie wanted to be buried in Blackpool next to her little girl, Kate. She didn't want a church funeral. Instead the service was to be at the Grand Theatre in Blackpool. It was the perfect showbiz send-off. So many greats from the world of entertainment had played there in the past – but few were as talented as Bernie, who was to take centre stage that day.

The day of the funeral came at last. Her coffin was placed in the back of a beautiful vintage Rolls Royce and then the whole family followed behind in a cortège of eight funeral cars. Driving through the streets of Blackpool, the streets where me and Bernie had played as kids, then down the promenade where we'd hung out after performances during our teens, was surreal. How could we now be driving through those same streets on the way to Bernie's funeral?

All along the route crowds gathered to pay their respects. Shoppers and day trippers stood with their heads bowed at the side of the road. Even kids were taking off their baseball caps in respect. It was incredibly moving. Bernie would have been so proud.

By the time we pulled up outside the Grand Theatre there were thousands of people all applauding. Bernie was the ultimate performer and this was some performance. We'd had to have a password for guests to get into the theatre because so many people wanted to come. In total there were more than seven hundred people in there, all desperate to say goodbye to Bernie.

Brian made an opening address and then Erin read a poem. She'd practised the poem in front of Bernie and was word perfect. Then Maureen read out a letter Bernie had written before she died. It was so full of hope, so full of Bernie. 'Don't be crying too much for me,' she had written. 'Obviously I'd like a bit – I think I'm worth a little crying – but not too much.'

And then it was my turn to say some words. I was terrified I might break down so I screwed up all my courage to walk up to the front and get every word right. The way Bernie would have wanted.

'We all knew Bernie as the fabulous singer and entertainer that she was,' I said, looking out on the crowds of family, friends and former colleagues cramming into the theatre. 'But today I want to speak about her not as those things, but as a fabulous sister. Today we are truly broken. We will never be the same again. Bernie, we miss your smile, we miss your laugh, we even miss your Les Dawson impression.'

As I went on I could feel the emotion threatening to overwhelm me. Coleen stood right behind me and knowing she was there helped me keep going. I got to the end of my speech and was so relieved – I'd done good for Bernie.

There was just one person Bernie had missed out as performing in her running order for the 'show' – herself. But we couldn't have that. We thought it would be great to hear her there singing one of her songs, so right at the end as it was time to leave the theatre we played her singing 'Run to You'. It was a recording of a live performance from a show she did in Blackpool and, as usual, she was amazing.

As our brothers Tommy and Brian and nephews Shane Jnr, Jake, Tommy Jnr and Danny lifted up the coffin to take Bernie from the theatre there was a standing ovation.

Steve and Erin were incredible. They were utterly destroyed but they were so dignified and brave through it all.

After the service we went to the crematorium and then back to the hotel in nearby St Anne's where Bernie and Steve had held their wedding reception. Just seventeen years apart – but a world of difference.

That night we all drank and laughed and talked about Bernie. It was a great night. But the morning after a funeral is always hard. The outside world goes back to normal, yet for those lost in grief it feels like nothing is ever going to be normal again.

Sixteen

Celebrity Big Brother

I was standing in Tesco trying to decide between salad or pizza for tea. (It wasn't really much of a decision.) Then I heard my phone vibrating in my bag. It was my friend and agent Melanie. 'Just ringing for a chat,' I thought, putting the phone to my ear.

'Hiya, Mel,' I said, still more focused on whether it'd be a pepperoni or Hawaiian.

'OMG – guess who wants YOU,' Mel screamed down the phone.

'Who? Who?' I replied. I was desperate for work and had been hoping I might get another touring show or maybe just a couple of nights at a local theatre. To be honest, anything right then would help pay the bills.

'Only the BIGGEST show on TV,' Mel laughed. '*Celebrity Big Brother*.'

I'd like to say I squealed in delight but I was so totally, completely and utterly shocked that my jaw actually dropped half an inch and I let out a sort of strangled gurgling noise. I dropped my basket on the floor and felt other shoppers turn round, wondering what the crazy lady was up to. But I really couldn't care.

'*Celebrity Big Brother?*' I croaked.

'Yes,' Mel replied. 'They want you.'

'Oh my God, oh my God, oh my God,' I started yelping into the phone as I became slightly aware of all these passers-by staring at me on the verge of hyperventilating, surrounded by my up-ended shopping basket.

After years of feeling that my life was lurching from one sadness and disappointment to the next, I'd finally got my opportunity. It was my chance to start again. Bernie had only been gone a few months and the loss was still raw but losing her had certainly made me realize life isn't a dress rehearsal. And if I had a moment's concern I'd think: 'What would Bernie say?' I knew the answer to that: 'Go for it, girl!'

The months that followed Bernie's death had been tough. After I'd spent every waking hour for ages worrying about her, I wasn't sure what I was supposed to do next.

Initially I kept in constant touch with Steve and Erin in Surrey. Erin had enrolled in a performing arts summer school with a final production planned for the end of August and before she died Bernie had asked that we go to watch it. She knew she wouldn't be around herself by then. So we did that and it was great to spend time with Erin. But relations between myself and Steve had become strained. We're quite different people and there had been differences of opinion when Bernie was still alive. Nothing major, just little frictions. But with Bernie gone there was nothing to pull us together. Life felt emptier than ever, which was why the *Celebrity Big Brother* call was the most wonderful surprise in every possible way.

I'd always been a massive fan of *Celebrity Big Brother*. For me, watching the way people interact with each other is the basic stuff of all great entertainment. I'd followed every series and been utterly hooked on it when Coleen had been a contestant the previous year. I knew that watching other people on the show was very different from actually laying your whole life open to inspection by the public twenty-four hours a day for a month. But I was willing to give it a go. I was massively flattered to be asked, considering I'd barely been on television in years. And, once again, I desperately needed the money. *Celebrity Big Brother* pays very well and it would mean I'd be able to pay off my credit cards and set myself straight once and for all. Once the contract was signed one of the first things I did was ring the benefits office to sign myself off as I was finally about to start earning again.

But I wasn't daft enough to think it would be easy. I was pretty petrified having seen what Coleen went through in there and knowing the public can really take against a contestant for no good reason at all. I knew I would certainly be earning my money – but oh my, what a great opportunity.

The whole process of going into *Celebrity Big Brother* is a bit like joining the FBI or going into a witness-protection scheme. Once my agent had told them I was definitely up for it I was invited to London for a meeting where they would explain everything to me and do publicity photographs for the show. Because it is vital that news doesn't leak out early about who the contestants are it is absolutely top secret. We even had to have code names. Mine was Lamb Chop. Hilarious!

I took the train in mid-November from Blackpool down to London for the first meeting. I'd been sent a message with the registration number of the cab which would be picking me up at Euston station but under no circumstances was I to tell the driver my real name.

So there I was walking up to the car at Euston and as the

driver wound down the window, I leant in and said, 'Lamb Chop.' It's probably the closest I've ever come to being Miss Moneypenny.

I got into the car and couldn't help but laugh with the driver. It was so exciting but hysterically funny.

When we got to the photographic studios they did my hair and make-up and then there were a couple of hours of photography where I had to pull all the funny faces and poses they use for the opening credits. Then I was interviewed by the production staff for research purposes.

One of the questions was: 'Who would your worst possible housemate be?'

It didn't take me a moment to respond: 'Some horrible old male chauvinist,' I replied. Having grown up in a house full of strong women I can't bear men who think they're somehow superior and put women down. 'In fact,' I said, 'someone like Freddie Starr or Jim Davidson.'

I'd worked on the road with both of them in the past and knew exactly what they were like – totally full of themselves and thinking women were only good for one thing!

Now, I'll be honest. I didn't know anything for a fact but I had an inkling Jim Davidson might be in the series because I'd heard a rumour that he'd been all set to be in the last series but then had to pull out at the last moment. So, yeah, it may have been a little bit mischievous of me to say Jim's name. Just a tinsy bit perhaps. I immediately saw the spark in the eyes of the producer who was interviewing me and it was an instant confirmation that Jim would be in the *Big Brother* house with me.

Not that it really bothered me at the time. I didn't like him, never had done much. But I thought we'd be able to get on just enough while we were in the house.

Why didn't I like him? Ah, well, that is a long story. Back when I was doing summer seasons around Britain I'd worked with Jim dozens of times. He was decent enough sober but when he'd had a drink he'd be a nightmare. He was just obnoxious and rude to everyone around him. He used to call my Brian 'Mr Nolan', purely to piss him off.

And then there's his attitude to women. I think he's simply a misogynist who loves women in terms of making him feel good but doesn't respect them at all. I decided that the best plan was to forget about all that while I was in the house – and keep as far away from Jim as possible. Which isn't how things worked out. At all.

Before I had that to worry about, though, I had to get through Christmas. I was able to spend it with the family at Brian and Annie's house. Christmas without Bernie was tough for everyone, and things weren't any easier between me and Steve. I'd been determined to make a big fuss of Erin, knowing the first Christmas without her mum was going to be tough. I bought lots of little stocking fillers – girlie bits and bobs, underwear and smellies. Then I bought lots of bits for Steve too, wrapped them all individually and placed them in Christmas bags.

'You've spent too much,' Steve said.

I knew I had, but I'd wanted to do it. Still, there was something about Steve's attitude which didn't feel right. It all became clear when Coleen called me a couple of days later to tell me Steve had been less than kind about me behind my back. Apparently he thought I'd tried to take over after Bernie died. I was really shocked to hear it. Coleen had only told me because she didn't want me making a big fuss of Steve, given what he'd been saying.

I was so hurt and angry that I had it all out with Steve and there was a big row. I felt terrible afterwards because I knew Bernie would have been devastated by that but at the time I think we were both lost in our own grief and lashing out.

It meant, though, that as I packed my suitcase for *Celebrity Big Brother* on New Year's Eve 2013, I was definitely ready for a change. The following morning I was all set to be whisked to the 'holding hotel' on the outskirts of north London where they keep all the contestants locked away from the outside world before entering the house. Again, I felt like a spy. I received an email telling me that a driver would arrive at my house, knock on the door and then I should get in the back of the car saying only my codename.

I followed the instructions to the letter, even scanning my street suspiciously as I stepped into the back seat of the black limousine. Although goodness knows why. It was New Year's Day morning in Blackpool and the place was deserted after everyone had been out on the town the previous night.

Inside the car, I leant forward and whispered to the driver: 'Lamb Chop.'

'All right love?' he replied cheerily. 'You on your way to *Celebrity Big Brother*?'

I had to laugh. It seemed perhaps it wasn't so top secret after all. The driver and I had a good old chat all the way down the M1 – until I realized I'd left my medication at home. There was no way I could go into the house without my antidepressants and Tamoxifen, which I have to take for ten years after having cancer.

Big Brother was great though, and as soon as I got to the

hotel they sent someone to go and pick up a prescription for my tablets. This was going to be stressful enough – I didn't fancy coming off antidepressants at the same time.

I'd been signed off by Dr Briggs a couple of months earlier but had seen the *Big Brother* psychologist when I signed my contract for the show. I was feeling emotionally stronger than I had been in ages. The thought of being watched all the time and being surrounded by people didn't actually bother me at all. When you've grown up in a four-bedroom house with Mum, Dad, two brothers and five sisters you're pretty used to not having much privacy. And I love the noise and energy of having lots of people around.

All my family had been full of encouragement about me going into *CBB* – they thought it was just what I needed to pick me up. And Coleen of course had been through it the previous year and was right behind me all the way.

'You're going to be great, Lin,' she said. 'There's nothing in that house you can't cope with – except perhaps the heat!'

It's a standing joke in our family that I get the most terrible hot flushes – have done ever since chemo brought on an early menopause. And inside the house you are dealing with TV lights which get very, very hot. A friend of mine from one of the cancer units where I still went for check-ups told me about a 'chillow', which is a pillow you fill with cold water to keep you cool at night. I bought one and *Big Brother* agreed I'd be able to take it in. So that was one less thing to worry about.

When we arrived at the holding house things got even more bizarre. I was met by two burly security guards (one of whom was drop-dead gorgeous) and told to put on a hat and cape so no one would recognize me on my way in. That was when

I had to hand over my mobile phone too – it was goodbye to the outside world, my sisters, friends and all the support network I'd depended on so heavily over the past six years. This was scary. But exciting.

I was introduced to a young woman called Faye who was to be my chaperone for the next two days until we actually went into the house. She sat me down and said the first thing the team would do would be to check my suitcase for any items which were banned and any clothes that might have designer labels on which mustn't be seen on screen.

'The only labels they'll be finding on my clothes will be "Made in China",' I laughed. I'd been on a massive shopping spree over the past two weeks trying to find clothes for tropical conditions in January which would look OK on the telly. But it was definitely Primani not Armani!

What I didn't know then were the names of any of the other contestants also staying in the hotel – Sam Faiers from *The Only Way Is Essex*, Lee Ryan from Blue, Lionel Blair, the journalist Liz Jones, Luisa Zissman from *The Apprentice*, Ollie Locke from *Made In Chelsea*, singer Dappy, the models Casey Batchelor and Jasmine Waltz, boxer Evander Holyfield . . . and Jim Davidson. We were all kept totally isolated. We stayed in our rooms eating room service meals. I even had to hide in the bathroom while they were being delivered.

First off we had to do a press conference with reporters who'd print the stories after we'd been unveiled to the public. I was sitting on my hotel bed surrounded by ten young journalists all firing questions at me and we had a great laugh.

'You're favourite to win,' one of the reporters said. I just laughed – that seemed too much to imagine.

After the interviews I was checked over by a doctor and

then sat around watching movies and reading magazines until the evening of 3 January. It was show time.

A long line of limousines with blacked-out windows were queued up outside the TV studios in Elstree. My hair and make-up had been done for me. I had scarlet lips and was wearing black trousers, black boots and a bright red cape with fur around the edge. There was no way I wasn't going to be noticed. (That cape went viral on Facebook and Twitter with people wondering if it was designer and where it was from. None of them knew it was £10.99 from a shop in Blackpool!)

Leaving my hotel room I'd teetered down the corridor with a blindfold covering my eyes and headphones over my ears so I still had no idea which other celebrities were sat in the back of the other limousines.

'You feeling OK, Linda?' said Faye, the chaperone.

'Yes, I'm fine,' I lied. My stomach was in knots and the palms of my hands were sweating. I thought I was dying but I was so excited as well.

'In a moment the bodyguards will open the door and then they'll practically drag you out and push you into the house,' Faye said. 'Good luck.'

'Thanks,' I squeaked as the car door was flung open and I felt myself being yanked to my feet. The blindfold meant it was all incredibly disorientating but there was no mistaking the roar of a huge crowd.

My introductory tape was playing, and as I said the bit about my worst possible housemate being Jim Davidson there were howls of laughter from the crowd. Moments later my blindfold was whipped off and there was Jim standing right behind me.

'Ah, hello, Jim,' I said laughing.

'Hi, Linda,' he replied. We hugged and it all seemed fine. But then we were handcuffed together and led into the house. As a first-night twist all the housemates were handcuffed to one other. And of course they'd put me and Jim together.

Inside the house we met all the other housemates – some I'd never even heard of before, but it was great. Then Jim announced he was desperate for a wee. But we were still handcuffed together! I had to stand in the bathroom with a towel over my head while he relieved himself.

We even had to share a bed.

'No, I can't do this,' Jim said after we'd lain next to each other for twenty minutes. 'I can't lie in bed with another woman while my wife's watching.'

We laughed and he got up and slept on the floor.

The first time Big Brother spoke was incredible. 'Wow, I really am here,' I thought. It was a million miles from my little semi in Blackpool in every possible way.

It's incredible how quickly you get used to living in the *Big Brother* house. I guess that's how people become institutionalized. I ended up sharing a bed with Sam Faiers who was lovely. After a while I could forget I was being filmed all the time and I very quickly got used to constantly having other folk around. The bathrooms and toilets didn't have locks but we had a system of always knocking before we went in and everyone respected each other's space.

There was hardly any room for storing our belongings and some of the contestants' areas looked like bombsites – but we got used to it. The hardest thing was when the doors were locked at night as there was no getting out then. A few of the housemates suffered panic attacks and claustrophobia, which was understandable, although luckily I felt fine. The thing I found hardest was never knowing exactly what time it was. Big Brother woke us every morning with the bright studio lights and an alarm but we didn't really know whether it was four in the morning or midday.

Sometimes we'd be exhausted but Big Brother would still demand we get up.

'Sod this, I'm staying in bed,' I said one morning, pulling the duvet over my head. But then Big Brother just blasted out the sound of a baby crying until we had to get up. Other times they whacked the air conditioning up to boiling or down to freezing to force us out of bed. When people warn you not to mess with Big Brother, they really mean . . . don't mess with Big Brother.

Dappy was lovely to me in there and each morning he'd bring me a cup of tea in bed. Then after we'd got up and showered we'd just hang around chatting all day or do whatever tasks had been set for us.

I'm constantly on my phone when I'm at home but I didn't even really miss talking to my brothers and sisters, which I do every day normally. I'd mentally prepared myself for what it would be like being away from them so I tried not to think about the outside world and just got on with having a good time inside the house.

If any housemates ever wanted to talk privately we'd go into the bathroom, take off our microphones and cover the mic hanging from the ceiling with a towel. It wasn't like we were talking about anything scandalous – just having a gossip away from the rest of the world. But we soon got found out and were told off by Big Brother and ordered out of the toilet.

Probably the worst aspect of life in the house was the food. It was grim – a lot of chickpea mash! If we wanted bread, we had to make it from scratch. Fortunately Ollie Locke volunteered to do this and the fact he was usually baking topless made the hunger a little more manageable! At one point I lived on Weetabix for three days because I was sick of the sight of chickpeas. Most of the time we were all pretty much starving-hungry.

I quickly became close to Sam and Casey but I felt like I got on with everyone. The youngsters called me Momma Lin because I suppose to them I was a protective, motherly figure in the house. I loved it. I wasn't nominated for three weeks and was having the time of my life.

I even got on pretty well with Jim at first. But then the real Jim became apparent to everyone in the house – even if the way the show was edited meant it wasn't quite so obvious to viewers watching at home. If he was cooking he'd sometimes only cook for the men. And once he flatly refused to take part in a challenge eating dog food and biscuits. 'I've done enough,' he said. I ended up doing it instead of him – and was repeating Pedigree Chum for the rest of the day!

The thing about Jim was he was all about the show. He is a showman and knew how to create a scene where he was centre of attention during all the trials we were set. And that irritated me. A lot of people thought we had a love/hate relationship because we were of a similar age and maybe there was some kind of sexual chemistry going on. But my God, I'd rather be shot than poisoned – not a chance.

There were times we got on brilliantly and we'd be hysterically laughing with each other at some of the craziness the younger contestants got up to. Once we were in the kitchen and Jim was shouting at me: 'Come on! You know you want me!' He was funny and we really weren't bickering and biting all the time. Realistically though, *Big Brother* pays celebrities a lot of money to appear on the show and for that money you have to accept you're in their hands and have a part to play. Jim went in there for the money and to rejuvenate his career after a difficult few years but I think *Big Brother* always had the intention of portraying him as the down-to-earth good guy. I had been selected to be the older, grumpy woman who held a grudge against Jim. And in many ways that's fine. Because we were being paid to do a job – even if it wasn't that realistic about our characters.

Then came the night when Jim and I had an enormous bust-up, which made days of newspaper headlines – and changed everything in the house.

When I'd watched *Big Brother* in the past I'd never understood how contestants managed to get so drunk so quickly. But when you're in there booze is rationed – and as the food is too, drinking on an empty stomach soon has an effect. I guess what I'm building up to saying is we'd all had a bit too much to drink on the night of the big row.

It all began when I was in the bedroom and Luisa came in and told me she'd been chatting to Jim in the other room. Apparently he'd said to her: 'Linda's been having a go at me over nothing again. Well I'm going to mention her husband and Frank Carson.'

Of course Luisa had no idea what he was talking about but he refused to tell.

'Go and ask Linda if you want to know,' he said. Which, of course, she did.

As soon as Luisa told me what Jim had said I could feel a red-hot rage explode inside me. I knew exactly what Jim was referring to. Years ago, back in the mid-1990s, Brian had been accused of stealing £20 from Frank Carson's dressing room at a show where we were performing together. Brian swore to the day he died that he didn't take it – he just wasn't the type of person to do that. But the police were called and it was due to go to court. And of course because Brian was known publicly as 'Linda Nolan's husband' it got a lot of attention in the papers at the time.

Brian was devastated because of his own reputation – but more because of the damage it might do me. One of our friends at the time told Brian: 'Just plead guilty and it'll all be over, otherwise the court case will go on and on.'

Looking back, it was bad advice but Brian didn't know what to do so he pleaded guilty. It was all over £20 but it was a horrific time for us. For Jim Davidson to bring it up now in the *Big Brother* house when he knew millions of people were watching, and Brian wasn't even alive to defend himself, was disgusting.

I was furious. I stormed towards the room where Jim had been sitting. 'Momma Lin, don't,' Luisa was shouting, chasing after me across the room. But nothing was going to stop me. I stormed over to Jim and called him a revolting little shit. I could feel the tears starting to burn in my eyes from pure rage. I went back to the bedroom and couldn't help but cry and cry.

The girls all came over and hugged me and sat with me but nothing could take away from my anger at what Jim had done. I couldn't bear to be near him.

After a while I went to the diary room.

'I want to go home,' I sobbed. 'I've watched the show for years and I knew exactly what I was getting myself into but

I didn't sign up for this.' The more I spoke, the more the tears kept falling down my face.

'I haven't come here to have my dead husband's name vilified by such an awful human being.'

Big Brother said I should go back downstairs and see how I felt in the morning. That was the hardest part. Going back knowing I was going to have to sleep in the same room as a scumbag who'd said that about the man I loved more than anyone in the world. I didn't want to be anywhere near him.

Jim played the innocent over what he'd said to Luisa. She was gobsmacked. How else could she have known about that incident? What's more, millions of viewers saw him telling her when the episode was screened.

After a while I managed to stop crying and was sitting on the bed when Jim came over to me. He knew he'd overstepped the mark. I couldn't even look at him.

'Fuck off, Jim,' I said. 'Just go away, I don't want to talk to you.'

I had a terrible night's sleep and the next morning when I walked into the bathroom the first person I saw was him in there, shaving. He opened his arms as if wanting to give me a hug. I walked straight past him to the shower.

From then on he made a few attempts to be friends but I couldn't do it. I made sure I always nominated him for eviction and there was no doubt the house would have been a nicer place without him. But I think how I responded to the row afterwards was what changed the viewers' opinion of me. Up until then I'd been doing really well and was popular. But afterwards I think people thought I should have forgiven him and moved on. But I couldn't. Not when it was about my Brian.

One eviction night I was carving up some chicken after the live show had finished. Jim handed me a knife, saying, 'This one will be sharper, Lin.'

'It's Linda,' I replied bluntly. I guess he was trying to help but I couldn't forgive.

At the beginning of our third week in the house we were called to the diary room individually. Big Brother told me to take off my microphone and then I was taken through a door into another room. It was all very mysterious and I was instantly terrified something must have happened to one of the family back home. Instead it turned out that the series had been getting the highest ratings ever and they wanted to extend it for an extra week. 'Would I be happy to stay in longer?' they were asking.

Would I? Of course. Apart from the run-ins with Jim I was having the time of my life. And I was delighted the British public were enjoying it too. Then I had to put my microphone back on and go downstairs but not mention anything to the other contestants as the viewers at home knew nothing about the extension. One by one all the housemates were called up and asked the same question. Everyone wanted to stay.

Unfortunately for me, though, my time was running out anyway.

On the next eviction night I received two nominations. Jim had nominated me, which was hardly a big surprise. But I was disappointed that Dappy had followed Jim's lead. During the first week or so I'd said something to Dappy like: 'Why are you always so tired? You're a young man.' He hadn't liked it but we'd had a long chat afterwards where he explained how busy he'd been recording before he came into the house. We cleared the air and were good mates after that so I was very disappointed he'd turned against me.

My fate now lay in the hands of the public. I was so nervous I felt sick waiting to hear who'd be going home. I desperately wanted to stay.

And then it happened. 'And the next person to be evicted from the *Celebrity Big Brother* house 2014 is . . .' – the pause seemed to go on for a lifetime – '. . . Linda Nolan.'

My heart dropped. But then Big Brother was telling me to get out and it was all such a rush and a hurry I didn't have a chance to think about it any further – or what the response would be in the outside world. It was all so frantic I even kissed Jim goodbye. Afterwards Eamonn Holmes asked why I kissed him. Who knows? Maybe in all of it I was the bigger person.

The doors of the *Big Brother* house slid open and I stepped out into the freezing night air. But if that was cold, the reaction of the public was sub-zero. The crowd were booing and hissing at me. I reckon if they'd been allowed to stone housemates that's what they'd have done to me.

I was horror-struck. 'What had I done that they hated me so much?' I was thinking. Everything that had happened over the last few weeks raced through my head as I tried to understand what the hell was going on. It was only later I realized that the show has warm-up guys before filming starts who whip up the crowd into a frenzy, so by the time the evictee comes out they're ready to kill.

I could feel myself wobbling as I walked down the stairs towards the host, Emma Willis, who quickly ushered me away from the baying crowds. I was shaking and using every ounce of energy I had to hold it together.

The exit interview with Emma was tough.

'Why did you get so upset with Jim?' she asked. I felt she was judging me and it seemed clear this was the kind of thinking that had turned the crowd against me. It irritated me that Emma was sitting on the fence and making no judgement at all about Jim's appalling behaviour.

'Well how would you feel if someone spoke about your husband Matt the way Jim spoke about my husband?' I snapped. She didn't answer. At the end of the interview she referred to me as a 'tough cookie'. Maybe I am. I'd never thought of myself that way before but I've had plenty to toughen me up over the years.

I was pleased I stood my ground in the interview but afterwards I was seen by Gareth, the show's psychologist, and I pretty much fell apart.

'I just felt I had to be strong and not let Jim bully me,' I explained. 'I thought if I gave in and showed weakness he'd just keep coming back for me. I knew what he was capable of and I had to keep up this front that I was tougher than him.'

Gareth was amazing to talk to and of course that was when I started to cry, my mascara running down my cheeks.

'Whoa, hold on,' said Gareth. 'I'm a psychologist not a make-up artist!' I was then ushered onto *Celebrity Big Brother's Bit on the Side*. Rylan and the audience gave me an amazing reaction, so I began to feel a little better.

They took me to a hotel nearby that night and I was straight on the phone to my brothers and sisters who couldn't have been more supportive and lovely.

'You were amazing,' said Coleen. 'But one bit of advice – don't look at Twitter for a while.'

So of course what did I do straight away? It was horrific – how can people write such vile stuff about someone they've never met? There were comments like, 'You grumpy evil cow' and 'You scrounging bitch, get back on Benefit Street.' And it went on and on. But actually there were some really supportive comments about me too – and some people were horrified that Jim had been so out of order as to mention Brian the way he did.

It was only a few more days until the final night of the show so I stayed down in London with Brian's son Lloyd and his family. One afternoon I decided to go to Westfield shopping centre in Stratford to get a new phone charger as mine wasn't working. I'd been mooching around the shop for a while when I became conscious there was a big crowd of people standing near me. I thought a new shop must be opening nearby or something. Then gradually I realized they were looking at me.

At first it was scary, as I thought they were all about to start booing like the crowd outside the *Big Brother* house. But then this group of boys came up and asked if they could have their picture taken with me. After that it was one person after another, all wanting selfies and saying how much they'd loved me on the show. Shop assistants were asking for all the gossip from inside and saying how badly they thought Jim had treated me.

Then the shop manager asked if I'd like to have a chat in his office while his staff served me. All I wanted was a phone charger! It was hilarious. It gave me an enormous boost to think that maybe not all the public were against me.

But the thought of going back to the house again and seeing the crowds as well as Jim on eviction night was horrific. I'd have rather licked the back of my fridge than spend one more evening with Jim. In the end it wasn't so bad and it was great to have a final catch-up with the other housemates – I'd loved getting to know them. Jim was like the cat who got the cream when it was announced he was the winner. He came over to me at the end of the final show.

'Well done . . .' I said.

He just smiled. 'I know,' he replied. 'Fooled them all, right to the end.'

I couldn't tell if he was joking or being serious, but as far as I was concerned, I wanted to take his words at face value. To me, hearing him say that was almost a relief – I hadn't imagined what he was like after all. I'd been absolutely right.

At the end of the day, I did have the most incredible time on *Big Brother*. It was something entirely different which I'll never experience again. I wouldn't have missed it for the world.

Seventeen

My Shame

'Linda Hudson. You do not have to say anything. But it may harm your defence if you do not mention when questioned something which you later rely on in court. Anything you do say may be given in evidence.'

How on earth had it come to this?

A thick-set council official was sat opposite me across a wide desk, reading out the caution. Next to me was my solicitor with a pile of official-looking folders in front of him. It was the sort of thing I'd only seen on the TV before – but now it was happening to me.

My stomach was churning and my heart pounding. 'I'm going to be sick,' was all I could think.

It had all begun when I came downstairs one morning in my dressing gown, picked up an envelope lying on the hall mat, and my world collapsed once again.

At the top of the letter in big black letters was printed: 'Benefit Fraud'. Underneath, it said the letter was to inform me that I was being investigated for claiming benefits while working.

'But I haven't. I wouldn't,' I shouted at the letter I was holding in my hands. I was utterly horrified as it's the last thing I would ever intentionally do – take money I wasn't entitled to. I was shaking but the more I thought about it the more I became convinced it must be an admin mistake; there was no way I'd done anything wrong.

I'd never, ever wanted to go on benefits in the first place, as I've said. I'd only done it after Brian died as I was totally skint and too unwell to work. I guess sometimes people think because I've been on the telly and had a successful career I must live in a gated mansion with a swimming pool and croquet lawn. But that couldn't be further from the truth. I was still in the same rented two-bedroom semi which Brian and I moved into the year before he died. It's certainly no mansion but there's nowhere I'd rather be. And I've never been materialistic or one for flashy clothes and swish holidays so the money didn't go on anything like that. I don't even have a car. The benefits just meant I had enough to live on and pay my bills.

And ever since I'd gone on benefits I'd stuck to the rules religiously. Or so I thought. When we did the *I'm in the Mood Again* tour at the end of 2009 I informed the authorities so my benefits stopped, and I did the same each time I worked from then on to make sure I was never taking money when I was earning. Which was why I couldn't understand how they now seemed to think I'd been on the fiddle.

As ever in a crisis I was straight on the phone to my brothers and sisters. Then I rang my best friend Sue, who works as an usher at the magistrates court in Blackpool.

'You need a solicitor,' she said without pausing for breath.

'But I haven't done anything wrong,' I replied.

'All the more reason why you need a solicitor,' she went on.

Which is why a couple of weeks later I was sat in the council offices with the solicitor at my side and the guy in the grey suit reading me my rights like in an episode of *The Bill*. I still couldn't believe this was happening to me.

'I don't want to swindle anyone,' I said. 'I'm not a bad person. Or a liar.'

It was then they started questioning me and I was able to see what they thought I'd done. It turned out the 'working' they were talking about was writing an occasional agony aunt column for a local magazine and appearing on one episode of *All Star Family Fortunes* with Coleen. They also counted some appearances I'd done for charities and going on television talk shows to discuss cancer and depression as 'working'.

It dawned on me that some of the things they thought of as 'work' just hadn't occurred to me. I thought working meant doing a stage show, not quick interviews on the television. The first time I'd done one of those I had rung the benefits people to check it was all OK. The lady on the phone said unless my circumstances changed permanently, I didn't need to ring every time I had an offer like that. I took that to mean it was all OK. But of course it turns out I should have let them know and then my benefits would have stopped or been changed, depending on how much money was coming in.

As for the magazine column, I did it on my laptop sitting on the sofa. I'd never thought of that as work for a moment. They were all small amounts of money – £100 here and £100 there. But there was no getting away from it: it was all my mistake – and I felt horrified and ashamed that I'd made it. I should have thought about the whole thing much more carefully before agreeing to do anything at all.

The council was investigating me for claiming housing

benefit and council tax relief between April 2012 and December 2013 (so it was for a period before I even went into *Big Brother*). Meanwhile the Department of Work and Pensions who paid my income support were also investigating. In total they reckoned I'd fiddled around £12,000. It was horrific.

'I'll get you all the paperwork you need,' I told the man from the council. 'Please believe me – I'm not trying to hide anything from you.'

That night I could barely sleep. I spent hours going back through my diary to list every engagement I'd done over the past few years and any paperwork I had which showed any earnings.

From then on the case was the last thing I thought of when I went to sleep at night and the first thing I thought of in the morning. As soon as I opened my eyes, the awfulness of it all was there on my chest like a dead weight. I knew that sometimes people are sent to jail for benefit fraud and the thought of that was too much. I'd start having anxiety attacks again. I'd never once been in trouble with the law in my entire life – I'm the sort of person who's frightened when they see a policeman in the street!

I tried to fill my time by getting together all the paperwork that the investigators wanted. And I actually felt a little proud of myself for managing to do it without Brian. I wouldn't have been able to do it in the past.

A couple of weeks later I was back in front of the investigator being read my rights for a second time.

'I'll pay back anything you think I owe,' I said. And I was determined I would, however hard it would be to scrape the money together. Finally they came up with a monthly repayment plan which I immediately agreed to – I set up direct debits and began paying back as much as I could every month.

It was in the run-up to Christmas and I'd just put up the tree and a bit of tinsel round the door when my phone rang. It was a lady from the Department of Work and Pensions.

'Hello, Mrs Hudson?' the voice said.

'Yes.'

'I'm just calling to inform you that our investigation into yourself is now closed. We won't be taking any further action.'

'Yes,' I screamed. 'It's over.' They believed me at least!

It was the best Christmas present I could have hoped for. Finally I could start again – and maybe the New Year would really be my new beginning.

There wasn't much time for celebrating, though, as that Christmas I was performing as the Wicked Queen in *Jack and the Beanstalk* in St Helen's, Merseyside.

'They're desperate to have you,' my agent Amanda (who works with Melanie) had said when she first called about the job. 'In fact they want you so much you can choose between the roles of the Good Fairy or Wicked Queen. But, be warned – there's quite a lot of 10 a.m. shows.'

Amanda knows I'm not a morning person.

'In that case,' I laughed, 'I'd better be the Wicked Queen – there's no way I'd be able to smile at small children at that time of day!'

The panto was fabulous and received great reviews. So as 2015 began I really did feel as if things were improving. But as I've said, my sisters don't jokingly call me Linda 'Lucky' Hudson for nothing. And in May I had another letter drop on my mat – which was the worst yet.

It was a court summons to Blackpool Magistrates' Court for failing to disclose earnings and for overpayment of housing and council tax benefits. I was being charged with £12,000 of benefit fraud by the Department of Work and Pensions and Blackpool Borough Council. Even though I was repaying the money, they'd decided I should be punished for what I'd done.

I was gobsmacked and horrified. When I'd received the call at Christmas saying the investigation was closed I really believed that was the end of the matter. But this meant that they really did think I was a criminal – they hadn't believed me at all when I'd said it was an accident. And it seemed the fact I was scrimping and saving to pay back anything I'd wrongly received meant nothing at all to them.

I was still reading the letter when the tears began to slide down my face and onto the lines of black type. 'I just can't do this any more,' I said to myself.

After everything that had happened – losing Brian, losing Mum, losing Bernie, getting through breast cancer, trying to get through the depression – this was too much. There was a very real possibility I could be sent to prison. How on earth would I cope with that? It felt like I was never, ever going to get me a break. It was hardly as if I was jetting off to Barbados or drinking champagne every weekend. I was struggling to get by.

I was devastated, terrified and angry. But there was something else too. I felt utterly ashamed. Up until then only close family had known what was going on but this would get in the newspapers now and everyone would think I was a cheat. I'd brought shame on the whole family.

That night I lay in bed and wished I could go to sleep and

be with Bernie and Brian and it would all be OK. I wanted it all to be over. I picked up the phone and started typing out a text.

'I don't know what I'm going to do, but I do know what I could do,' it said. I didn't want to frighten them but I was just pouring out everything in my head. 'I've never been in trouble in my life and the thought of going to court is horrifying and frightening. I have thought of another way out but I'm holding on with my fingernails, trying not to slip back down the ladder.'

I was sobbing hysterically. I knew I had enough tablets in the house to end it all if I could bring myself to do it. I just wanted some peace.

Within minutes my sisters were all on the phone to me. They were amazing, talking me through.

'Look, Lin,' Col said. 'You're going to be OK – we are all going to be in court en masse behind you. And you haven't made us ashamed – you make us very proud.'

I cried all night and the next morning I rang my GP, who referred me back to counselling and prescribed sleeping tablets.

My psychologist, Dr Briggs, was once again utterly amazing. She'd helped me so much since Brian died, and she was there for me again.

'Come on, Linda. You haven't done anything dishonest and you've got through a lot worse than this in the past. You'll just have to compose yourself and hold your head high.'

I just had to cling on a little longer. But then the story came out in the newspapers. 'Linda Nolan Benefits Shame' was the headline. I felt physically sick when I saw it. For five days I wouldn't go out of the house and depended on my sisters to bring supplies round. I couldn't face people staring and pointing at me, thinking I was some kind of crook. When I went bankrupt it was awful and humiliating but this was a million times worse.

'You coming to bingo tonight?' Maureen called up to ask one Sunday.

'No way,' I replied. 'Absolutely not.' I couldn't ever imagine being able to go to bingo again.

But then I started receiving letters of support. Within a week I'd had more than a hundred letters, most simply addressed to Linda Nolan, Blackpool. I was scared to open the first one in case it was full of abuse. But letter after letter was so kind and supportive.

One card came from a couple in Manchester. It said: 'Dear Linda, we just feel the need to send you this card to let you know that many people have been through similar experiences as yourself. We can really understand and empathize with what you're going through and the pain, distress and sleepless nights it causes. Please know that you are not alone, you are appreciated and very much loved. Please stay strong and thank you for all the wonderful years of entertainment you have given us.'

It touched me so much. And gradually I built up the courage to go down to the shops or out to see friends. Everywhere I went people were saying: 'We believe you, Linda. We all make mistakes and we believe you.'

It really was those people and all that support which kept me alive.

A couple of weeks later I received a call saying the DWP were dropping their charges in regards to £8,000 of the money, saying it was no longer in the public interest to prosecute. But Blackpool Council insisted it was continuing with their own legal action, relating to £4,000 of wrongly claimed housing and council tax benefit.

A court date was set and I counted down the days towards it, feeling more and more hopeless and sick. After all that, it was postponed at the last moment. But my friend Sue, who was still working as an usher at the court, said the place had been packed to the rafters with journalists and photographers ready to cover the story. I knew when my date did arrive I'd have to walk into that bear pit. I suppose people like reading about things going wrong for people who've had fame, it's a human drama. But the thought of being watched by all those reporters was terrifying.

And that was the least of it. Although everyone told me a prison sentence now seemed unlikely, what if the magistrates wanted to make an example of me? Anything could happen. There was no way I could survive going to jail. Or I could end up with community service or a curfew.

I wanted the opportunity to show in court that I was innocent and had made a simple mistake – but the thought of court terrified me. And a criminal record meant there'd be no hope of me fostering ever again. The one good thing in my life in recent years and I was going to lose that as well.

My solicitor said he thought I might be offered the chance to accept a caution. That would mean I signed a piece of paper to admit I'd done wrong but there would be no court appearance or criminal record. If that was an option the whole nightmare would be over. But still Blackpool Council seemed intent on having their day in court.

It was July and I was due to accept a cheque from a chemist's shop in Blackpool for Hug In A Bag – a breast cancer charity of which I'm a patron. I was going with Debbie Marr, who works for the charity and who has become a great friend over the years. Attending events like that with the court case hanging over me was torture, but I'd made the commitment to go and I couldn't drop out and let down the charity. It was a case of getting on with it.

Debbie and I had just pulled up outside the chemist's shop when my phone rang and my solicitor's name popped up in the Caller ID.

'Oh God,' I said. 'I'm sorry, Debbie, but I'm going to have to take this.'

'Hello,' I said nervously into the phone.

'Hi, Linda,' my solicitor said. 'Where are you?'

It didn't sound like good news. Were they coming to lock me up straight away?

'I'm in town?' I said. 'Why?'

'Where in town?' he replied.

'I'm outside a chemist's, about to go and accept a bumper cardboard cheque for charity. Whatever it is, just tell me now.'

'OK,' he said. 'They're offering you the chance to accept a civil caution. You won't have to go to court. It's all over.'

I could barely speak. The sense of relief was overwhelming.

'Oh, thank you,' I choked. 'Thank you so much.'

I turned the phone off and could feel tears welling in my eyes.

'Is everything OK?' Debbie asked, looking concerned.

'Yes, it's OK,' I said. 'In fact, it's amazing. They're not taking me to court.'

By then the news had sunk in and I was feeling quite hysterical with relief. It was like a ten-ton weight had been literally lifted off my shoulders. I wanted to go dancing off down the high street but first Debbie and I had to go through with accepting the cheque as if everything was quite normal.

Afterwards I immediately phoned my brothers and sisters to give them the good news. They were all thrilled for me. Maureen was working in Spain and just replied with one word far too rude to write here!

Debbie and I walked back to her car through Debenhams. It was then I spotted the most beautiful pair of court shoes.

'Hey, these could be my not-going-to-court shoes,' I laughed to her.

'Go on, treat yourself,' she replied. 'You deserve it.'

That was an incredible day. This time it really was all over.

Eighteen

Another Goodbye,
and an Old Hello

Maureen helped me lift my darling dog Hudson onto the vet's table.

I buried my head into the soft folds of his fur, my tears sinking into him as they'd done so many times before. But this time Hudson didn't have the energy to lick them away or cheer me with a wag of his tail. Hudson was old and tired. It was time for him to go.

But knowing that he had to be put down was breaking my heart that hot August afternoon.

Brian and I had adored Hudson from that moment Coleen turned up with him under her arm seventeen and a half years earlier. He'd been with me through everything that had happened in the years in between. When I had cancer and Brian was ill it was Hudson who gave me the impetus to get out of bed and take him for a walk. When I was at the lowest ebb with my depression it was Hudson who licked the tears from my face when I woke in the morning.

But during his last few years he had slowed down. When we went for walks, instead of him pulling me along, I was having to encourage him to keep going. He developed cataracts in his eyes, was a little bit deaf and increasingly confused. Sometimes he'd fall asleep in the lounge then wake up and look around and appear totally bewildered.

'You don't know where you are, do you, darling?' I'd say. 'Don't worry, Mummy's here.'

Then he became increasingly frightened and it was as though he had some form of dementia. And he became incontinent. A friend of mine who worked at the vet's surgery said one day: 'I think Hudson is getting towards the end of his life.'

I knew it had been coming but it was still heartbreaking to face up to.

And so on 19 August I woke early and cooked Hudson his favourite sausages for breakfast. And then there was roast chicken for his lunch. Afterwards we sat out in the garden in the sunshine like we'd done hundreds of times before.

'We're going to take you to the vet's this afternoon and then you're going to see Daddy,' I said. 'You're going to go for lots of long walks together again.'

It was another piece of Brian going and I was desperately upset.

Maureen and Sue had come with us to the vet's. By the time we got there I couldn't even speak. We lifted Hudson onto the surgery table and I put my arms around his warm fur while the vet injected him. 'It's OK, Hudson, there's nothing to worry about,' I said. 'Mummy's here.'

I was sobbing, Maureen was sobbing, the two surgery receptionists were sobbing. Sue had to stand with her fingers in her ears because it was all so upsetting.

And then Hudson just laid his head down and it really was like he had gone to sleep.

He'd been such an amazing friend to me through everything that had happened. I couldn't have asked for anything more.

A few days later I went back to the surgery to collect his ashes, which I placed into a beautiful wooden box. When I got home Sienna and Ava had arrived, as I was looking after them.

'Auntie Linda, Auntie Linda, have you got Hudson's lashes?' they asked. 'That's a big box for his little lashes.'

I think they'd got the wrong end of the stick!

Soon after losing Hudson I was off to Ireland to appear in a major tour across the entire country of the hilarious stage show *Menopause the Musical*. I'd done a tour of the show in England the previous year and loved it. But this time touring meant spending three months away from home. Just a year or so earlier there was no way I'd have managed that without my sisters with me, but I was feeling far stronger mentally. It would be the longest I'd been away on my own since Brian had died but I now felt I could do it. I was ready.

Having family in Ireland helped enormously. We've always been close to our cousins and see each other whenever we can but staying over there for three months meant I'd get to spend even more time with them. Towards the end of September it was my cousin's wedding in Dublin so I went over for that and then was due to go straight into *Menopause* rehearsals.

I was going to be away for so long that I had tons of packing to do and filled two enormous suitcases right to the brim. I even got myself to the airport and all was going brilliantly until the plane just lifted off the runway and into the air. Suddenly I could be heard yelping: 'Oh my God!!!!'

I think the man next to me must have thought I was terrified of flying. It wasn't that – it was that I'd just remembered my wedding outfit was still hanging off the bedroom door in Blackpool where I'd left it. There was nothing to be done except turn up at the wedding in black leggings and a top. My nails looked fabulous though!

Then it was straight into rehearsals for the musical alongside Mary Byrne, who'd been in *X Factor*, and a couple of other fabulous actresses. It was a great show about a group of women who really had nothing in common other than they were all going through the menopause. It was hilarious and the audiences loved it.

But there was sad news while I was in Ireland too. One morning Maureen rang me as I sat in my hotel room.

'Hi, Linda,' she said. 'I'm afraid I've got some bad news. Ritchie and I are splitting up.'

'Oh, Maureen. No,' I said. I knew things hadn't been great between them for a while but I didn't realize it was this bad. 'I'm so sorry.'

Maureen really struggled to talk about it. They'd both known their marriage had come to an end but it was still devastating. And suddenly Maureen was faced with a future that was nothing like the one she'd imagined. It felt like they'd been together for ever. They might only have been married seven years but they were engaged for seventeen years before that.

I think it is very hard to hold down a relationship in showbiz when you both have to spend so much time away from home. Maureen had been touring in different shows for years and Ritchie was on the road a lot too as Roy Chubby Brown's production manager.

At one time, me, Anne, Denise, Maureen and Ritchie would all go to bingo together every Sunday night. Then afterwards we'd go back to one of our houses and watch an episode of *X Factor* that we'd recorded. We had such a laugh. But then Ritchie stopped coming. And with both of them usually working during the week they saw less and less of each other. I guess they just drifted apart.

I was anxious to fly straight back to Blackpool to be with Maureen but I had to finish the rest of the tour. And I was loving *Menopause the Musical*. It was a very special time for me because finally I'd fallen in love with performing again. Me and the others in the show had such a laugh together and after each performance we'd go back to each other's rooms for chicken legs and Prosecco. It wasn't so much R&R as M&S!

By the time I got back to Blackpool that Christmas I was feeling good. One afternoon I spent hours decorating my front room, putting up my little tree, prettying the fireplace with tinsel and fairy lights and then hanging up all my Christmas cards. When I'd finished I collapsed on the couch, slightly out of breath from climbing up and down on chairs to get everything in the right place. But the finished result was pretty good. It looked sparkly and Christmassy.

'You know what, Brian,' I said out loud in the empty room, 'I think you'd be proud of me.'

And for one of the first times since Brian's death I really believed it.

Finally I felt happier. The desolate feeling which had followed me constantly for years was subsiding. The dark cloud was lifting. Finally I felt I was back to the Linda Nolan I'd been before Brian and I both got ill. And now I'd decorated the house for Christmas all on my own.

For the first time in a very long while I felt contentment.

Then, in the New Year, I landed another great stage role in a new musical called *Rumpy Pumpy!* It was a great story about how a local Women's Institute decided to improve conditions for a group of prostitutes, with some fabulous music. It was starting in Windsor then moving to London, which was great for me as it also meant I was able to spend time with Brian's children Sarah and Lloyd. By then Lloyd had married and he and his wife Kam had a gorgeous little daughter, Mia.

I'd been at the cinema with a friend to watch the movie *Australia* when I came out and saw a message on my phone saying Mia had been born. I instantly burst into tears. I was so delighted for Lloyd and Kam but I was so upset Brian wasn't here for that moment. He would have been over the moon. After Mia was born I was always nipping down to London to see her so the opportunity to stay with them for a few weeks while doing *Rumpy Pumpy!* was too good to miss.

I'd been in rehearsals for the show in London all day and was walking back to the tube one afternoon, a bit tired and bedraggled, when a lady stopped me on the pavement.

'I saw your sister on *Loose Women* today,' she said, staring me straight in the eye. 'And she's right, you know. You will find someone.'

My jaw fell open slightly as I looked at her totally bewildered. I didn't have a clue what she was talking about.

'I'm going to kill her this time,' I muttered to myself as the woman darted off. I pulled my mobile out of my pocket and immediately rang my friend Melanie, who is agent for both me and Coleen.

'OK, Mel, what's she gone and said now?' I asked. Having a sister who gets paid for talking on one of telly's most popular shows means you're ready for anything to be made public!

'Oh, you've heard then?' said Mel.

'Not exactly, but I have had a complete stranger wandering up on the street to discuss my love life,' I replied.

'It was fine,' she laughed. 'They were having a general conversation on *Loose Women* about people moving on after grief and all Coleen said was that you were devastated after Brian died but she desperately wishes you could meet someone else now. She said you deserve to be happy.'

'Oh,' I said quietly, feeling tears prickling in my eyes.

I suppose it was hardly a radical thing to say but none of my sisters had ever said anything like that to me before. I guess they were too worried that I'd fly off the handle at the mere thought of any man other than Brian. But what upset me most when I thought about it later was how worried Coleen appeared to be about me. It was a reminder of how supportive she and all my family had been through everything. They'd always had my best interests at heart – could they possibly be right that meeting someone new might be in my best interests?

I began to wonder if it might actually be nice to have a little romance one day in the future. Maybe.

I shocked myself even thinking it. There was absolutely no way any man would ever mean to me what Brian did – and still does. But it would be nice to have someone to spend time with, go to the cinema or pop out for a pub lunch. Maybe . . . One day.

I was to find out far sooner than I could have imagined. In fact it was only a few weeks later I was sitting on a tube train and looked at my reflection in the window to see myself grinning like a Cheshire cat. It was nearly eight years since I'd sat in an almost identical place on a tube train in the dark shortly after Brian and Mum had died. Back then, in the reflection I saw a woman who looked sad and broken. But this evening, looking back at me was a woman with a huge grin stretched across her face. Yes, I looked tired, older and worn from the way life had buffeted me over the past decade. But there was no mistaking that smile.

I'd been on what can only be described as . . . a date. And we'd kissed, albeit fairly briefly. What's more, I didn't feel consumed with guilt about Brian. Or upset. I was happy.

It had all come totally out of the blue. The autumn is always a difficult time for me because it is Brian's anniversary on 26 October. I couldn't quite believe that eight long years had passed without him there. So it was a tough time, but since Coleen had said what she did about me on *Loose Women*, I'd been thinking differently.

And then one evening I received a message on Facebook from one of the guys my sisters and I used to hang out with when we first moved to London in the 1970s. He was one of a group of croupiers we'd go out with after we'd finished work. We'd end up at four in the morning, wandering down the Embankment singing, before going for breakfast at Mike's Diner as dawn was rising.

He'd emigrated to Australia years earlier but in his Facebook message he said he was back in England for a family funeral and would I like to meet up?

I knew he'd fancied me back then, but that was forty years ago so I put any idea of romance firmly out of my mind. 'It's not a date – just a pleasant evening,' I told myself as I messaged him back, agreeing to meet. On the day we were due to meet I went into rehearsals with butterflies in my tummy.

'I'm going out for dinner tonight,' I said. 'With a guy.'

There was lots of screaming and giggling. 'But it's not a date.' And then I explained the whole history of it all.

'Definitely not a date,' the other girls repeated.

'Yep,' I said. 'Definitely not a date.'

To get me ready for my Definitely-Not-A-Date the girls took me for a drink straight after rehearsals. I was so nervous I had two large gin and tonics before setting off to meet the man (remaining nameless to avoid any red faces) at Covent Garden tube station. I recognized him standing beneath the tube sign straight away. He was older of course, we both were, but the way he smiled and the ease with which we chatted made it feel like it had been just days since we'd last met.

We went to a beautiful restaurant all decked out like a theatre inside. I had another large gin and tonic to calm my nerves and then we chatted for hours over dinner. There was a singer performing in the restaurant and much to my embarrassment he came over to the table and asked if I would like to sing.

'Oh I couldn't,' I said. But he was insistent so eventually I got up and did 'I've Got You under My Skin'.

Afterwards all the diners applauded, although I'm not sure if that was just because they wanted rid of me!

We looked at old pictures and talked for hours about the old times and about everything that had happened in our lives in the intervening years. Then after we'd finished dinner he walked me back to Holborn tube station where I was going in one direction back to Lloyd's house, and he was going in the other.

'Right, well, thanks for a lovely evening,' I said nervously in the ticket hall.

'Thank you, Linda,' he replied. 'Er, would you like to come back to my hotel?'

'Oh God no, no, I couldn't,' I replied, smiling. 'It's been wonderful – but I couldn't do that.'

I paused and then said: 'But you can kiss me.'

'I don't think I've ever been ordered to do something like that before,' he laughed.

'Well, there's no pressure,' I said, 'but it will be the first time I've kissed anyone since Brian.'

He leant forwards and kissed me and it was lovely. I felt sixteen again. Goodness knows what passers-by must have thought – we were like two young kids saying goodbye after a night on the town. But I didn't care. It was fabulous but there was still absolutely no way I would be taking it any further than that.

He promised to call me the following day and then saw me onto my train. And that's when I caught my reflection in the glass, grinning with sheer joy. I immediately thought of Brian but the remarkable thing was I didn't feel guilty, which is what I'd always assumed I would feel in that situation. Instead, I thought to myself: 'I reckon he's up there now with Bernie and they're having a whisky and Coke and saying: "Go on, girl!"'

When I got back to Lloyd and Kam's house I couldn't find my key anywhere in my handbag so had to knock on the door to get in.

Kam opened the door, whispering: 'Did you have a good time?'

'I did,' I replied. 'And I kissed him!' She pushed me into the front room so we wouldn't wake up Mia as we fell about laughing.

'Don't tell Lloyd,' I laughed. 'He'll be like my dad about it all!'

Obviously she went and told him straight away because next morning over breakfast Lloyd stood up and announced: 'Right, now I don't want you thinking you can bring any strange men into this house.'

And then he and Kam fell about laughing.

The following day there was lots of texting backwards and forwards between me and my new romance. He was keen to meet again but I wasn't sure. It had been a lovely evening but that was enough for me. And besides, he was about to return to Australia and I felt certain he had another very happy life back there.

He sent another message saying goodbye before his flight left and we have kept in touch, even though there won't be any more romance there. He's on the other side of the world! But the whole experience showed me that romance could be possible in my life again one day and made me think it would be nice to have some male company. I'm not talking marriage or anything like that – just someone to watch a film or go for a drink with.

I knew I'd already had the love of my life and had been incredibly lucky to have that. But perhaps there could still be someone else out there for me too . . .

Nineteen
Feeling Good, Looking Good

I sat at my bedroom mirror putting on my make-up for a night out with Maureen and the girls. Since I'd been feeling better in myself I loved our nights out. We'd have such a laugh. Often it felt like we were teenagers all over again. Except that certainly wasn't how I looked in the mirror any more. I applied my foundation, then blusher, eye shadow and mascara, the way I'd been doing for years. Yet nowadays no amount of make-up seemed able to cover up the tiredness and sadness I saw in my face. Sometimes I barely recognized the woman looking back at me at all.

And yet, while I looked tired and sad on the outside, I no longer felt that way inside. I wanted my face to reflect how I was finally feeling – optimistic, hopeful. And, yes, happy. A couple of days later I was chatting to Maureen.

'I want to have a facelift,' I suddenly blurted out.

'What?' she spluttered.

'A facelift.' I repeated. 'My face looks tired, saggy. Like an old woman. I want to look like me again.'

'You look great,' she said. 'Why now?'

'I'm ready,' I said. 'It would have been all wrong for me to do it a few years ago because I really was sad then. If I'd done it then I'd have just been putting a mask on the real me. But now the real me feels younger and happier and I want my face to show it.'

'Well that makes sense,' Maureen said. 'You'd better just go for it!'

I'd never thought about having plastic surgery before but I wasn't one of those people who are dead set against it. In fact every time I watched *X Factor* I'd joke: 'Look at Sharon Osborne – she's amazing. Get me the number of her plastic surgeon NOW!'

Over the next few weeks I ran the idea past my brothers and sisters and friends. Most of them, lovely as they are, said the same: 'You look great, what are you worrying about that for?' But when I explained, they seemed to understand. The only person I didn't tell was Coleen because she's always been strongly opposed to plastic surgery. She thinks people should grow old naturally.

I was particularly conscious about the little creases on my top lip which I'd developed from twenty years of smoking. Make-up would get clogged in them and I hated it.

I set about researching a few clinics online which had good reputations before making an appointment with the Harley Street Clinic in London. Because I'd been working hard for the last few years I had a little bit of money set aside for rainy days. This was how I wanted to spend it.

The clinic invited me down for a free consultation with the surgeon there, Mr Cumbo. I sat in the ornately decorated consulting room, surrounded by vases of lilies and gilt-framed paintings, while Mr Cumbo handed me a mirror and asked me to take a long hard look at myself.

'Now, Mrs Hudson,' he said, 'you do not need anything doing to your eyes or your forehead.'

'That's a relief,' I thought. 'At least he's not just after my money.'

'But we could help you with the "marionette lines" running down either side of your nose and give you a lower-face lift to address how the skin has become saggy with ageing. And then a chemical peel would give you a brighter, fresher complexion. Afterwards you'll still look like you. Just a bit fresher.'

'That's exactly what I want. But what about scarring?' I asked, thinking of some of those dreadful Hollywood facelifts people used to have in the 1980s.

'No, all scarring will be inside and around the back of the ear so none of it will be visible. Oh, and did I mention that we can do all this without a general anaesthetic while you are awake?' he added.

'Whoa. Whoa,' I yelped. 'I don't think so. Did I mention to you I am still scared of going to the dentist and this is way worse than that,' I laughed.

He explained that it would always be better to avoid the risks of general anaesthetic.

'You'll be sedated though, and won't feel a thing. Trust me. I have done this many times. You'll even be able to go home the same day.'

It certainly sounded remarkably easy. 'OK, I'll go ahead,' I said.

The operation wouldn't be until the New Year, though, after I'd finished the panto season I'd been booked for in Preston.

'We'll call you as soon as we have a date,' Mr Cumbo said.

I returned home to Blackpool excited about what 2017 held. I could feel a new life beckoning. And for my new life I wanted a new face. But understandably some of those closest to me were concerned.

'Oh I don't know whether it's a good idea, Linda,' my brother Brian said, worrying about me as ever. 'Is it really worth the risk?'

'Look, Brian,' I said, 'thanks for worrying about me but I'll be OK. And don't panic, I'm not expecting to come out looking like Miss World. I just want to look a bit more like this,' and then I pushed the skin back either side of my face. And I think even Brian could see then what I'd used to look like ten years ago before everything fell apart.

By that point there was no changing my mind anyway. I wanted finally to be able to look in the mirror and see a woman once again full of life. All I had to do was get through the next few weeks in panto without a hitch. But you'll remember my nickname . . . Linda 'Lucky' Hudson!

It was the second day of rehearsals for the pantomime in Preston and I'd taken the train to make sure I was there in good time. At Preston station I ran over the bridge and was just going down the steps on the other side when I felt myself starting to tumble.

'Oh God,' I cried as I fell the entire height of the iron steps.

I ended up face down at the bottom of the steps. I was conscious of people huddling around me and a voice saying: 'Don't move, love, keep very still.' And a woman was gasping: 'Oh that was a terrible fall. Do you think she'll be OK?'

I certainly didn't feel it. The next thing I knew, two policemen were there. One of them knelt down next to me.

'Where does it hurt, madam?' he asked.

'My leg,' I said. It was agony.

'OK, let's lift your trouser leg up and I'll take a look,' he said.

'Oh God,' I thought, '. . . And this is why you should always shave your legs before you leave the house!' I may have been in agony but I still didn't want to terrify this young policeman! My leg, hip and arm were all badly grazed and I was still feeling a bit befuddled.

'Can you name the Prime Minister?' the policeman asked gently.

'Oh goodness, yes,' I replied. 'It's that woman, you know. I can't remember her name but I think that's probably because I'm menopausal rather than concussed.'

He laughed but said he really ought to get me to hospital to be checked over.

'Oh no,' I said, 'I can't go to hospital, I've got to get to rehearsals.'

I limped into a cab then sat with my leg raised and packed in ice for the entire rehearsal. I just about managed it home at the end of the day but as soon as I took my shoe off my ankle swelled up so badly I couldn't walk. I rang Maureen.

'Could you pop round and take me to the hospital?' I asked. 'I fell down the steps this morning and now I can't walk.'

'For goodness' sake, Linda,' she said. 'Why didn't you go to hospital straight away?'

'I had to get to rehearsals,' I repeated for the second time that day.

At the hospital they placed my neck in a brace because that had started hurting too, then they X-rayed my leg, hip, head, shoulder, elbow, pelvis, knee and ankle.

'Well I think you've used up your nine lives this time, Mrs

Hudson, because, incredibly, nothing is broken,' the nurse said. 'But really, why didn't you go to hospital immediately?'

'Because I had to get to rehearsals,' I said for the third time that day.

Maureen just raised her eyes to heaven.

I was off work for three days but was back in plenty of time for the opening show. It was a wonderful pantomime and my nieces loved seeing Auntie Lin flying through the auditorium like a real fairy.

On New Year's Eve I went to bed truly looking forward to 2017. I felt more in control of my life than I had in a long time, I was working regularly, had money in the bank, was paying off my debts, was getting a new face and felt almost, well . . . hopeful: 2017 was going to be a good year.

The pantomime finished on 2 January and I was just getting back to normal at home a day or so later when the phone rang. It was Melanie.

'*Loose Women* has been on,' she said, 'and they want to film your whole cosmetic surgery procedure. They reckon it will make great telly.'

I thought about it for a couple of moments. Could there be anything more embarrassing than letting the world see me lying on a surgeon's table having my skin sliced off? Probably not.

'OK, I'll do it,' I said. The *Loose Women* show has been very good and had me on to share some of my darkest times: losing Brian, having depression and calling the Samaritans. It seemed only right that I should share the journey now I was on the way back up. Plus, they were prepared to pay me . . .

Two days after that the phone rang again. This time it was the Harley Street Clinic.

'Mrs Hudson, we have an appointment for you on 11 January,' the receptionist said.

Suddenly I froze. 'Errrr, I'll call you back,' I said, dropping my mobile like a hot brick.

Oh no – now it was really real. It's one thing having consultations and giving it a load of chat about having a facelift. It's a whole other thing actually having it done. Did I really have the courage to go through with it? I made myself a strong brew and thought it all through from the very beginning. Inside me I could hear a little voice saying: 'Come on, Linda, be brave. Go for it.' I rang back, confirmed the appointment, and got ready for action.

Coleen had just gone back into the *Celebrity Big Brother* house and as I still hadn't told her about the op it felt like that was meant to be.

My other sisters were all working so couldn't come with me. Denise would have done but, like I said before, it's a standing joke in our family that she is terrible around pain. She actually faints, so she'd be no good. Then my wonderful sister-in-law Annie volunteered to take a few days off work and come with me. I booked us both into a hotel near Hyde Park and on the Monday morning we set off.

That day I was a guest on *Loose Women* to talk about what I was doing and why. Stacey Solomon was on the show and she was lovely. She put her arms around me and said, 'Oh, I'm so nervous for you.'

I was nervous for me too! That evening I treated Annie and myself to tickets to see the musical *Dreamgirls* in the West End. Afterwards we queued at the stage door for autographs – I'm still as in love with showbiz as I ever was! We were walking back to the hotel when this cab-load of students drove past. 'Good luck with the surgery,' they yelled out of the window. They must have seen me on *Loose Women*. Me and Annie laughed all the way back.

On the Tuesday I did a slot on a show about Paul O'Grady and then prepared myself for the following day – operation day.

'Are you all right?' Annie kept asking that evening as I became quieter and quieter. It was just nerves – but by the following morning I could barely speak. Brian always used to say I was very quiet on the first day of a big show. And today was no different.

Annie and I took a cab to the clinic and sat nervously in silence in the waiting room. Annie wasn't even having the operation and she looked as white as a sheet – so goodness knows what I must have looked like. Next I had to change into my theatre scrubs and sign my life away in case of some terrible medical disaster. Then Mr Cumbo came into the room holding a lip-liner pencil. I looked at him suspiciously. I lay on the bed as he drew lines across my cheeks and lower face and tried to stop myself imagining that in a few minutes' time a razor-sharp scalpel would be cutting my face where those pencil marks had been drawn.

After that Linda Robson from *Loose Women* came to interview me.

'How do you feel?' she asked, as a camera focused on my face that looked like a kid had been at it with their felt pens.

'Well at the moment I feel pretty ridiculous,' I said, laughing nervously. The truth was I was terrified but I was desperately trying not to show it.

'Good luck, it's going to be great,' Linda said, giving me a big hug.

'Ready?' asked Mr Cumbo.

'As I'll ever be,' I squeaked.

I had a cannula in my arm already and the lady anaesthetist started pumping the drugs into me. One moment I felt a bit drowsy and the next moment I was gone. I was sedated for five and a half hours and felt nothing at all. It was more traumatic for the poor camera guy from *Loose Women* who was filming the whole thing. Annie went out shopping for a few hours but when she got back he was saying to her: 'It was unbelievable, they've taken half her skin off then pulled it right back.'

'Oh, don't tell me,' Annie yelped. 'I don't want to know.'

When I finally came round in a bright little room in the clinic I didn't actually feel that bad. I was able to eat a biscuit and drink some orange juice and although my face and ears felt swollen, it was OK. I didn't dare touch them. Annie walked in to see me, looking a little nervous.

'Oh,' she said, 'you don't look as bad as I thought you would. Here, I bought you a jumper.'

She handed me a beautiful dusty-pink jumper.

'Ah thanks, Annie,' I said. 'It'll match the bandages round my head! I'll call it my I've-had-a-facelift jumper.'

Although I didn't look too shocking at first, over the next few hours the swelling got worse and worse until I looked like one of those babushka dolls with a big fat round face and slit eyes. When I tried to eat a slice of melon I nearly choked because I couldn't chew it.

I was still pretty woozy and don't remember much about getting back to the hotel but we were back there by 7.30 p.m. and I was starving as I hadn't eaten all day, so we ordered room service.

'You'd better hide in the bathroom,' Annie said when it arrived. I was covered in bandages and didn't want to terrify the poor waiter.

I just about managed to eat some soft penne pasta and then Annie and I lay on the bed and watched Coleen in *Celebrity Big Brother*. Every now and again Annie would give me a worried look and then dart into the bathroom and return with cold wet cotton wool for my eyes. I didn't know it then but she could see my face swelling up like a balloon and my eyes were just tiny little slits.

The pain seemed to be getting worse by the hour. The clinic had given me co-codamol painkillers but I didn't want to take too many. I'd had them before and anyone who's ever taken them knows they give you terrible constipation. I decided the pain was preferable. Finally I drifted off to sleep but woke in the night to use the loo. I walked into the bathroom, put the light on and saw myself in the mirror. 'What have you done?' I thought. I looked horrific. My entire face looked like it had been battered. My nose was all across my face – and I hadn't even had anything done to my nose. And my whole head felt intolerably tight and painful.

It became too difficult to sleep and I could feel a sense of anxiety building up inside me. I began gasping for breath and realized I was having a panic attack. I hadn't had one for ages but all the symptoms were there again – not being able to breathe properly, sweating and feeling uncontrollably panicky. I focused really hard on breathing in and out and gradually calmed myself down.

By 6 a.m. Annie was on the phone to the clinic to see if this was normal. Of course they just told me to do what I should have done all along: take the correct dosage of painkillers. Once I did that it was much more manageable.

We spent the Thursday cooped up in our hotel room, hiding from the room service guy each time he knocked and trying everything possible to distract me from the throbbing sensation in my face.

I'd wondered why the clinic had told me to buy a children's toothbrush before the operation but by then I knew exactly why. I could barely open my mouth wide enough to get the baby brush inside. Annie nipped out to a local shop and bought some instant porridge and a teaspoon. It was the only thing I could eat. Lloyd works for the chain of hotels we were staying in and arranged for us to be brought some miniature bottles of gin. Annie only let me have one – and I had to drink that with a straw!

On the Friday morning we returned to the clinic for a check-up. When I knocked on the door, my face still covered in bandages, the receptionist took one look at me and said: 'Ah yes, let me take you straight up to the consulting room.'

'She doesn't want me in the waiting room terrifying the other patients,' I giggled to Annie.

Even Mr Cumbo looked a little surprised when he saw my still enormously swollen face.

'Oh, you poor thing,' he said.

'Er, please tell me it's normal,' I laughed, slightly nervously.

'Oh yes,' he assured me, 'you'll soon be back to normal.'

He took off some of the bandages and replaced them with a large white support stocking for my face. Not a good look. After that Annie and I were free to go home. There was no way I could go on the train and frighten young children, so we had booked a car instead. We went straight to Denise's house as she had offered to look after me for a few days.

'Oh my God,' said Denise, when she looked at me.

Maureen was there too. She looked as though she was going to faint. She was sat on the couch, and as she looked at me she squeezed her legs under her chin in horror.

Denise had made a fabulous stew, just like one of Mum's, for dinner. She mashed it up for me and gave me a teaspoon to eat it with. It was delicious, but two minutes later I threw it all up again. I hadn't eaten anything much for three days and it must have been too much for my stomach to cope with.

After a couple of days with Denise, though, I was soon on the road to recovery. I lived on strawberry jelly but the swelling soon subsided and by the Sunday I was off the painkillers. I still had to put special emollient cream on my face every day as the effects of the chemical peel kicked in. At first I thought I must have a nasty attack of dandruff when I saw lots of white flakes all over my blouse. But then I realized – that was my skin falling off.

That weekend little Sienna and her mum Maddison popped round to visit. Sienna came running round the corner but as soon as she saw me she just froze.

'What have you done, Auntie Lin?' she said.

'Oh, it's all right, darling,' I said. 'You remember I said I was having a little operation on my face? Well this is it. But it's all fine. Now, can I have a kiss?'

She put her arms around me and ever so gently kissed me.

'You don't look the same any more,' Sienna said.

'I know, darling,' I laughed. 'And that's good.'

Twenty

It's Back

SpongeBob SquarePants, my great-nieces' favourite cartoon, was blasting from the television. Six-year-old Sienna, her sister Ava, who's seven, and two-year-old Roma were snuggled up on my sofa watching it for the umpteenth time, and merrily charging their way through the bag of sweets I'd got us for our sleepover treat.

Like I've said, I've been close to the girls, who are Maureen's son Danny's children, since they were born. Sienna in particular brought a sliver of hope and happiness into my life when she was born in the midst of my despair after Brian's death. She and her younger sisters often come round to play or for a sleepover at Auntie Lin's if their mum and dad are working or just fancy a night off.

That evening – Saturday, 2 March – we'd had tea and played some games and the girls were just going to get ready for bed so I nipped upstairs to get their pyjamas from their overnight bag. I was halfway up the stairs when my foot slipped taking the next step and I tumbled forward. My body slammed down and immediately I heard a loud cracking sound. There was no mistaking this. It was bad. The pain in my hip was excruciating and I started screaming and crying: 'Sienna, Sienna!'

I must have been screaming pretty loudly because after a minute the girls even managed to hear me above the racket of *SpongeBob*!

'Hey, Ava, Auntie Lin is playing a game,' Sienna said. 'She's lying on the stairs pretending to cry.'

'No, Sienna,' I wailed. 'I'm not playing – I really am crying.'

The two girls came darting up the stairs to find out what was going on. Ava, the older of the pair, immediately took charge.

'OK, Sienna,' she said, 'I'm going to hold Auntie Linda up, I want you to go downstairs, find her mobile phone, ring Mummy or Nanny and then unlock the front door so they can get in. Then come up here and look after Roma.'

By this point Roma had got herself to the top of the stairs and was teetering at the edge. I was thinking, 'Oh my God, Akela from the Boy Scouts is here taking charge.' Ava was absolutely amazing.

The girls managed to find my phone and I rang Anne, who immediately said, 'I'm on my way.' She then rang Denise who lives just five doors away.

Minutes later Denise came sprinting up the front path in her pyjamas. She could see I was in terrible pain and couldn't move and immediately rang 999. Then followed the standard questions:

'Is she conscious?'

'Yes.'

'Is she bleeding?'

'No.'

'I'm afraid it could take between one and four hours.'

But the pain was indescribable. Even moving a fraction was

making me scream. As I howled in pain Denise held the phone nearer to me so the operator knew I was not making this up.

There was nothing I could do but stand at the top of the stairs and wait – surrounded by my sisters, my brother Brian who also rushed round, and three little great-nieces. It was then Sienna began to cry.

'Oh, don't cry, Sienna,' I said, trying to comfort her through my pain. 'Auntie Lin is going to be just fine.'

'No it's not that,' Sienna sobbed. 'I really wanted our sleepover and now you've got to go to hospital.'

In the end we only had to wait twenty minutes before an ambulance turned up. I'd never been so pleased to see anything in my life before. They took me straight to Blackpool's Victoria Hospital, where I was lifted onto a trolley and taken to A&E. There I was put on gas and air for the pain, which was amazing. Having never had children I hadn't tried it before – but it was incredible and I quickly felt more comfortable.

As I lay on the bed I cursed myself for being so clumsy. That was the third time I'd fallen in a matter of months. There had been the time at Preston station and another occasion at home too. That time had been just before I was due round at my brother Brian and Annie's for dinner. When I got there I told them what I'd done.

'Have you hurt yourself?' Annie asked.

'Well my hip's aching,' I said.

'You ought to get that checked out,' Brian instructed like the older brother he is.

'Yeah, I will,' I said.

But of course I hadn't done anything about it at all. And

here I was having fallen over again and now it was REALLY hurting.

It was mayhem in the hospital with ten beds lined up in the corridor and staff running in all directions, but the doctors and nurses were wonderful. After a short wait a porter pushed me on the trolley to get the hip X-rayed. When the doctor reappeared half an hour later with a large X-ray in his hand and a grim look on his face I knew it wasn't good news.

'Good evening, Mrs Hudson,' he said. 'I'm afraid to say you have a crack in your hip which we are going to have to operate on. And we're also going to do an X-ray on the femur bone in your leg because of your medical history.'

I knew instantly what 'medical history' meant. He meant cancer.

As he walked away I turned to Anne, who was sitting next to me on the bed. 'Well,' I said. 'I never saw that coming.'

And I really hadn't. Yes, of course every woman who's had breast cancer always knows there is a risk that it may appear as a secondary cancer at some later date. And if it does then it cannot be cured. But I'm just not the kind of person who thinks about things happening until they actually do. So in all those years since my first cancer I'd never once wondered about it coming back.

But now, eleven years after the first time, the black cloud of cancer was being held above my head in another hospital ward. I instantly felt a terrible sick feeling run through me. But then I managed to suppress it because all the doctors and nurses around me were acting so matter-of-factly about it all. I was still being treated very much for my cracked hip. Even the way the doctor talked about the additional X-rays I needed made it sound like it was entirely standard. Just procedure.

They kept me in overnight and Anne stayed with me the whole time. We didn't discuss my 'medical history' as the doctor had so delicately put it. We didn't need to. We knew from Bernie exactly what that meant.

Anne had breast cancer back in 2000 and, as I write this, is seventeen years clear, but she would often tell me over the years that she worried about it coming back and everything that would mean. I was worried about her worrying. But I'd never worried about it for myself.

I'm not proud that I left it so long to deal with my breast cancer the first time and that I ended up with it at stage three with a 9cm-by-5cm lump. I know that was entirely stupid and the wrong thing to do. But from that you can tell something about my reaction to such things – I stick my head in the sand. I was very, very lucky to survive that first time because it had become so serious. But maybe that's all the more reason why I couldn't imagine what it would be like for it to return.

The doctors told me they wouldn't operate on my hip until they knew exactly 'what was going on'. They'd done some other scans and tests and for a few days there was nothing I could do but stuff myself with grapes and try to stop my brain from wandering to the scariest places where all these additional tests might lead. Fortunately my family were almost always at my bedside, keeping up my spirits.

It was a couple of days later and I was lying in bed alone on the ward when I saw the consultant walking towards me, flanked by a registrar and a nurse. I'd been in enough hospital situations to know it's serious when you get a consultant, a registrar and a nurse.

'Uh oh,' I thought. 'Here we are.'

The consultant picked up my notes and started speaking slowly.

'Now, Mrs Hudson,' he said. 'We've looked at the X-rays and there is a crack, but it seems to be through quite a large cyst . . . or something.'

He didn't say 'the word' but he didn't need to. I knew. And for a moment I thought I was going to die on the spot. He meant tumour. I didn't really think about being brave or angry or any of those other things you're supposed to be at moments like that. I simply began to cry. I knew exactly what a tumour would mean. Secondary breast cancer is a death sentence. Maybe not this week, this year, or even this decade. But that's what it is.

The consultant said they'd need to do more tests to discover if it actually was a tumour and secondary breast cancer. There was always the chance it was a brand spanking new cancer! Or it was a non-cancerous tumour. Anything was possible but in my mind I was already convinced it was going to be secondary breast cancer.

My sisters and brothers descended on the hospital within hours.

'Oh, I'm so sorry, Maureen,' I said. 'I can't bear to put you all through this all over again. After Bernie and Mum and everything that's happened I didn't want it to be me causing more problems for you all.'

As each of my brothers and sisters came in to visit I collapsed in pieces all over again. I could see the devastation in their faces. And I desperately didn't want it to be me who put them through this again.

Coleen was down in London filming *Loose Women* and I

decided I didn't want to break the news to her over the phone when she was so far from home. But every couple of hours she was texting me saying: 'Had your results yet?'

'No – later I think,' I lied in reply.

'You must have had them by now,' she texted again a couple of hours later.

And so it went on.

Then she rang and was joking that if the doctors didn't get a move on, she'd out them on TV. She was mucking around but I could tell in her voice there was something else, she was searching for reassurance. But I couldn't bring myself to tell her, I knew she'd be devastated all over again.

The following day Coleen was still texting for news and I knew I couldn't keep the truth from her for ages. I rang Mel first. She was in London and I wanted to be sure Coleen would have a shoulder to cry on should she need it.

Then I plucked up my courage and rang Coleen's number.

'Hi, Col,' I said as cheerily as I could manage.

'Hi, Lin,' she replied, already a note of wariness in her voice. 'What's the news?'

'I'm sorry,' I said. 'It's not good. It's a tumour.'

'Oh Linda, no,' she said, her voice cracking. Again all I could think of was Coleen as the little baby of our family and here I was upsetting her all over again. 'But you're going to be fine,' she went on, desperately trying to keep both our spirits up.

'Of course, Col,' I replied. 'I'm going to be fine.'

I don't know whether either of us really believed that at that moment. But it was the line we were sticking to.

'I'll be over to see you at the weekend,' Coleen said. 'Love ya.'

'Love you too, Col,' I replied, tears brimming in my eyes.

At night when all my visitors had gone for the day and I was left alone, I struggled to sleep. Believe me, none of the irony was lost on me. For years of my life – for pages of this book – I was so depressed and sad I wanted to die. But now, facing the reality of death, I wanted to live more than I'd ever wanted anything. I kept thinking: 'After all those years of going through life, making plans and trying to get by and then suddenly I'm *here*. I'm here and it's all out of my hands.'

Now there seemed so very much to live for.

Two days later, on the Wednesday, the oncology team returned to see me again. Again, it was bad news.

'We've looked at your test results and we are now 99.9 per cent sure that you do have secondary breast cancer,' the consultant said gently. 'I'm afraid it's not curable. But we must be optimistic – it is treatable.'

'That's what you said to my dead sister,' I snapped back. It was unfair of me to say it but I wasn't feeling very fair right then. And it was true, that was exactly what Bernie was told when her cancer returned. Just over a year later she was dead.

It felt like history repeating itself. I'd spent so much time with Bernie when she was battling that secondary cancer so hard. But in the end it still got her. And if someone as strong and determined couldn't beat it, then really . . . well, there was a lot of stuff I still couldn't even think about.

The consultant asked me about what had happened to Bernie.

'Your cancer is very different to your sister's,' he said. 'Yours is located in just one place – your hip.'

That was true, by the time Bernie's secondary was found it had spread to her lung, liver and bones. And there had even been a tiny bit in her brain. Mine really did seem to be confined to quite a small area. For now.

'I reckon that was Bernie pushing me over on the stairs to get it discovered before it was too late,' I laughed to Coleen one day. 'Typical Bernie – she was always pushing me on!'

My breast-care nurse, Sarah, who'd been with me every step of the way first time around was one of the first in to visit. She'd become like my sixth Nolan sister over the past decade, getting me through every obstacle along the way.

'I just don't know whether I can do this all over again,' I said to her one day.

'You can, Linda,' she replied. 'You've done it before, so you know you can do it again.'

But this time felt so different because I knew there was going to be no 'all clear' at the end of it. This really was going to be a fight to the end.

Sarah came to visit me while I was in the hospital almost every day. I'd know she was there when an arm popped into the room waving a white handkerchief. She knew I'd be about to start crying at any moment so she was all prepared! But even when I was crying, Sarah and I would be laughing at the same time too. Even in the very darkest times there is always something to laugh at too – if you're prepared to see it. One day I was moping around feeling very sorry for myself again.

'Ah, don't screw your face up like that, Linda,' Sarah joked. 'Not after you got all that expensive work done on it.'

'I don't know why I let you come in to see me,' I laughed.

'It's because we've got the same low sense of humour,' she shot back.

And she's right. Love and brilliant care and a lot of drugs

got me through those terrible first few weeks. But so did laughter.

'The thing is, I've got cancer whether I laugh or cry,' I said to Coleen one day. 'So I might as well laugh.'

At first I couldn't understand why the cancer had come back now – after eleven years clear. Where had it been hiding all that time?

Sarah explained it. 'I'm afraid cancer is a bit like fairy dust,' she said. 'But bad fairy dust. When you've had it once it's like someone has blown it and it can land anywhere else in your body. It sits there quietly and then one day – though not always – it can start to grow again.'

But of course when it comes back a second time there is nothing that can be done to totally eradicate it. It's taken root for ever then.

The week I'd been taken into hospital I was supposed to be going to see little Sienna's first dance show.

'Why can't Auntie Lin come?' she asked her mum, Maddison.

'She's still really poorly at the hospital,' Maddison replied.

'Well I'll have to take my show to her then,' she said.

And she did. Straight after her dress rehearsal she turned up at the hospital with her mum in her full dance costume and did the entire routine at the bottom of my bed. It was fantastic. At the end I clapped and whistled.

'You were amazing, darling,' I said.

As I watched her spinning and skipping, just the way I used to do when I was her age, I thought to myself: 'This is it. This is what staying alive is all about.' And it's true. I could see it so clearly from that point onwards – enjoying the most simple things in life with the people you love most is what it is all about. Actually they are the only things that really matter.

After three weeks in hospital in Blackpool the doctors announced I was to be moved to a hospital more than an hour away in Oswestry, Shropshire.

'It's a specialist orthopaedic unit,' the doctor explained. 'When we get you there the team will be able to decide on the best course of treatment.'

'Oh, OK,' I replied. I still tend to go with whatever the doctors tell me to do. Ignorance is bliss in my book but my sisters and friends are much more inquisitive. When I told Suzanne I was being transferred to Oswestry she was immediately suspicious.

'Why are they sending you there?' she said. 'It's in the middle of nowhere.'

Within twenty minutes she'd texted back.

'I've googled it. It's the best place you could be – a centre of excellence for orthopaedics and your consultant is at the top of his game.'

'Oh great, thanks, Suzanne,' I replied.

I guess it's good I've got other people asking all the questions for me.

The hospital in Oswestry was all new and bright and clean. I had a room to myself and there were views out over fields in the distance. On arrival I was introduced to my consultant, Mr Kool.

'Pleased to meet you, Mr Kool,' I said. 'Now that's a show-biz name!'

He laughed and I knew we were going to get on well – even if this was most likely to be one of the worst weeks of my life.

Mr Kool said that despite the diagnosis I'd already had, to be absolutely certain what kind of tumour I had, he would have to take a bit of the bone for a biopsy.

'Although we think there is a 99.9 per cent chance you have secondary breast cancer, you could be the 0.1 per cent. Only a biopsy will tell us for certain and help us work out the best form of treatment.'

That would mean a general anaesthetic while they took the sample they needed. Even the thought of that terrified me.

I came round from the biopsy sobbing in the arms of the recovery nurse. I suppose I must have started coming to and the worry of it all, mixed with the drugs and anaesthetic, was just too much for me. The nurse was fabulous and kept her arm round me as I cried. She stayed with me until I was allowed back onto the ward where Tom, Denise and my lovely friend Liz Emmett were waiting.

Oswestry was a long old trip from Blackpool, but Denise and Tom stayed with me for the week and Liz came over too. All the others – my brothers and sisters, nieces and nephews – created a WhatsApp group titled 'Linda's treatment', which had forty people on it supposedly swapping times that they'd be visiting but mainly sending ridiculous messages to drive each other bonkers. They were hysterically funny.

When I was first in hospital, every day one of them would turn up with a bagload of food. I asked Tommy for a bag of Walkers cheese and onion crisps as I was really craving them and he bought a massive multipack. Then a couple of hours later Denise arrived with two enormous bags of wine gums.

'If I beat this cancer they'll be moving me straight into the gastric-band ward,' I laughed as Coleen turned up with another big box of chocolates the following day.

It was as if they were bringing in food to feed the entire ward! But I knew why they did it. None of them knew what they could do to help me – feeding me felt like something.

'If there is anything you want, Linda, anything at all, please just ask,' Maureen said to me one day. 'Because then that doesn't just help you, it helps us too by thinking we're being useful.'

Tom and Denise even moved into a hotel near Oswestry so they could visit me every day. They are such caring people – I really don't think I would have managed that long stay so far from home without them. But when all my visitors went home at the end of the day it was terribly quiet. Night times in that hospital became the longest time in the world as I was left alone with my thoughts.

I tossed and turned for hours thinking about Brian and Bernie and Mum. And then I'd start panicking about what was now happening to me. What would it really be like to join them?

I told my doctor I wasn't sleeping and was feeling anxious all the time and he suggested sleeping tablets. I was worried about getting back into the habit of taking a pill to sleep. But I knew if I was going to give fighting this disease my best shot I had to get some rest – and that meant going back on sleeping tablets.

The first night I took them I was asleep by eleven thirty and went right through until seven o'clock the next morning without waking once. Still, the first thing I thought when I woke up was: 'I've got cancer.'

But having had a good night's sleep meant that the second thing I thought was: 'But I'm still alive. And I'm going to fight it.'

Twenty-One

Groundhog Day

I never really thought Linda 'Lucky' Hudson would be in the 'Oh, you'll never guess what, it wasn't cancer after all' 0.1 per cent which Mr Kool had spoken about.

And sure enough, the results of the biopsy only confirmed what I'd already known in my heart – I really did have secondary breast cancer.

'I'm sorry,' said Mr Kool sombrely.

'It's OK,' I replied. 'I think we all knew what the outcome would be – although I guess there was just one moment when I hoped that for once I might be in the fortunate 0.1 per cent.'

He smiled. 'Right, now we just need to decide what to do for you next. I don't think we can operate to remove the tumour because of where it is situated on your pelvis. It would be a massive operation and there would be a lot of risk involved – you could be left with a permanent disability. You'd only see me doing an operation like that for you if I thought it was the absolute last resort.'

'Oh,' I said, forcing a smile. 'Well, let's hope I never see you again then.'

Mr Kool grinned back. Cancer humour was going to get me through this, even if surgery wasn't.

'So will I need radiotherapy and chemotherapy?' I asked.

The thought of going back to chemotherapy was horrendous. All those months of feeling terrible and losing my hair again.

'No, it definitely won't be chemotherapy,' said Mr Kool. 'You will need radiotherapy. But we can't do that until the crack in your hip has started to heal. We need your bone to strengthen as quickly as possible before we can begin, because radiotherapy weakens bones and we certainly don't want yours to be any weaker at the moment.

'The most important thing now is to get the crack in your hip to heal as quickly as possible. We'll put you on calcium tablets to strengthen your bones and then you just need plenty of rest. You are more than welcome to stay here for as long as you like while you recover, or you could go home to Blackpool. I'm not throwing you out but in my opinion I think you would benefit from trying to get back to some kind of normal.'

'Oh, but I'm so scared of suffering that pain again if I fall,' I said. 'Or being on my own and hurting myself – the pain was horrific.'

'I understand,' Mr Kool said, nodding. 'But we will give you painkillers and if it gets too bad just call an ambulance. But you have to go back to getting on with life as best you can. Otherwise what are you going to do? Stay in bed for the rest of your life?'

That was probably exactly what I needed to hear. I'd been in hospital for about four weeks altogether by then, being scanned and tested and waiting for results. And although I hardly loved being in hospital, it did feel safe. A kind of padded cell. I had nurses on hand if I needed to walk any distance and all my medication was sorted for me. Leaving hospital was going to be a return to the real world.

My brothers and sisters were worried about me leaving hospital too.

'But isn't there a risk your hip could just snap if you try walking on it too much?' said Denise when she next came in to visit.

Mr Kool explained to both of us. 'If you see a building with a crack in it, it doesn't mean it is going to fall down at any minute. Unless it's a supporting wall, a building can survive with cracks for centuries. And that's what Linda's crack is. It may be a bit uncomfortable at first but using the crutch for support will help.

'And gradually,' he said, turning to me, 'you will be able to walk just fine again.'

I was booked in for physiotherapy sessions with a young guy who taught me how to walk up and down stairs again. He was wonderfully patient and within a couple of days I'd mastered it.

And so, after five days at the hospital in Oswestry, I was ready to go home.

I was scared the morning I packed up my belongings, went downstairs and tentatively eased myself into Denise's car for the journey back to Blackpool. In hospital everyone had been so lovely and it had all seemed so safe. I knew that there, if I fell or was in pain, I could call a nurse and they'd be with me within seconds. At home I could be struggling on my own for hours.

Denise was adamant that wouldn't be happening.

'You're coming to stay with me and Tom,' she said.

'I don't want to be a burden,' I bleated. But Denise had made up her mind. Secretly I was delighted my big sister was happy to take care of me.

Denise and Tom looked after me like I was the Queen. They had a downstairs loo and a walk-in shower, which made things easier, and they made me up a bed in their back room so I didn't have to worry about trying to climb stairs. In fact I didn't have to worry about anything. Every time I so much as tried to get up to put the kettle on, Denise was jumping out of her chair and offering to make a cup of tea for me.

I didn't have to cook, put the laundry on or wash up a cup. And even more than that, I felt safe and secure and loved. At a time when I'd had the worst diagnosis it's possible to have, that meant the world. All my brothers and sisters, nieces and nephews were fabulous too. I was never left alone for a moment. There was always someone there to make sure I was doing OK both physically and emotionally.

Back in Blackpool there was another appointment to discuss my treatment. The oncologist held up the scan picture of my hip as he talked me through it all.

'So that's it, is it?' I said, frowning at the circular blob on the scan – the cancerous tumour resting on the crack in my pelvis. It looked like a little lump of Blu-tack on the scan – how could something so small possibly threaten my entire life?

'How long do you think it has been there?' I asked.

'Could have been years,' the consultant replied. 'Or it could have just appeared before you had the fall. It's impossible to tell. But what we can tell from all the tests is that it hasn't spread anywhere else in your body. And we are confident that with radiotherapy and the right drugs we can hopefully contain it.'

Within a fortnight I was back for my first new course of radiotherapy at the Rosemere Cancer Centre at Preston Hospital. I walked through the same Lancashire drizzle, down the same whitewashed corridor and into the same brightly lit reception area as I had done eleven years earlier when I'd been there for my last radiotherapy treatment.

Then I sat myself down in the same waiting room with the same free tea and coffee (I guess they reckon there have to be some benefits to having cancer). It was like being in a particularly sick version of *Groundhog Day.*

The first day was spent entirely in drawing the indelible marks on my hip where the radiotherapy would have to hit. They have to be so exact that it takes ages making sure they've got it absolutely right.

'OK, so just a couple of things we have to warn you about,' the nurse said at the end of marking me up.

'The radiotherapy can cause a form of sunburn on your skin because it is vicious stuff. And because the cancer is near your bowel it could cause diarrhoea too.'

'This just gets better and better,' I muttered to myself.

'But we can give you tablets to alleviate the symptoms,' she smiled. It is incredible – they can give you tablets for literally anything these days.

When the actual treatment started it was very quick – just like last time. There's about ten minutes, fiddling around trying to get the machine into exactly the right position, but then it only takes a couple of minutes to be blasted with the rays. My course was every day, five days a week for two weeks.

Because of the position of the tumour it meant having to lie waiting for the scan with a medical gown hitched up and not much else on. I know that's the sort of thing that shouldn't bother you when you've got cancer, but actually it did. I may have done all those saucy pictures in the *News of the World* when I was in my prime, but I've always been a bit of a prude about nudity and having to lie like that was just one more humiliation.

'It'd have been too easy for it to have been in my ankle, I suppose,' I grumbled to myself.

The first time I lay on the bed waiting for the beams to start blasting at that bloody tumour in my hip I felt more alone than at any point since my diagnosis. Because the rays are so strong no one else is allowed in the room when the treatment is happening. So I lay there, utterly alone, surrounded only by the buzzing and whirring of machines.

The first time I'd had cancer Brian had been by my side for these radiotherapy appointments. He'd driven me to the hospital then sat waiting outside the treatment room before taking me home and making me endless cups of tea. I knew my sister was waiting for me outside this time, but oh I missed Brian at that moment.

'You will get through this because you are strong,' Brian had told me that first time cancer came for me. 'I am here and your family is here, we'll do it together,' he'd said.

Except Brian wasn't here any more. Thank God I still had my family.

And so the tears fell from my face onto the bed as the radiotherapy machine blasted its rays into me once again that morning.

When the nurse bustled back in a couple of minutes later she looked worried as she saw my mascara-streaked face.

'You OK?' she said kindly.

'I'll be fine,' I sniffed. Somehow that first blast of radiotherapy and the familiarity of the hospital had made everything feel horribly real. Yep, this really was happening to me all over again.

Some of the staff at the centre remembered me. 'Hello, Linda,' one lovely nurse said. 'I'm sorry you're back. But it's lovely to see you.'

It was lovely to see the team there too. Although if I'm honest I was hoping and praying that when my two weeks of treatment were up I would never have to see any of them ever again. I really couldn't face doing radiotherapy for a third time, which I knew I might have to if this course didn't work.

My family all rose to the occasion as ever and arranged a rota to make sure someone picked me up every morning, drove me the thirty minutes from Blackpool to Preston for my treatment, waited with me, then drove me home again. They were utterly incredible.

But the treatment was tough. The radiotherapy scorched my skin and left it red-raw. Clothes rubbed against it and walking was even more painful than ever.

As I got up off the scanning bed after my last session I was delighted. It was another stage completed in this ongoing battle I was locked in.

By then it was just days before the second Bernie Nolan Celebration Charity Ball which we plan to hold every year. However rotten I was feeling I was determined to make it there that night. The idea of the ball is for friends and family of Bernie to get together and remember her and raise money for breast cancer charities. The first ball, in 2016, had been a huge success and we had sold hundreds of tickets for the 2017 one.

I was still using a crutch and finding walking incredibly

difficult when I hobbled into the ballroom at Towcester Race-course. But I was so glad to have made it for Bernie. The previous year I had danced the night away but this time I was in too much pain to even leave my chair. That felt terribly sad, as if one more thing – the chance to have fun – was being taken away from me.

The thought of not seeing the little ones, and all my nieces, nephews, great-nieces and great-nephews, grow up hit me all over again and it was devastating. But I held myself together and made it home. It was a great night for Bernie.

The doctors were certainly throwing everything at their disposal at this cancer. I was on seventeen tablets a day. If you shook me I'd rattle. There were the anti-cancer drugs and calcium tablets, which were like chewing on chalk, to build up my bones. And then on top of that I was booked in for injections into my stomach every month to also strengthen my bones.

After the radiotherapy there was nothing really to do but sit and wait to find out if it had worked. The doctors said I'd have to wait six weeks before I could be scanned again to check whether the radiotherapy had contained the tumour – or, ideally, shrunk it.

That was a difficult time. Being in hospital had been busy with the constant stream of visitors. And then radiotherapy was hectic with daily appointments to be attended. But now there was nothing to do but sit at home. That was when my mind started spiralling out of control and I thought about exactly what I was facing.

I'd been due to start a new stage show called *Our House* based on the music of Madness but of course I had to pull out of that. I wondered if I would ever go back on stage again. Performing had been my life. Without the prospect of doing it again, life seemed very empty.

And without wishing to sound like a child, I couldn't help but think how unfair it all was. After everything I'd been through – Brian falling ill, me having cancer, Brian dying, Mum dying, Bernie dying, my depression, the benefits case – things had finally started looking up for me. And now I was being slapped back down again by cancer.

I missed Brian so much at that time.

My doctors referred me back to the consultant psychologist, Dr Jean Briggs.

'Here I am again then,' I said to Dr Briggs as I sat in her consulting room, tears sliding down my face. 'The funny thing is, after all those times I sat here telling you I didn't want to be alive, here I am now desperate to stay alive.'

She smiled. And listened. Just like she had always done. And I talked to her about everything, how scared I was about dying, how angry I was about what was happening. There was so much I could say to Dr Briggs that I couldn't say to my family because I was too frightened of worrying them.

The irony of my whole situation wasn't lost on me at all. For so long I'd wanted to die, had wanted just to be wherever Brian is. But now I had an almost violent desire to cling to life.

I was still in quite a bit of pain in my hip and struggling to walk with a crutch. The crack in my bone meant that sitting for any length of time felt like being perched on the world's most uncomfortable chair. Denise bought me a special cushion to sit on which helped a little, but there was a constant nagging pain. That only made me feel more down than ever.

My family could all see I was struggling again and there was someone with me most of the time, but there were times when they were gone, late at night, and I was in bed alone when I felt utterly terrified. So much that's written about cancer is about people being 'brave' and 'fighting' and being an 'inspiration'. And that's fantastic if they can be like that. But there's a lot about cancer which is just very, very frightening. Sometimes I wish people spoke about that too and were allowed to be a bit more honest about how cancer affects them.

When people say to me, 'Oh, you're so brave' it drives me mad. I'm not 'being brave' at all. I'm simply getting out of bed in the morning and getting on with things the best I can. Because there is no alternative. And a lot of the time I've felt scared stiff. I just wish there was a little more honesty around that. Because not every woman with cancer suddenly turns into Wonder Woman with hot pants and super human spirit.

Often I would wake in the middle of the night and the first thing I'd remember was that I had cancer. And it was then I craved Brian's arms around me to comfort me and calm me down. I knew Denise was only in the next bedroom and I could always go into her but I wouldn't do that to her. And I don't want to upset my brothers and sisters with my illness any more than I already have done.

Being so dependent on them again was upsetting too. For ages I had leaned very heavily on them but in the past year or so I'd picked myself up and managed to stand on my own two feet again. Now here I was, back to feeling like a burden on my family.

'You're not a burden,' Denise said. 'Tom and I love having you here.'

But it still troubled me that once again I'd become something else for my brothers and sisters to worry about.

Twenty-Two

A Life Worth Loving

I was just putting on some make-up for a night out at a local restaurant with my brothers and sisters when a message pinged up on my Facebook Messenger. As I read the words I felt a wave of sadness sweep through me.

It was from a girl called Mia telling me that she and her friend Emily had been victims in the Manchester Arena bomb attack the previous month, which had killed twenty-two people. Mia said Emily had such serious shrapnel wounds that she was in danger of losing her leg and was being taken in for surgery the following day.

'She's a massive Nolans fan and if you could call her before the surgery it would mean the world to her,' the message said.

'Of course,' I typed back into my phone without even thinking. 'Send me her number and I'll call her in an hour.'

The entire country had been horrified by the attack, mainly on young people leaving the Ariana Grande concert. And it felt so close to home. My nieces had been there only the week before and I'd been to see dozens of concerts there myself. Ringing a teenage victim of the attack seemed the very least I could do.

Later, when I was at the restaurant with my family, I nipped outside to make the call. Emily sounded breathless and incredibly poorly on the phone.

'How are you feeling?' I asked. 'I hear you are being really brave but you're going to be just fine.'

The poor girl could only just reply, she sounded in terrible pain.

The next day I received another message from Mia saying Emily had pulled through the surgery well. From then on I started messaging Mia frequently, and then we spoke on the phone most days. I was still feeling quite down about my cancer and it helped me to have someone else to worry about.

Mia talked about Emily but also told me about her own life. She told me about problems she'd had at home, how her dad had left when she was a kid and all the traumas she'd had with a string of boyfriends. She even told me her mum had died of secondary breast cancer. We chatted about my treatment and I hoped I was able to provide her with some comfort after everything she'd been through.

Some days I'd speak to Emily, who was still in hospital. She often sounded drowsy and in pain and she told me the doctors were still struggling to deal with her injuries. I sent a bouquet of Milky Bars and other little gifts to the hospital which I hoped would cheer her up.

As the weeks went by I became more and more keen to meet Emily. She'd been through so much and I thought maybe a visit might cheer her up. My brother Brian said he'd drive me over to the hospital in Manchester.

'I'm thinking I'd like to visit Emily,' I told Mia on the phone one evening.

'Oh, er, great,' she replied. 'When?'

'Next Wednesday,' I suggested.

But that weekend I received a message saying Emily had

taken a turn for the worse. I called her on the phone but she sounded so weak and breathless she could barely talk.

'I don't want to put you through all the upset of visiting me,' Emily said.

'Don't be daft,' I replied. 'I want to see you.'

I put the phone down in tears. There was little doubt from what Mia was telling me that I would be saying hello and goodbye to Emily in the same meeting.

'The doctors say there is nothing more they can do,' Mia told me on the phone.

'Oh God, I'm so sorry,' I replied.

Then at five o'clock on the morning I was supposed to be going over to see Emily I received a message saying she had passed away. I was devastated. I'd never even met the girl but it seemed such a terrible waste after such a dreadful tragedy.

Denise offered to come with me for the funeral and I waited to hear from Mia about the details. But for a few days I heard nothing at all. Then I got a message from another of Emily's friends thanking me for making her final days so special.

But I didn't hear a word from Mia.

What I didn't realize then was that two of my lovely nieces – Laura, who's Tommy's daughter, and Amy, who's Anne's daughter – had become suspicious. They felt there was something which just didn't add up about the girls' stories – and there had been no news in the press about another victim of the stadium bombing having died.

Laura and Amy are brilliant on computers and Facebook and all that and they started researching Mia and Emily. Within a few hours they'd discovered the whole story had been a terrible, cruel hoax.

Mia and Emily hadn't been anywhere near the Manchester

Arena that night – but they were regulars on a website for trolls who get their kicks out of hoaxing people in the public eye. It's about as sick as you can get.

Laura phoned Denise and told her what she'd discovered. Then Denise had to break the news to me.

'I don't understand,' I said to Denise. 'How can it be made up?'

But the more I thought back over the things they'd told me, the more improbable the stories sounded. And the fact that Emily had 'died' the day I was supposed to visit her was highly suspicious.

I rang my niece Laura.

'Why would they do that?' I asked her.

'I'm so sorry, Auntie Lin,' she replied, 'but you've been trolled. These people think doing this sort of thing is funny.'

I felt physically sick. How could I have been so gullible? I felt stupid and embarrassed. But I also felt violated – I'd trusted these people and they'd betrayed me in this terrible way. On top of that they'd used the most awful event for their wicked plan.

I sent a message with just one word to the number of the girl who called herself Mia: 'Why?'

I didn't hear a thing back.

I called the police, who were very sympathetic and kind but said there was nothing they could do. Because the hoaxers hadn't asked me for anything they hadn't actually broken the law. All I could do was block their number and if they continued to contact me then it would be deemed harassment.

The whole incident left me feeling sickened about some aspects of human nature.

'I've been such an idiot,' I said to Maureen one night.

'No,' she insisted. 'You were being nice. Don't ever apologize for being nice. It's these complete sickos who have the problem.'

I guess there are always risks when you live some of your life in the public eye but I'd never considered anything like that happening before. And I was determined that the next time someone asked me for help supporting a charity or a friend in need it wouldn't put me off. Otherwise those sickos really would have beaten me.

I was also determined the experience wouldn't put me off speaking publicly about issues which might help other people. That had been the reason why I'd agreed to allow *Loose Women* to follow my cancer journey, filming regular updates on my progress. Because Coleen had talked on the show about my cancer returning, the editor thought viewers would be interested in watching how I was getting on.

'Oh, I'm not sure I really want the ins and outs of my illness all over national television,' I said at first. 'Let me think about it.'

But the more I thought about it the more I thought it might be helpful for ordinary women to see up close the realities of cancer treatment. And somehow I might be able to make them feel their fears were quite normal and maybe help some of them feel a little less alone.

And that was what made me agree. So six weeks after my last radiotherapy session I had a *Loose Women* camera crew with me when I went back to the hospital for the results of a scan to see if the cancer had spread during or after my radiotherapy. That really was scary. Terrifying. Because if it had spread it meant radiotherapy wasn't working. And I'd be coping with the worst possible news in front of a TV camera.

They would be in the consulting room when I got the results, waiting to record my reaction. It wasn't live but, still, my immediate response would be recorded for everyone to see.

My sister-in-law Annie, my niece Alex and my breast-care nurse, Sarah, came with me. Then when we got to the hospital another nurse from the cancer unit said she would come in to see the consultant oncologist with me too.

'Oh God, she knows something,' I thought, instantly feeling sick. 'Why else would she be in the meeting unless it was because she knew it was going to be bad news?' I was shaking when I said goodbye to Alex and my friend Sue who were going to wait outside the consulting room.

My oncologist Dr Dankwatta had been a junior doctor at Blackpool Victoria Hospital the first time I had cancer. Now he was a consultant. And although it was a horrid situation, it was comforting that I knew him from before.

When I walked in the room this time he looked more serious than I'd ever seen him. My stomach hit the floor and I could actually feel my knees start to wobble. My palms were sweating as I sat in the chair in front of his desk and straightened my skirt.

Dr Dankwatta looked up from his notes and smiled across the desk at me.

'Mrs Hudson, it's good news. We are very pleased with the scan results. I'm very happy that the tumour hasn't spread.'

I nearly jumped over the desk and kissed him. If it hadn't been for my dodgy hip I would have done.

'Oh, thank you, thank you,' I blubbed.

By the time I got outside the room I was in floods of tears again – but this time tears of joy not sadness.

'It's OK,' I choked. 'It hasn't spread.' Alex and Sue jumped up and hugged me and the TV crew all started clapping. It was amazing.

I don't think I had realized how stressed I had been waiting for those results. And for them to be good was an amazing sense of release.

I returned home to Denise who continued to look after me with incredible love and care. There wasn't much I could do but rest my hip, which I could feel was gradually healing. Some days it could still be painful but bit by bit that was easing. Then it was just a case of waiting until the next scan on the last day of July.

I was still nervous when I went to pick up those results on 19 August, but the fear was far more under control than the first time.

When you are waiting for results like that people have a habit of saying to you: 'Oh it'll be fine.' It's meant to be comforting but it isn't really as it's based on no knowledge at all.

I talked to Sarah, my breast-cancer nurse, about it.

'But what if it isn't fine?' I said to her. It was such an odd feeling because I felt I had this horrible maggot-like creature living inside me which could start growing at any moment, and then there might be nothing that could be done to stop it.

'If it's not fine,' Sarah said as calmly as ever, 'we will deal with it then. We'll sort it.'

She was so sensible and calming that she stopped my panic going off the scale. I'd be lying if I said the nagging sense of anxiety ever totally went away but I did give myself a good talking-to about the best way of dealing with it.

'If this is how it's going to be every three months for the

rest of your life, Linda,' I told myself, 'you're just going to have to find a way of dealing with it.'

I really didn't want to spend what time I do have left in a constant state of anxiety about my next set of scan results. Although sometimes it was a lot easier to keep that anxiety in check than others.

Again, the August results were good. Another reprieve.

By September I was feeling emotionally stronger. Strong enough to make a few big decisions about my future.

I decided to talk to Dr Briggs about it.

'I want to get all my affairs "in order", as they say,' I explained. 'I've caused my family enough worry over the years and so I want everything possible decided now so they don't have to if I become very poorly.'

And then I talked through the list of things I wanted agreed. I want to be DNR (Do Not Resuscitate) if it is near the end of my life. And I want to go to a hospice rather than be looked after by one of my brothers and sisters. I saw how well Bernie was treated in a hospice and I'd be happy with that. And then when I'm dressed and fed and cleaned my brothers and sisters will be able to visit me with a bag of sweets and a movie but none of the worry.

I have chosen the songs for my funeral too. I would like 'There You'll Be' from *Pearl Harbor* sung by Faith Hill. The words couldn't be more fitting for the moment when I'll finally be going to meet Brian again. It's the song we played at his funeral. The song we'd jokingly rowed about years earlier as to which of us would have it at our funeral. A row in the days when we thought dying was a million miles away. Goodness, how things have changed.

And there's a Neil Sedaka song too, 'Our Last Song

Together'. It's beautiful and by then it really will be our last song with my wonderful family.

Now I've made these decisions and talked them through with Dr Briggs I just need to put them down in writing. I'll do that soon.

I've talked to Dr Briggs a lot about how I've been feeling. About the cancer now and my immediate future – but about the past as well. Sometimes I feel desperately sad about what has happened in the past, and what's happening now. Sometimes it's just raw anger. I'm still angry Brian isn't here. Angry that drink took him from me. And I'm angry about cancer too. That it took Bernie and it's trying to take me as well. Sometimes I feel I want to go out and find cancer and kill it with my bare hands.

Those feelings are within me, but I'm trying to contain them. I don't want anger and sadness to overwhelm me. For if I haven't got a long life left ahead of me I want to live it well. Knowing I may not have much of it left has certainly made me appreciate it more than I ever have done.

Some women live with secondary breast cancer for ten or twenty years. Others don't. I don't know what will happen to me. What I do know is I can choose how I spend the time I have available.

And I want to spend it appreciating the simple pleasures in life, like spending time with my family and doing little things which make my friends and family happy.

I bid for tickets for my brothers to go and watch Barcelona play at the Camp Nou Stadium, because they're huge football fans and they'll love that. And I booked a special booth for twenty-two of us from the family to watch the fireworks on the pier in Blackpool at the end of September. Now I'm trying to take my nieces to see Little Mix in concert, because they're huge fans. Seeing the delight on their faces is all I want. Because after everything I've been through I've learned that making memories and seeing happiness in the eyes of those you love really is what life is all about.

In day-to-day life we can all go through weeks and even years without giving much thought to what really matters or remembering how blessed we are to be alive. But this disease has made me do that. When people say, 'Live every day as if it is your last,' they generally just think it sounds good then carry on as they always have done. But I actually do that now. I have to.

At the start of October I was at a charity ball in aid of the local hospice and I even managed to get up for a dance. 'Uptown Funk' was on and me, Denise, Anne and Annie were up on the floor like we were in our teens all over again. And I was in my best Louboutin shoes, which are pretty impossible to dance in even if you haven't got a blasted tumour buried in your hip!

Those Louboutins are my pride and joy. My friend Liz Emmett, who organizes the Bernie ball, arrived with them as a gift when I was in hospital, just after I was told the cancer was back.

'You'll soon be up and about and wearing these,' she said, handing me a box holding the purple velvet shoes.

'They're beautiful, Liz,' I said. But at that moment I really didn't believe I'd ever wear them.

So that night when I wore them to dance with my sisters was a huge step forward in my recovery. It proved to me I really am living, not dying, with cancer. And I'm not just living, I'm laughing and dancing too.

On 11 October I went back in for another scan. Once again I got the all clear. I told myself that for the next three months, until I had my next scan, I wouldn't worry but of course there are always going to be times when I find myself wondering, is the cancer growing? Is it creeping around my body without me even knowing?

Before Christmas 2017 I started suffering headaches almost every day. They weren't as severe as a migraine, just a constant nagging pain. At first I tried to ignore them, but after a while I couldn't.

It wasn't the pain that was the real problem, it was the fear that cancer had spread to my brain. Just like it did with Bernie. Sometimes I'd wake in the night panicking that the cancer was on the march. I'd start crying, desperate for Brian to tell me, 'Don't worry, you're doing great Lin, now go back to sleep.' But he wasn't there so I did worry and I couldn't go back to sleep.

'I think it's spread to my brain,' I told my palliative nurse at my next appointment.

'Hmmm . . . well let's try Specsavers first.' She smiled.

An eye test didn't flag up anything untoward so my doctor suggested I should see a neurologist, 'because of your medical history'.

And then the neurologist recommended an MRI scan, 'because of your medical history'.

How I hated that phrase. We all knew exactly what it meant – cancer. So why not just say it?

The neurologist was very optimistic though. He was convinced the real cause of the headaches was a fairly common reaction to co-codamol, the painkiller I was on for my hip.

'I'm pretty sure taking you off the tablets cold turkey will cure the headaches,' he said. 'But we'll do the MRI anyway because of your . . .'

'I know, I know.' I laughed. 'Because of my medical history.'

I hated the thought of an MRI scan because they've always made me feel horribly claustrophobic in the past. But at least I felt reassured that the neurologist didn't believe my headaches were due to cancer in my brain. Even when I'm told not to expect the worst, there's always going to be that anxiety living with me night and day now – that the worst might actually be about to happen.

I'm getting stronger all the time though and, while a year ago I'd have been a gibbering wreck being wheeled into the MRI machine, this time I was feeling really quite calm.

And they'd even managed to fit a mirror inside the machine – a bit like a periscope – which meant I could see out when I was inside it. It made me feel a lot less claustrophobic and panicky. It really wasn't too bad at all. And even better . . . the scan came back absolutely clear.

The doctors took me off co-codamol, replacing it with two different painkillers, and the headaches disappeared instantly.

I felt fantastic.

By New Year's Eve I was even able to host a charity ball and dance the night away in a pair of sparkly stilettos.

And yes, there are still days when I feel a bit hopeless about it all but those days are becoming fewer and fewer. I keep my fear deep down now. I won't let it near the surface to ruin the time I have left.

I'm getting my house painted and decorated so I can move back and finally leave Denise and Tom in peace. They've been fabulous caring for me all this time but it's time for me to look after myself again. I'm able to walk without the crutch and the pain in my hip is far less. I'm keen to start doing a bit of gentle exercise too, as I feel like I've put on so much weight since I've been immobile.

I'm even hopeful I may be able to work again sometime soon. Standing on stage for long periods might be tricky but there must be some sitting-down roles I could do.

Writing this book has allowed me to look back on my life and think about it all. Yes, there have been some terrible lows . . . Of course I wish Bernie were still here. There are still times when I'm out in the town and I'll see something and think: 'Oh, I must call Bernie when I get home and tell her.' And then it hits me all over again that I'll never be able to call her. I'll never hear that cheery 'Hiya, Lin' on the end of the phone.

And there is the never-ending sadness of life without Brian. He was the love of my life, my soulmate. And while I can now get through days or even weeks without crying that he's gone, I still think of him every day.

I wish too that Mum hadn't had that terrible Alzheimer's disease and that our family had avoided some of the fall-outs we've had over the years. And my one big regret is that I never had children – I would have loved to be a mum.

But despite all that I think what a wonderfully blessed life I have had. I've had some incredible experiences, like touring with Frank Sinatra and working with Morecambe and Wise and appearing on *Top of the Pops*. But even more importantly, like I said at the start, I've known what it is to love and to be loved.

I have the most incredible family, who've always been there for me. And now I have my wonderful great-nieces and -nephews, who enable me to see the future. I keep in touch with Bernie's daughter Erin, who has grown into a fabulous young woman. And I have a fantastic relationship with Brian's children Sarah and Lloyd and their children, my step-grandchildren. Sarah's daughter Lucy came to stay recently and I see Lloyd and his family every time I go down south. Spending time with all the children gives me such joy.

I'm not particularly religious but if I pray now it is to plead with God for just a little more time. Time to live, to spend with my family and watch the children grow a little older. They're not big things or expensive things, but they are all that matter.

Perhaps I'm repeating myself now. 'You're rambling . . . and you're not even dressed for it,' as Bernie used to say to me.

I hope you've enjoyed this ramble through my life. The memories of the good times and the bad. The laughs and the tears. And above all I hope I've helped you see, as I've had to learn the hard way, that life is a wonderful blessing. And that however bad the bad times can be, it is one fabulous adventure.

Acknowledgements

Thank you to:

My brothers and sisters – 'The Cavalry' – I wouldn't be here without your love! A special thank you to Tom and Denise, who I lived with for nine months. You can change the locks now! To all my nieces and nephews – big and small – who have shown me that life *is* worth living. Auntie Teresa, you never cease to amaze me with your unconditional love for all of us.

Annie, 'my buddy'. Love you.

Clinical Nurse Specialist Sarah Middleton and Consultant Clinical Psychologist Dr Jean Briggs. Who knew that we would have to do this journey again? I just wouldn't be able to without your help and support. (Your tissues are STILL rubbish though!)

Sue, Graham, Suzanne, my best friend of over forty-five years who's only a phone call away 24/7, Liz Emmett, Debby and Jaqueline, in fact all my wonderful friends who have made me smile on my darkest days and have been there to support me when I needed their strength.

To our fans, your continued support is so appreciated.

Ingrid and all at Pan Macmillan, for your belief that my story should be told.

Alison Phillips, whom it has been a pleasure to work with. I knew you were the one I wanted to help me on this emotional journey.

Amanda Beckman, not just my agent but my friend. You are a joy to work with. (Still going to find you Mr Right!)

Last but not least, Melanie Blake. Thank you just doesn't seem adequate. When I lost my Brian, I also lost my way. I grieved for my career, but you gave it back to me. Your belief and faith in me has helped me realize that the dark days can brighten. Your guidance has helped me to reinvent myself and your friendship is one I will cherish always.

PICTURE ACKNOWLEDGEMENTS

All photographs are from the author's own collection, with the exception of the following:

Page 2 © Associated Newspapers / Rex Shutterstock
Page 3 top © Press Association
Page 3 bottom © Dezo Hoffmann / Rex Shutterstock
Page 4 top © Ted Blackbrow / Associated Newspapers / Rex Shutterstock
Page 4 bottom © Mirrorpix
Page 5 top © Michael Putland / Getty Images
Page 5 bottom © Mirrorpix
Page 8 top © Chris van de Vooren / Sunshine / Rex Shutterstock; bottom left © John Paul / Scope Features
Page 10 bottom © Krestine Havemann / *Evening Standard* / Rex Shutterstock
Page 13 © Paul Mitchell / *Woman* magazine / IPC + Syndication
Page 14 top © Mark Campbell / Rex Shutterstock
Page 16 © Nicky Johnston